BOX OFFICE ARCHAEOLOGY

REFINING HOLLYWOOD'S PORTRAYALS OF THE PAST

JULIE M. SCHABLITSKY
EDITOR

Left Coast
Press Inc.

Walnut Creek, California

Left Coast Press Inc.

LEFT COAST PRESS, INC.
1630 North Main Street, #400
Walnut Creek, CA 94596
http://www.LCoastPress.com

ISBN 978-1-59874-055-4 hardcover
ISBN 978-1-59874-056-1paperback

Library of Congress Cataloging-in-Publication Data available

Printed in the United States of America

∞™ The paper used in this publication meets the minimum requirements of American National Standard for Information Sciences—Permanence of Paper for Printed Library Materials, ANSI/NISO Z39.48–1992.

07 08 09 10 11   5 4 3 2 1

Cover photograph of John DeBry gathering artifacts from Richard Condent's ship the "Fiery Dragon" which sank off Madagascar.
Photo by Nick Caloyianis courtesy of the Discovery Channel.

Cover photograph of mummy recovered from an excavation in the Theban necropolis. Photo by Stuart Tyson Smith.

CONTENTS

PREFACE

Several years ago, I researched and excavated a 19th-century, ethnically heterogeneous, working-class neighborhood in Virginia City, Nevada. I had never watched the classic Western television series *Bonanza* but I knew the series was set in this world-famous mining district. After becoming intimate with the history of this once urban town, I watched a few episodes of *Bonanza*. The connection to the mining industry was tenuous and overshadowed by handsomely dressed cowboys and brightly colored Indians. Virginia City, Nevada, was only a backdrop to play out life lessons taught and learned by the affluent Cartwrights. From this experience, I became interested in the way history was collected for use in films and how gilded Hollywood history affected society.

To explore this interest, I organized a session, Screening the Past: An Archaeological Review of Hollywood Productions, for the Society for Historical and Underwater Archaeology Conference in York, England, in 2005. When archaeologists begin to explore their discipline's subject matter and its representation in popular culture, they are initially concerned with physical inconsistencies and facts. As expected, during the session many of us focused on older movies and Hollywood's telling of the past. Vergil E. Noble, one of the session discussants and chapter author, re-centered us through a discussion of the differences between archaeology and movies.

One comment, in particular, resonated with all of us, "Hollywood does not need to accurately tell a story if they can effectively teach the lesson." Since then, we have realized that archaeologists and Hollywood directors have different ways of delivering messages. Therefore, their stories need to contain certain elements (such as romance and violence), while purging others (ordinary people and the mundane). Archaeologists do not have the luxury of ignoring uninteresting or ambiguous information, so they can easily become excited by the discovery of a broken toothbrush.

On Thanksgiving Day, 2006, I watched an interview between Mel Gibson and ABC correspondents about Gibson's movie, *Apocalypto.* This production is based on the decline of the Mayans and their disturbing ritualistic response to an overstressed environment. To understand the Mayan culture, Gibson solicited the help of archaeologist Richard Hansen; however, not all of the professional guidance was followed in the movie. Toward the end of the ABC interview, Gibson revealed that *Apocolypto* held a lesson. The Mayans were guilty of using every resource from their environment and ultimately, conspicuous consumption led to their demise. The behavior of our modern culture, Gibson warned, is a mirror image of this ancient society.

Reflecting back, Vergil's revelation that Hollywood movies teach lessons is correct. The fact that archaeologists contribute detailed information needed to translate these lessons is also true. Although movies and archaeology have two separate purposes, they often tell the same stories, albeit in different formats. By the end of this book, I believe we will collectively realize that archaeology and Hollywood share common ground and perhaps this is why our conversation on movies began.

CHAPTER 1

THE WAY OF THE ARCHAEOLOGIST

Julie M. Schablitsky

• •

No one should have illusions about television. It is never going to be primarily an educational and cultural medium.
—*Eric Sevareid (CBS correspondent, 1960)*

Scholarship that focuses on the accuracy of Hollywood's portrayals of past events, places, and people is short sighted and ineffective at encouraging film producers to adhere to historical truths. For the past thirty years, historians have berated producers of movies and television shows for "getting it all wrong." Unlike modern movie budgets, television and movie production companies had limited funding, sets were simple, and intensive research on a historical-based story was the exception rather than the rule.

Today's Hollywood productions are savvy, the sets are impressive, and the wardrobes are impeccable. Movie producers take the time and allocate funding to hire historical consultants and employ prop masters to fine tune their sets. Before the film begins to roll, the actual setting is visited by production personnel; photos are taken, historical documents are copied, and historians and/or archaeologists are consulted. Within weeks, a mirror image of a historic town or building interior can be replicated from this research.

When Hollywood seeks out experts for use on the creation of their productions, they commonly solicit the knowledge of the amateur historian. Often, their published material is geared toward the public and their approach to the subject is filled with specific details rather than broad themes like those provided by professionals (Carnes 1996:21). When professional archaeologists are called on, they are used for specific aspects of the movie such as the reconstruction of lost languages. In other instances, their laboratories may be visited so that the film sets can be dressed with historically accurate tea sets, lighting, and decorative pieces.

A large part of this new attention to historic detail by producers is the direct result of a newly educated public. Active participation in historical reenactor groups, access to museums, and an increase in the number and variety of documentaries have created audiences who can discern between 19th- and 20th-century fashions and regional differences between American Indian homes. Although the cinematography and accuracy has dramatically improved over the years, filmmakers have not been inspired to capture an absolute past. Instead, Hollywood takes risks, pushes the envelope, and exercises creative liberties with our history. Unlike the archaeological community, their success is not measured by a scholarly panel but by the number of viewers who buy tickets and tune in to their stories.

As scholars of history, it is acceptable to acknowledge that our past played out on stage is limited, simplistic, and often witnessed from the majority's perspective. Many popular culture experts, along with members of the public, wonder why intriguing details, historical figures, and events are left out of movies when the truth is much more fascinating and effective at capturing our imaginations (Toplin 2002:1). Screen writers defend their approach, saying that when too many details and dimensions are placed within a film the audience is alienated; therefore, characters remain one dimensional, plots are kept simple, and details are ignored (Carnes 1996:13).

Another critique is the director's concentration on the lives of the social majority. One could argue that audiences want to see characters they can most closely identify with, thus Hollywood's main characters are primarily privileged White men and women. Hollywood, however, should not be blamed for providing moviegoers with what they want—an opiate that removes them from their own worlds and transports them to other places and times.

In Hollywood's defense, movie producers are hired to entertain and not teach history; the function of the big screen is different from the goal of scholars who tell the past as fully, completely, and unbiased as humanly possible. Inadvertently, the public is influenced by a gilded past flickering across the screen. Although some may find an ethical debate within an embellished true historical event or person's life, education can and does stimulate people to learn more about subjects highlighted by Hollywood. Often, positive audience responses to historical movies and television shows can be measured in increased tourism to a recently viewed historical location, purchases of biographies, and historical research. Hollywood productions do create a desire and interest in the public to learn more about what they watch on television and in movies (Carnes 1996:9). Producer, director, and writer Oliver Stone claims that "movies are just the first draft. They raise questions and inspire students to find out more" (Carnes 1996:306).

As a group of archaeologists who study the physical evidence left behind by people who lived hundreds of years ago, we propose to step beyond the current debates by popular culture historians on berating Hollywood or congratulating moviemakers (Toplin 2002). Instead, we will explore the past and discuss its complexity by using Hollywood productions as our stage and archaeology as our narrator. Through these chapters, archaeologists will lead the reader through the tombs of Egyptian mummies, sail them into tales of pirates and Vikings, and escort the uninitiated through the Wild West.

We hope that this book inspires the public, students, and scholars to recognize the differences between the mission of the archaeologist and the movie director, yet appreciate the way we learn more about our past from the study of crumbling ruins, dusty archives, and yesterday's garbage. Our duty, as archaeologists, is to bring the past alive and create a tangible link between us and those who lived before, resurrecting the past and reconnecting us on a personal and human level. The *way of the archaeologist* can confirm documented history, add new information and complexity to well-known stories, and contradict previously held popular myths. Do pirates bury their treasure? What was Pocahontas's life really like? Are there really secret Shanghai tunnels hidden beneath our cities?

This composition on archaeology and Hollywood begins with Stuart Tyson Smith "unwrapping the mummy," where he introduces us to the different types of Egyptian movie genres and uses archaeological methods to give the ancient Egyptians a voice. By far the most popular of the film genre, mummy movies have been with us for over a hundred years and continue to be blockbuster hits. Tyson's expertise as a movie consultant lends incredible insight into Hollywood mummy movies. In addition to movie references, he uses years of scholarly research to illuminate the lesser-known aspects of mummification and humanizes these final rites for the dead.

From Egypt, we travel to Iceland where Mark Axel Tveskov and Jon M. Erlandson expose us to popular misconceptions of Vikings found in movies, commercials, and cartoons. Referring to several films, the authors identify the homogeneous behavior of Hollywood Vikings. Using archaeological findings, Tveskov and Erlandson effectively deconstruct the stereotypical child-like warrior icon to rebuild the Norse as industrious people whose travels outside of the village were congruous with global trader rather than world conqueror.

Peg legs, parrots, and buried treasure are descriptors that can only be used to identify one thing ... pirates. But, how do underwater archaeologists differentiate a sunken pirate ship from thousands of other wrecks? Charles R. Ewen and Russell K. Skowronek discuss pirate imagery and their popularity in American culture over the last three generations. The history of piracy on the high seas is revealed, along with a confession on the challenge of identifying a pirate ship from a merchant vessel. Ewen and Skowronek dock their discussion on pirate archaeology by recognizing the need to not only identify artifact patterning to differentiate shipwrecks but to study the global impact of piracy.

Continuing our focus on underwater archaeology, James P. Delgado sails the reader through an amazing fleet of wrecks discovered and studied on the ocean floor. He acknowledges the fascination that Hollywood holds for these lost ships, particularly *Titanic*. Delgado describes a galley of films produced on this ship and reflects on our fascination with its sinking. Perhaps the most exciting part of his chapter is the description of the archaeologist's discovery of the *Titanic* and how findings such as these help reconnect us with the past. Delgado's contribution also warns us about the personal and ethical challenges we face with the awakening and revisiting of such tragedies.

Marching us back in time to the U.S. Civil War, Robert S. Neyland launches his story on the *H.L. Hunley* submarine with historical background on the construction, sinkings, and eventual loss of the vessel in Charleston Harbor, South Carolina. Although only two films and a handful of documentaries were produced about the *Hunley*, the author incorporates numerous examples of how archaeology has contributed new information on the history of the submarine. Discoveries within the *Hunley* are discussed, including the romantic tale woven around a bullet-bent gold coin and forensic details that reveal the arduous lives of the Confederate sailors.

Arriving at the first landing site in Virginia, Randy Amici introduces us to the timeless Pocahontas. We learn that history has painted a Western view of the Powhatan culture and fabricated Pocahontas's romantic interactions with John Smith. Much of what is told in popular culture is a result of the misinterpretation of Native American customs by the British, who carried these experiences back to England. The author unveils a vignette of the Powhatan culture through archaeological and historical discoveries. The most fascinating revelation of the chapter is when Amici exposes the true impact of Pocahontas on America.

Continuing the conversation on tribal representations in Hollywood and what archaeologists have learned from these sites,

Charles M. Haecker focuses on battles between Native Americans and the federal government. Most importantly, he illuminates the misinformation and propaganda that surrounded violent encounters with Indians and effectively demonstrates how archaeological work has unveiled the true nature and outcomes of these battles. Throughout the chapter, Haecker revisits Hollywood accounts and representations of the Native American to demonstrate the perpetuation of stereotypes by the film industry and how archaeology is relieving us of this racist, silver-screen past.

Paul Mullins's Imagining Blackness chapter probes deeply into the complex world of racism and the representation of African Americans in popular culture. Besides visiting Hollywood portrayals of African Americans, he also discusses the way archaeologists try to understand their world and culture. The author encourages us to question the origins of Hollywood's simplification and stereotypes of ancestral groups and cultures. Furthermore, Mullins underscores the challenge of archaeologists who may become so entrenched in the details of human culture that they become ineffective at moving toward historical truth.

The ubiquitous nature of archaeology is explored with Rebecca Yamin and Lauren J. Cook's excavation of New York City. The colorful representation of the Five Points Neighborhood in Martin Scorsese's *Gangs of New York* stepped into the slums and used a string of violent scenes to communicate the social and economic frustrations of newly arrived immigrants. The authors express disappointment with this homogenized and stereotypical portrayal of the poor, who are shown without employment or aspirations. Yamin and Cook illustrate how the archaeological record speaks for these impoverished families through discarded dinner bones, chipped plates, and personal belongings.

Emigrating from east to west, Julie M. Schablitsky introduces us to the people who lived and worked in 19th-century boomtowns. She uses the classic television series *Bonanza, Tombstone* the movie, and the current HBO series *Deadwood* to demonstrate the evolution of Westerns. In addition, this essay recognizes Hollywood's complacency with exposing viewers to the wide diversity of people who accumulated to form boomtown communities. Schablitsky ultimately demonstrates how archaeological findings illuminated an international culture of hard-working people who believed in superstitions, sunk their money in fashion, and took their drinking seriously.

The public's perception of 19th-century American Chinatowns is limited to a vice district formed through years of racism and perpetuated through Hollywood movies. Bryn Williams and Stacey Camp are breaking down this wall by identifying how and why these misconceptions were formed in America. Furthermore, they are using material culture to better understand the use of space in these neighborhoods through the analysis of stereotypical Chinese sojourner behavior, including opium smoking and gaming. With their intense study of San Jose, California's Chinatown, Williams and Camp are rebuilding a better understanding of these exotic communities.

Vergil E. Noble closes the book with a personal and scholarly reflection on historical movies and the chapters contained herein. His grasp on popular culture literature is obvious as he navigates us through a collection of movie classics. Common themes between the archaeologists' chapters are also discussed, such as our concern with Hollywood's complacency with the common man. Noble advises archaeologists to not be distracted by the unachievable goal of influencing Hollywood movies but to focus on the advancement of our own discipline.

References

CARNES, MARK C., EDITOR
> 1996 *Past Imperfect, History According to the Movies.* Henry Holt and Company, New York.

SEVAREID, ERIC
> 1960 *TV Guide Roundup.* "Big Rock Candy Mountain," pp. 15–18. Holt, Rinehart, and Winston, New York.

Toplin, Robert Brent
> 2002 *Reel History, In Defense of Hollywood.* University Press of Kansas, Lawrence.

UNWRAPPING THE MUMMY

HOLLYWOOD FANTASIES, EGYPTIAN REALITIES

Stuart Tyson Smith

● ●

Ancient Egypt is one of the most popular archaeological film genres. From epic blockbusters to Grade B thrillers to soft porn, Egypt provides an exotic setting for a wide range of stories. This Hollywood Egyptomania draws heavily on the popularity of ancient Egypt in the fine and decorative arts, a phenomenon that goes back to the fascination of a future emperor, Napoleon Bonaparte, for past glories. The first multidisciplinary team of scholars accompanied his 1798 military expedition to Egypt. The magnificent publications of 1802–1828 sparked a timeless interest in all things ancient Egyptian. Newly opened national museums and wealthy collectors *had* to have something from Egypt. Architects built in pharaonic style, and Wedgwood made tea sets with Egyptian themes (Humbert et al. 1994).

No trip to a museum or Egypt was complete without a close encounter with a mummy. Mummies were so popular by 1833 that

Egyptian ruler Mohamed Ali's advisor, Father Géramb, could say: "It would be hardly respectable, on one's return from Egypt, to present oneself in Europe without a mummy in one hand and a crocodile in the other" (Ikram and Dodson 1998:67). Tickets were issued to mummy unwrapping parties, which became all the rage in affluent society. When a new popular media, motion pictures, entered the scene around the turn of the last century, films with Egyptian themes were among the first produced, including 1899's *Cléopâtre*, which involved the revival of Cleopatra's mummy by a villain with diabolical plans.

The ancient Egyptian mummy in film, by far the most popular Egypt-themed genre, recently burst into theaters again with Universal Studios special effects-driven remake and sequel, *The Mummy* (1999) and *The Mummy Returns* (2001). A comparison of the portrayal of ancient Egypt in these and selected other films with the insights gained through archaeology and Egyptology will illuminate the differences between Hollywood's mummies, popular imaginings about Egyptian beliefs and practices, and the reality of death and burial in ancient Egypt, where mummies did take a central, if generally less mobile role.

Reel Mummies—Ancient Egypt in Film

Egypt, 4000 years ago, a land of strange rituals and savage cruelty ...

—*trailer for* The Mummy *(1959)*

Ancient Egypt–themed films fall into three basic genres that often overlap: (1) biblical/costume epics, (2) Cleopatra, and (3) mummies. Cecil B. DeMille's two productions of *The Ten Commandments* (1923 and 1956) created lavish sets that emphasized the epic quality of the biblical narrative, setting the benchmark for this genre. A huge success at the box office, the later version was shot on location in Egypt and boasted a stellar cast of academic advisors, including Egyptologists William C. Hayes and Labib Habachi. Unfortunately, this did not prevent significant inaccuracies in costume, props, and sets, the most notable of which are the garish costumes. Egyptians did not have access to color-fast dyes, therefore they mainly wore white linen and never, ever gold lamé! Although set in 1936, *Raiders of the Lost Ark* (1981) sought to revive the grand epic qualities of these films, using a surprisingly plausible biblical archaeology premise connected with Pharaoh Sheshonk's sack of Jerusalem in 925 BCE, but otherwise with little historical accuracy. The recent science fiction epic *Stargate* (1994) also played off of the lavish sets, costumes, and "cast-of-thousands" scale of the biblical tradition, again using ancient Egypt as an exotic and especially sensual backdrop (Figure 2.1). This film is surprisingly accurate aside from its clever Erich von Däniken–inspired space aliens premise.[1] *Stargate* also drew on films centered on the life of Cleopatra, which accentuate these qualities in Egypt's last queen, only rarely recognizing that as a descendant of Egypt's Macedonian conquerors, she was more Hellenistic than Egyptian. This image of the exotic East goes back to antiquity in the Roman view of Cleopatra and eastern Mediterranean civilizations in general, but was also recognized in Said's (1978) characterization of Orientalism. This Western view of the Eastern Other colors most Egypt-themed films, as the tag-line quoted above illustrates.

Mummy films combine elements of the other genres—the sensual, mysterious East with exotic settings and costumes. They also set the pattern for the archaeologist as adventurer encountering the unknown and macabre. The emergence of the genre is often credited to the notoriety surrounding Tutankhamen's tomb, especially rumors of a curse that supposedly killed people associated with the archaeological project (Cowie and Johnson 2002). The literary trope of revived mummies, however, goes back over a hundred years before Howard Carter's astonishing discovery in 1922 and the production of the iconic Universal film *The Mummy* in 1932.

Most mummy films draw inspiration from tales that emphasize the mysterious and horrific, like French Orientalist Théophile Gautier's (1840) "The Mummy's Foot." Two stories written in 1890 by Arthur Conan Doyle, who was fascinated by the occult, have

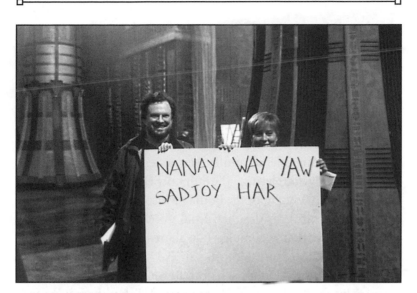

Figure 2.1. The author on the set of *Stargate.* Cue cards like this one, which translates "I am not amused," helped Jaye Davidson remember his lines.
Photo courtesy of Stuart Tyson Smith.

contributed the most to the mummy genre. "Lot 249" involves an Oxford Egyptology student who uses spells from a papyrus to revive and control a mummy with deadly consequences. In the end, the hero forces the evil genius to burn both the mummy and the papyrus scroll. An Egyptologist stumbles on an ageless Egyptian who unwraps a mummy in the Louvre in "The Ring of Thoth." He is not actually a mummy, but has stayed alive for 3,000 years through a special elixir. The mummy is that of his long, lost love, who he wants to rejoin in death, not revive. The former was clearly the inspiration for the shambling, horror film mummy Kharis, and the latter for Boris Karloff's masterful portrayal of the cursed Egyptian priest Imhotep, but Conan Doyle's contribution to the mummy genre went uncredited (Lupton 2003).

After *Cléopâtre* (1899), no less than two dozen mummy films came out *before* the discovery of Tutankhamen's tomb, but the understated creepiness of Karl Freund's Universal production *The Mummy* (1932), starring Boris Karloff, sets the basic plot elements as well as supplying a benchmark for later films. In the film, archaeologists find the tomb of Egyptian prince

Imhotep, who was cursed and buried alive for stealing the Scroll of Thoth in order to resurrect Princess Anckesenamon. Heedless of the curse, one of the archaeologists reads the scroll aloud and revives the mummy, who searches for his lost love, finally finding her reincarnated in the half Egyptian heroine, Helen Grosvenor. Eventually, Imhotep is defeated and crumbles into dust when the goddess Isis burns the Scroll of Thoth.

The idea of mobile mummies was not entirely alien to ancient Egypt. The papyrus relating "The Story of Setna Khaemwas and the Mummies" was bought for the Boulaq Museum (now the Egyptian Museum in Cairo) on the then legal antiquities market around 1865. This remarkably complex tale shares a number of plot elements with *The Mummy* (Simpson 2003:453–469), and very likely served as an inspiration for screenwriter John Balderston, who as a journalist had covered the discovery of Tutankhamen's tomb and was well versed in Egyptology (Lupton 2003). Paleographic analysis dates it to the early Ptolomaic period (ca. 300–200 BCE), but the story may go back as far as the New Kingdom, when the protagonist lived (ca. 1250 BCE). In it, Setna tries to steal the cursed Book of Thoth from a tomb and is opposed by the mummy of Naneferkaptah and the spirits of his wife and child. Setna fails to heed their tale of the disastrous consequences of their sacrilege in possessing the scroll, which was placed in their tomb to keep it away from mortals. Later, Setna realizes his mistake and returns the scroll, agreeing as a penance to reunite Naneferkaptah's mummy with those of his wife and son, who were buried far away. In an episode strikingly similar to the scene with Karloff's mummy, Naneferkaptah appears as an old man and leads Setna to the tomb of his loved ones.

In *The Mummy*, Imhotep uses magic to attack, paralyze, and bend people to his will. These actions and Imhotep's fate share some similarities with real events in New Kingdom Egypt. Administrative documents discovered at Thebes relate how conspirators were caught and convicted of stealing a sacred book of spells and using them for similar purposes in the plot to assassinate New Kingdom Pharaoh Ramses III (ca. 1151 BCE). The papyrus trial transcripts reveal both the offense and "great punishments of death" proscribed for the criminals by the gods (Redford 2002). At least one of the conspirators, probably Ramses III's son Pentawere, may have been buried alive in an unmarked coffin found in the Deir el Bahri royal cache of thirty-seven mummies. Bound and tightly wrapped, "Unknown Man E" suffered the further indignity of being sewn up in a ritually unclean sheepskin (Brier 2006). This archaeological discovery clearly influenced Balderston's screenplay and had a major impact on the mummy genre.

Universal's later Kharis series of Grade B mummy movies, starting with *The Mummy's Hand*, differ from the 1932 classic in that Kharis appears always as a mummy—a kind of vengeful automaton directed by the high priest of a secret priesthood of Karnak, a plot line remarkably similar to Conan Doyle's "Lot 249" (1890b). In each film, the archaeologists who desecrate Egypt's tombs pay the ultimate price at Kharis's mummified hands. This avenging, shambling horror became the prevailing popular image of the mummy in film, including Hammer Studios 1959 revival *The Mummy*.

The fourth Hammer mummy offering, *Blood from the Mummy's Tomb* (1972), drew on Bram Stoker's novel *Jewel of the Seven Stars* (1903). This story also involves a cursed tomb, that of the immortality-seeking sorceress-queen Tera. Ignoring warnings, the archaeologists enter the tomb, releasing Tera's spirit, who possesses the Egyptologist's daughter at birth. When the heroine reaches adulthood, the queen becomes increasingly assertive, so the archaeologists try to return her soul to her mummy with disastrous consequences. In spite of a tendency to emphasize the mystical and occult, Stoker's novel contains many correct historical and archaeological details. The idea that an evil spirit could possess an infant is something that was actually guarded against in Egyptian magic (Pinch 1994:147–160)—the one exception to the absence of any idea of reincarnation in Egyptian theology. This is actually pointed out in the 1980 remake, *The Awakening*, arguably the most archaeologically accurate mummy movie.

Universal's recent blockbuster remake and sequel *The Mummy* and *The Mummy Returns* merged all of these elements, creating a mummy that was revived by a spell from the Book of the Dead, starts out as a horror, but ends up as a powerful magician intent on reviving his lost love Anckesenamon. Added to the basic mummy plot is a strong infusion of Indiana Jones archaeology adventure combined with a dash of biblical content—a kind of apocalyptic Exodus.

Real Mummies— The Archaeology of Life after Death in Ancient Egypt

Ya-HEY TIY-soo (Oho! Rise Up!)
SISH-poo en-ak TA-pak (Receive your head!)
YIN-qoo en-ak qes-AW-ak (Collect your bones!)
SIA-qoo en-ak 'ey-OOT-ak (Gather your limbs!)
WIKH-aoo en-ak TAA ya-RA ya-WEF-ek
        (Shake the earth from your flesh!)[2]

Hollywood's focus on forbidden magic, marauding mummies, and curses, although not entirely without Egyptological foundation, obscures the complex and nuanced realities of ancient Egyptian religious beliefs in the afterlife. To be fair, Hollywood's concentration on the sensational was influenced by Egyptology's early quest for spectacular finds and resulting focus on tombs of the elite, which filled European and U.S. museums. Ironically, Balderston's script for *The Mummy* has Sir Joseph Whemple, the leader of the British Museum's expedition, assert that "more has been learned from studying bits of broken pottery than from all the sensational finds—and our job is to increase the sum of human knowledge of the past, not to satisfy our own curiosity" (Riley 1989:A-3).

The spell above from the pyramid texts does give the appearance of being meant to revive a corpse, but in reality it was meant to revive the dead in the afterlife, not this life. Nevertheless, the deceased did not leave the earth permanently for a remote heaven. Instead, the ancient Egyptians believed that the dead remained tied to both worlds, traveling between them. They made mummies as a vessel for their souls to occupy in the tomb (Ikram and Dodson 1998). There they could receive offerings and appeals from the living. Around 3,000 years ago, the scribe Butehamun left a touching letter by the mummy of his wife, asking her "How do you fare? How are you? ... Woe you beautiful one, who has no equal ... you have been taken away from me. ... Oh Akhtay, you gracious one as woman" (Romer 1984:187).

More than that, archaeologists have found papyri, amulets, and ex-*votos* offerings to the dead in tombs, temples, and houses, reflecting a belief that the spirits of the dead could intervene in life in both negative and positive ways. They could assist people by helping expel demons that might attack them, but they could also inflict disease and bad luck on the living (Pinch 1994). In a plot that Hollywood should love, Naneferkaptah's spirit torments Setna Khaemwas with horrific-erotic dreams to get him to return the Book of Thoth (Simpson 2003:453–469). A spirit could also physically attack the living, particularly those who might violate their tombs. In an inscription placed prominently in his tomb, Ankhmahor threatens: "As for any person who will enter into this tomb of mine in their impurity ... I shall seize him like a goose (wring his neck), placing fear in him at seeing ghosts upon earth, that they might be fearful of an excellent Spirit" (Silverman 1997:146). A number of tombs had such curses placed on them. The most famous curse of all, however, is bogus. Novelist Marie Corelli invented a curse for Tutankhamen's tomb, plagiarizing an older Arabic account of an ancient curse that "they who enter this sacred tomb shall swift be visited by wings of death" (Silverman 1997:146).

The ancient Egyptians themselves were far more concerned with ensuring the soul's passage through the afterlife, conceived as a series of trials and obstacles that led up to a divine judgment. The Pyramid Texts (ca. 2300 BCE), which evolve into the Coffin Texts (ca. 2000 BCE), which in turn become the Book of the Dead (ca. 1500 BCE), were constantly evolving guidebooks and aids for the afterlife (Hornung 1999). Egyptian priests expended a huge amount of effort and creativity to provide the dead with better and better means of achieving this goal. Earlier generations of scholars were disappointed that the Egyptians expended so much energy on this activity rather than engaging in philosophical and scientific study. This cleverness and trouble the ancient Egyptians took for their dead can also be seen as a reflection of a touching love of life and family.

An increasing array of amulets helped to protect the body and soul of the deceased (Andrews 1994). Scarabs are particularly common, often found on the third finger of the left hand. They represent Khepri, the manifestation of the sun god Re who appears as the rejuvenated rising sun. As a result, the scarab was a potent symbol of rebirth in the afterlife, alluded to by Karloff as Ardeth Bey in *The Mummy* (1932) when he says that Helen "shall dawn anew in the East as the first rays of Amon-Ra dispel the shadows" (Riley 1989:L-57). The Egyptians believed that the soul resided in the heart, which, unlike in the recent *Mummy*, was left within the body.[3] As the seat of morality, the heart was placed on a scale against the feather of *Maat*, truth and righteousness. If they balanced, then the soul was judged "true of voice" and became immortal. If the heart failed to balance with the feather, then the fearsome, crocodile-headed demoness Ammut, literally "the gobbler," ate the soul. For those feeling a bit guilty, a spell from the Book of the Dead (Faulkner 1994:no. 30b) was written on heart scarabs, compelling the heart not to testify against the deceased before the divine tribunal or tip the scales during the divine judgment. Just to hedge their bets, Egyptian priests—who invented the notion of back-up systems—came up with the "Negative Confession," a list of crimes and sacrilegious acts that the deceased did not commit, including nibbling on the divine food offerings, something that must have been quite common!

Once justified, the deceased entered into the Fields of Reeds and Offerings, where they lived with the gods in a kind of bucolic paradise. This afterlife lifestyle was not all fun and games. The gods regularly called on the deceased to work in the fields and orchards of these divine lands. The ancient Egyptian priests were, however, up to the challenge, inventing Ushabtis. Literally "the Answerer," these mummy-shaped figurines were activated by another spell from the Book of the Dead (Faulkner 1994:no. 6), which caused the statuette to leap up and answer for the deceased "Here I am!" whenever the gods called on them to work. During the New Kingdom (ca. 1500 BCE), their numbers start to multiply, eventually resulting in a standard set of 365, one for each day of the year. The priests were always thinking, and decided that an overseer Ushabti, complete with little starched scribal kilt, was required to keep each ten normal ones in line, for a total of 401. By

Figure 2.2. Mummy recovered from an excavation in the Theban necropolis. The exceptional preservation is typical of mummification's highest development from the Late Period (ca. 600 BC) onward.

Photo by Stuart Tyson Smith.

the Late Period (ca. 600 BCE), sets were mass produced in molds for those on a budget (Ikram and Dodson 1998).

One unexpected and interesting result of a systematic study of intact 17th- and 18th-Dynasty (ca. 1650–1300 BCE) burials from the Theban necropolis, including the Valley of the Kings (Smith 1991, 1992), was that some practices and items that Egyptologists typically regard as a standard component of a burial were, in fact, restricted to the elite (Figure 2.2). For example, in *The Mummy* Dr. Muller exclaims in surprise (Riley 1989:A-3) that the "viscera were not removed—the usual scar made by the embalmer's knife is not there!" Muller should not have been astonished. In contrast to conventional wisdom, only those of the highest status had the procedure done. Even among these privileged few, the practice was not ubiquitous. X-rays show that the mummies of Kha and Merit show no evidence of evisceration, even though their burials are among the richest ever found (Curto and Mancini 1968). The same applies to heart scarabs, Ushabtis, and the Book of the Dead. Film and Egyptology share a common emphasis on elite culture and the spectacular that neglects the lives of ordinary Egyptians. The non-elite focused on the basics, simple mummification (drying with the desiccant natron and wrapping), the magical and physical protection offered by a coffin, along with a scarab or two, a few items from daily life, and food offerings to sustain the soul of the deceased.

An unusual burial was discovered next to an elite pyramid tomb in the New Kingdom colonial cemetery at Tombos in Sudanese Nubia that paints a more prosaic picture of mummies (Figure 2.3). The body of a child had a string of small amulets around his or her neck, including Bes, a popular protective dwarf god, and the hippo goddess Taweret, patroness of women and children. They were just simple things made of glass, but one can imagine distraught parents sending their beloved child into the Afterlife with the best protection that they could afford—mummification, a coffin, and a string of amulets. As excavation continued, it became apparent that the child was buried face down, an unusual treatment that also

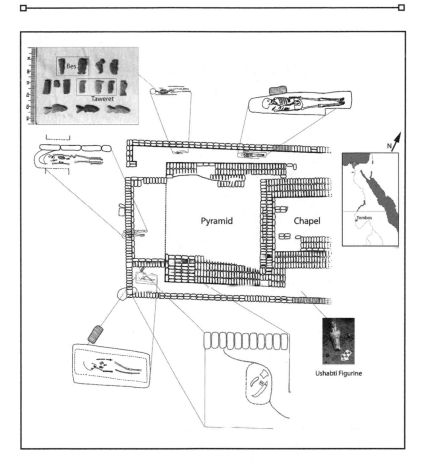

Figure 2.3. Burials of an adult and three children, one upside-down, around the pyramid of Siamun and Weren at Tombos in Sudanese Nubia, ca. 1400 BCE. Although their wrappings have decayed, they were all originally mummified.

occurs in Egypt (Smith 2003). The mummy of an elite man from Thebes named Boki shows that this was not deliberate but rather reflects human error. Boki appeared to be wrapped normally with obvious feet and a nose (Hayes 1935), but when the wrappings were removed Boki was lying on his face. The embalmers had clearly lost track of which side was up and picked the wrong side, adding padding to create artificial feet and a face!

It's a Wrap! Hollywood and Modern Mummy Mythology

The whole keystone of our old life in Egypt
was not the inscriptions or monuments
of which you make so much, but was our
hermetic philosophy and mystic knowledge of
which you say little or nothing.

—Sosra to the Egyptologist (Conan Doyle 1890a)

The recent success of the Universal remake and its sequel shows that the mummy genre still fascinates the public. To give an authentic feel to both movies, the Universal Studios production team hired me to re-create spoken Egyptian. The notion that no one knows how ancient Egyptian was spoken is a common myth going back to Roman misinterpretations of hieroglyphs as a symbolic system; in spite of their appearance, hieroglyphs do spell out words and thus represent the world's first phonetic script.[4] Vowels, which are not written, and accents must be reconstructed through a comparison between Coptic and transcriptions of Egyptian names into cuneiform and Greek (Loprieno 1995).

Coptic is a very late stage of Egyptian that is still used as a liturgical language in the Coptic Christian Church. It was written with vowels in a modified Greek alphabet starting around 200 CE. Some Egyptian words and grammar, usually embedded in names like Ramesses (literally, Ra-bore-him), appear in diplomatic correspondence written in Akkadian cuneiform (a syllabary), the diplomatic lingua franca of the era, in particular the Amarna Letters and Hittite Royal Archives (ca. 1400–1200 BC, contemporary with the ancient setting for the films). For example, Ramesses would originally have been pronounced something like REE-ah-ma-SAY-soo—quite different from the standard Egyptological pronunciation, which for convenience ignores both vowels and syllabic structure.[5]

Steven Sommers, the writer and director, kept my archaeological suggestions right next to his script during the shoot, using some of the information. For example, the heroine correctly calls the embalming place the *Sah-Netjer*. Sommers also avoided gemstones in the treasure and used bronze, not iron, for weapons. Finally, he adopted the use of the term *Medjay* for pharaoh's bodyguard—the subtlest Egyptological reference in the film. These Nubian nomads formed an elite police force during the New Kingdom, surviving appropriately in the film as a band of desert warriors who protect Hamunaptra.

Some plot elements, although appearing improbable, are consistent with archaeological discoveries. For example, although normal scarabs (dung beetles) eat dung and not flesh, a spell from the Book of the Dead does ward off the fearsome Apshai beetles that threatened to consume the deceased on their harrowing journey toward immortality in the Afterlife (Faulkner 1994). The scene where the villainess Ancksunamun battles the heroine Nefertiri (real queen to Ramesses II, Seti I's successor) combines Hollywood sensuality with the common New Kingdom court entertainment of bouts between soldiers and foreigners (but *never* scantily clad princesses!).

In other cases, accuracy is sacrificed. For example, I informed Sommers that the Book of Dead is the most common papyrus to survive from ancient Egypt with copies in museums all around the world; yet for effect, the film presents it as a legendary, unique hinged book and not the familiar scroll. Perhaps the most glaring mistake is in the scenes of mummification, where in spite of advice to the contrary, five, not four, canopic jars are used. Canopic jars held the separately mummified internal organs (Ikram and Dodson 1998), which never included the heart—the fifth canopic jar in the film was an idea likely inspired by the 1959 Hammer remake. Although in rare cases the heart was temporarily extracted during the embalming process, it was always replaced into the chest cavity.

Sommers' films were drawn from his imagination, inspired by dozens of mummy movies. The original films were informed by popular writers like Bram Stoker and Arthur Conan Doyle.

The fashionable spiritualist movement of the day and the notion of Egypt's "hidden wisdom" influenced both authors, leading to the idea of reincarnation and the physical revival of mummies. It would be easy to rail against Hollywood for planting misconceptions in moviegoers' heads, but these ideas extend back into antiquity. To the Hellenistic world, Egypt was a place of mystery, magic, and sensuality. As Jan Assmann (2003) points out, although misguided, this view of Egypt should not be dismissed out of hand. Hellenes observed and misunderstood the Egyptian culture of that time, blending it with their own to create hybrid philosophies and generate new mystery cults. Hermeticism comes from this milieu (Pinch 1994:161–177) and includes the concept of reincarnation.

Adherents of the occult insist that the beliefs reflected in the *Corpus Hermeticum* (ca. 100–200 CE) have deep roots in Egyptian religion. Conan Doyle (1890a:74) expresses this popular belief through Sosra's comment. This is a telling remark that reflects a fundamental break between the popular imagined Egypt and our archaeological and historical knowledge of Egyptian civilization. It goes back to the translation of Egyptian hieroglyphs in 1822 by Champollion, whose genius lay in recognizing that the signs were not symbolic and allegorical, in line with hermetic philosophy, but primarily phonetic, spelling out words. Since that time, there have been two intellectual tracks dealing with ancient Egypt: the occult, emphasizing mysteries and reincarnation, and the academic, informed by translations of often mundane inscriptions and the potsherds that Sir Joseph praises in 1932's *The Mummy*.

Films haven't really created mummy myths, but instead reflect deeply and long-held notions about the nature of ancient Egyptian civilization. Ancient Egypt provides rich textual, art historical, and archaeological records that, when integrated together, yield insights into not only the male elite, who speak to us directly through writing and representations, but also the ordinary men and women, often neglected by Egyptologists as well as filmmakers, who made up the bulk of Egypt's population. Archaeology can reveal the actions and beliefs of individuals who lived in the distant past but left no historical record for us to follow. Archaeology can give these people a voice, make them live again, and replace misconceptions of Egypt's mystical past in film and popular culture with an appreciation of their complex desires and beliefs.

Notes

1. Director Roland Emmerich, producer and writer Dean Devlin, and stars of *Stargate* were keen to get the ancient Egyptian language and background right, so I was brought into every stage of the production. Along with a genuine interest in Egyptology, they wanted to enhance the suspension of disbelief given the outlandish space aliens premise.

2. Pyramid Text Spell 373, ca. 2300 BCE (Faulkner 1969), pronunciation reconstructed by me for *The Mummy Returns* (2001). Capitals indicate accent—do not recite anywhere near mummies!

3. This was done despite my pointing out this error in comments on the script.

4. Sumerian is earlier but composed of logograms.

5. This fact provides a solid basis for the main conceit of *Stargate* (1994), that the protagonist could not initially understand the otherworldly language, but quickly learned how to communicate—as Egyptologist Daniel Jackson, played by James Spader, explains in dialog I wrote. Note that several films feature ancient Egyptian with Egyptological pronunciation, including *The Mummy* (1932), although Ardeth Bey only recites ancient Egyptian royal names instead of actual spells (Riley 1989).

References

Andrews, Carol

    1994   *Amulets of Ancient Egypt*. University of Texas Press, Austin.

Assmann, Jan

2003   *The Mind of Egypt: History and Meaning in the Time of the Pharaohs.* Harvard University Press, Cambridge, MA.

Brier, Bob

2006   The Mystery of Unknown Man E. *Archaeology Magazine* 59(2):36–42.

Conan Doyle, Arthur

1890a   The Ring of Thoth. Reprinted 1988 in *Movie Monsters, Great Horror Film Stories,* Peter Haining, editor, pp. 66–83. Severn House, London.

1890b   Lot No. 249. Reprinted 1989 in *The Mummy. Stories of the Living Corpse,* Peter Haining, editor, pp. 47–80. Severn House, London.

Cowie, Susan D. and Tom Johnson

2002   *The Mummy in Fact, Fiction and Film.* McFarland, Jefferson, NC.

Curto, S. and M. Mancini

1968   News of Kha and Merit. *Journal of Egyptian Archaeology* 54:77–81.

Faulkner, R. O.

1969   *The Pyramid Texts.* Clarendon Press, Oxford.

1994   *The Egyptian Book of the Dead.* Chronicle Books, San Francisco, CA.

Gautier, Théophile

1840   The Mummy's Foot. Reprinted 1989 in *The Mummy. Stories of the Living Corpse,* Peter Haining, editor, pp. 126–136. Severn House, London.

Hayes, William C.

1935   The Tomb of Neferkhewet and His Family. *Bulletin of the Metropolitan Museum of Art Egyptian Expedition* 30:17–36.

Hornung, Erik

1999   *The Ancient Egyptian Books of the Dead.* Cornell University Press, Ithaca, NY.

Humbert, Jean-Marcel, Michael Pantazzi, and Christiane Ziegler

1994   *Egyptomania: Egypt in Western Art 1730–1930.* National Gallery of Canada, Ottawa.

Ikram, Salima and Aidan Dodson

1998   *The Mummy in Ancient Egypt: Equipping the Dead for Eternity.* Thames and Hudson, London.

Loprieno, Antonio

    1995   *Ancient Egyptian: A Linguistic Introduction.* Cambridge University Press, New York.

Lupton, Carter

    2003   "Mummymania" for the Masses—Is Egyptology Cursed by the Mummy's Curse? In *Consuming Ancient Egypt*, Sally MacDonald and Michael Rice, editors, pp. 23–46. University College London Press, London.

Pinch, Geraldine

    1994   *Magic in Ancient Egypt.* University of Texas Press, Austin.

Redford, Susan

    2002   *The Harem Conspiracy: The Murder of Ramesses III.* Northern Illinois University Press, DeKalb.

Riley, Philip J., editor

    1989   *The Mummy.* Universal Filmscripts Series Classic Horror Films, Volume 7. MagicImage Filmbooks, Absecon, NJ.

Romer, John

    1984   *Ancient Lives: Daily Life in Egypt of the Pharaohs.* Holt, Rinehart and Winston, New York.

Said, Edward W.

    1978   *Orientalism.* Pantheon Books, New York.

Silverman, David P., editor

    1997   *Ancient Egypt.* Oxford University Press, Oxford.

Simpson, William Kelley, editor

    2003.   *The Literature of Ancient Egypt.* Third Edition. Yale University Press, New Haven, CT.

Smith, Stuart T.

    1991   They Did Take It with Them: Requirements for the Afterlife Evidenced from Intact New Kingdom Tombs at Thebes. *KMT Magazine* 2(3):28–45.

    1992   Intact Theban Tombs and the New Kingdom Burial Assemblage. *Mitteilungen des Deutschen Archäologischen Instituts Kairo* 48:193–231.

    2003   *Wretched Kush: Ethnic Identities and Boundaries in Egypt's Nubian Empire.* Routledge, London.

Stoker, Bram

    1903   *The Jewel of the Seven Stars.* Reprinted 1999 by Sutton, Phoenix Mill, Gloucestershire, UK.

VIKINGS, VIXENS, AND VALHALLA

HOLLYWOOD DEPICTIONS OF THE NORSE

Mark Axel Tveskov and Jon M. Erlandson

● ●

In the 8th century AD, sea raiders began to sweep out of Scandinavia to attack communities across northern Europe, terrifying the region for centuries. These raids were part of a remarkable historical process of conquest, exploration, trade, and cultural interaction that changed the face of Europe and the broader North Atlantic region. Commonly referred to as "Vikings," these pagan Norse people ultimately conquered much of northwest Europe, established colonies in Iceland, Greenland, and North America, and influenced a vast area of the North Atlantic through trading and raiding, conquest, exploration, and intermarriage.

The Viking expansion was ultimately stalled by the gradual assimilation of Norse peoples in their new homelands and the spread of Christianity through Scandinavia. Climatic deterioration, resistance from indigenous communities in North America and Greenland, and the increasing isolation of these distant colonies also confined their cultural expansion. Yet long after the end of the historical Viking Age, the Norse have maintained an iconic, ambivalent, and almost mythical stature, and popular culture invokes this archetype without need of explanation: Hagar the Horrible, the Minnesota Vikings of the National Football League, and the barbarian horde in Capital One credit card commercials are just three of a legion of examples (Orrling 2000; Ward 2000). Both scientific research and popular representations—including Hollywood movies—bear responsibility for the evolution of the modern Viking archetype, which continues to hold an important but ambiguous place in Western culture.

Our modern interest in the Norse evolved in concert with modern northern European and North American nations, as state ideology has always been buttressed by an appeal to a romanticized past (Roesdahl and Sørensen 1996; Orrling 2000:354; Ward 2000). By the 19th century, most of the ancient Icelandic sagas were available in modern translations, and Norse themes had entered contemporary Scandinavian artwork, literature, music, and theater. By the turn of the 20th century, as the pace of industrialization and rural development accelerated, many of the major Viking-age excavations had taken place, and classic images of Viking material culture, such as those offered by the Oseberg ship or the Danish site of Trelleborg, had entered the popular imagination (Orrling 2000).

The sustained power of Norse imagery was demonstrated during World War II, when Vikings symbols were used by the Germans in an all-too successful campaign to recruit young Danish and Norwegian men into the SS. Simultaneously, the Danes employed Norse symbols in their underground resistance to the Nazi occupation (Lönnroth 1997:247; Orrling 2000:356–362). To this day, an image from the rune stone at Jelling—the supposed 10th-century birthplace of the modern Danish royal dynasty—adorns the Danish passport. Academic research continues to contribute to the myth-making process; arguably few other archaeological subject areas generate as many popular magazine articles, books, and documentaries as Norse archaeology (Jones

1968; Fitzhugh and Ward 2000).

Norse imagery, as well as local Viking "finds," have also been embraced by Scandinavian immigrants to North America (Lönnroth 1997:244–245; Ward 2000:366). The 1837 publication of the *Vinland Sagas* in English was greeted enthusiastically and prompted a concerted search for Viking settlements and relics on the west side of the Atlantic (Wallace and Fitzhugh 2000:375). That the vast majority of these proved fraudulent seemed largely irrelevant, particularly within the Scandinavian American communities where most were uncovered. Even the National Museum of the United States was enveloped by the thought of ancient European exploration; one of the most famous finds, the Kensington Rune Stone, was displayed at the Smithsonian in 1948 despite nearly unanimous agreement among scholars that it was a fake perpetrated by a Swedish immigrant to Minnesota (Wallace and Fitzhugh 2000:381–384). The discovery of a real Norse settlement at L'ans aux Meadows in Newfoundland ultimately confirmed the saga accounts of Norse visits to the western Atlantic, and the site's fame and popularity attests to the appeal of academic research that reinforces the public's expectation to see Vikings as intrepid explorers (Wallace 1993, 2000).

The voracious public appetite for both academic and popular depictions confirms the mythic and ideological significance of the Vikings to North American and northern European people and the importance of the heroic and nationalistic themes that are reinforced in these representations. The ideology is often barely concealed, even in academic treatments: the preface of an English-language volume produced by the Viking Ship Museum in Roskilde, Denmark, points out that the authors deliberately selected "the year 1992—the 500th anniversary of Columbus's voyage of discovery—in which to present an exhibition and a book about Viking voyages to America" (Meldgaard 1993:5), and Hillary Rodham Clinton (2000:8–9), in prefacing a lavish Smithsonian Institution volume released in 2000, wrote:

> Our children and grandchildren will only learn about the courage and ingenuity of these explorers who came to our

shores one thousand years ago, and touched so many other shores as well, if we are prepared to help them learn. ... Because, after all, what the Vikings really convey to us over all these centuries is the power of the human spirit and the universal urge to find and cross new horizons.

The Viking of Hollywood Movies

Viking archetypes commonly inhabit Hollywood movies. Sometimes they are presented in highly fictionalized, fantastic, or satirical settings. For example, in Disney's *The Island on Top of the World* (1974), Victorian explorers encounter a lost Viking colony in an Arctic valley, and *Erik the Viking* (1989) presents an unfathomably silly portrayal of the Norse that includes Mickey Rooney as a Viking chieftain. Arnold Schwarzenegger's lead character in the Conan the Barbarian franchise and the Riders of Rohan in the *Lord of the Rings* take this further, as these characters live in wholly fictional worlds but are painted with Viking trappings. Alternatively, and perhaps more problematically, some movies place "Vikings" at the center of a fictional narrative but attempt to represent the Norse in a historically and culturally accurate way. The lavish production value, narrative power, and the obvious care taken in researching what Vikings were "really like" combine in these films to create a vehicle that powerfully innovates and reproduces the Norse archetype. Unfortunately, because of and despite their apparent "authenticity," problematic social relations and stereotypes are frequently legitimized in such films.

One of the earliest so-called authentic Hollywood cinematic representations is *The Vikings* (1958), directed by Richard Fleischer and based on a novel by Edison Marshall (1951). This star-studded Greek drama of a movie features Tony Curtis as Eric, the orphaned son of an English queen raped by Ragnar, a Viking chieftain played by Ernest Borgnine. Eric is taken as a slave by

Ragnar and raised alongside his half-brother Einar, played by Kirk Douglas, in a Norse village in Norway. Eventually, both Eric and Einar fall in love with Morgana, a captured Welsh princess played by Janet Leigh. In his quest to regain his birthright, Curtis ends up killing both his father and brother but gains both the throne of Northumbria and the hand of the lovely Morgana. A more recent but similar film, *The 13th Warrior* (1999), directed by John McTiernan and based on a novel by Michael Crichton (1988), features Antonio Banderas as a fictionalized version of Ibn Fahdlan, a 10th-century Arab writer who left us some of the most vivid first-hand descriptions of the Norse based on his travels on the Volga River (Jones 1968:164). The Hollywood Fahdlan also encounters Norse traders in Russia, but is surprised to find himself named the "13th" of a group of warriors mandated by a Norse witch, who, in a shamanic trance, commands the men to return north and rescue a Viking village from the depredations of a band of mysterious marauders known as the "Eaters of the Dead." They accomplish their mission with much adventure and mayhem.

These movies and others like them present a well-defined signifier—a consistent image of who the Norse were that is easily digestible to modern sensibilities. In almost all cases, Vikings are presented as fundamentally irrational: they compulsively shout "Hail Ragnor! Hail Einar!" whenever they meet one another and are prone to fits of laughter or explosive violence with little provocation. In the *13th Warrior*, for example, the Viking warrior Buliwyf arises from a drunken stupor to behead a rival at the funeral of his chief. Notwithstanding this machismo, Vikings are prone to child-like fits of tears over seemingly silly things and, despite their celebrated prowess as explorers, display irrationally superstitious fears of natural phenomena such as fog.

Gender roles are sharply inscribed in these movies, and Viking men are portrayed as heroic, physically adroit, and wily. One striking scene shows Kirk Douglas and other members of his crew running, with child-like enthusiasm, along the outstretched oars of their Viking ship. In *The 13th Warrior*, the character Herger wins a duel by initially feigning ineptitude, thereby lulling his much larger opponent into a false sense of security. Throughout the films, Viking men display brute strength, endurance, valor, and fortitude as well as supreme skill in sword fighting, archery, and other martial arts. Of course, they are also intrepid explorers and fearlessly pilot their ships to the ends of the earth through storms, jagged reefs, and whirlpools. A sea-sick Fahdlan can only raise his head up enough to catch a glimpse of Buliwyf and Herger manfully and proudly standing at the steering oar of their ship as it is lashed by a North Atlantic gale.

Viking women, on the other hand, are generally portrayed either as drudges, wenches, or healers (if they are young and beautiful), or as superstitious witches (if they are not). Both *The Vikings* and *The 13ᵗʰ Warrior* show older women as shamans who master supernatural forces amid much moaning, careening with the wind, and divination. The Viking men regard these women with reverence, awe, and resentment. Young women appear only to submissively serve mead, to offer bandages after battle, or to serve as objects to be conquered. It is notable that one of the few strong and independent younger female characters in the movies is Morgana in *The Vikings,* who is not Norse. Still, nearly all of her actions are motivated and dictated by her relationships with men.

The debaucherous ale- or mead-drinking party held in a Viking longhouse is a scene so common and stylized that it appears to be a mandatory component of any Viking movie. In this scene, all of the typical irrational, violent, heroic, and salacious behaviors are mixed together in one fun-filled evening. Apparently, Vikings were incapable of quaffing ale from their drinking horns without spilling it all over their beards, and a vat of ale the size of a hot tub—tended diligently by comely wenches—was standard equipment in any respectable Norse house. One wonders if in the Viking Age, such vats were available from Ikea, shipped across the North Atlantic Norse sphere of influence unassembled in convenient flat boxes.

The consistency of the images presented in these movies is

striking. What differs from film to film, however, is what the Norse had to offer civilized people. In *The Vikings,* the pagan Norse remain completely unredeemable savages. Throughout the film, Anglo-Saxons are generally depicted as civilized Christians living in castles and farming the land. In contrast, the Norse are almost never seen tilling the land or engaging in any "civilized" behavior. Instead, they are depicted as irrationally violent and, perhaps more tacitly but more powerfully, as rapacious. The movie opens with a rape scene and this rapaciousness is reinforced in another scene where a woman accused of adultery is placed in bondage while her drunken husband hurls axes at her. Ragnar explains that if the husband kills her, she is guilty. If her braids are cut, she is innocent. Ragnar later confides proudly to his son that he, in fact, had taken Einar's own mother by force, and gives him permission to rape Morgana, despite the fact that, thus sullied, she would be rendered unusable as a hostage. Morgana foils his advances and he remains childishly confused by her lack of response to his aggressiveness.

Eric, on the other hand, spends the entire movie using his innately civilized manner to overcome his adopted savage heritage. Despite his Norse upbringing, Eric is kind, circumspect, and intelligent. He easily and adroitly handles a hunting hawk when Einar can't—a simple metaphor of the successful "dominion over nature" valued by civilized people. Nevertheless, he is torn between the civilized nature of his ancestry and his loyalty to the savagery of his upbringing: loyalty, too, being a civilized quality. In one scene, the English king orders him to cast the captive Ragnar into a pit of ravenous wolves. Unable to allow even his former slave master such an ignominious death, he disobeys. He cuts Ragnar's bindings loose, gives him a sword, and allows him to die as a Viking should. This loyalty to his adopted pagan heritage is costly; the English king, as punishment, has Eric's hand cut off. Mutilation is also used as metaphor for the price of being a savage earlier in the film when Einar's handsome visage is horribly defaced by a hawk.

In stark contrast to *The Vikings*, produced in the 1950s, *The 13th Warrior*, released in 1999, presents the Norse as the antidote for civilization and everything civilized man is *not* but that, deep down, he really *needs*. Fahdlan is disillusioned and at odds with his civilized upbringing and seeks his rite of passage and true manhood by immersing himself in the savage ways of the Vikings. Initially, the effeminate Fahdlan is dismayed and offended by the sheer savagery of the Norse, their elemental violence, poor hygiene, and superstition. This is a quest for Fahdlan, however, and over the course of the movie the Norse are revealed to be the salt of the earth: intelligent, egalitarian, crafty, noble, loyal, and even gentle. Many scenes in the movie involve Banderas reflecting that, "Hey, these guys aren't so savage after all."

Interestingly, the sexual violence of the *The Vikings* is left out of *The 13th Warrior*, despite a terrific opportunity: The historical Ibn Fahdlan provided one of the only surviving eyewitness account of a dead Viking's burial in a burning ship (Jones 1968:426–430). In the historical account, the throat of one of the dead man's female slaves is cut as she is sacrificed into the funeral pyre, but only after all of his surviving shipmates have sex with her. The historical accuracy of this account has been debated, but it seems telling that neither the sex nor the sacrifice is portrayed in the movie.

Despite the patina of authenticity offered by these movies, their portrayals of rationality, social relations, and gender roles are clearly more about the present than the past. In *The Vikings*, Norse men are used to celebrate the achievements of civilization and to be successful, the characters must shed and reject their savagery—sentiments that surely resonated in postwar North America. In the more recent *The 13th Warrior*, on the other hand, civilized man has clearly lost something … something not fully appreciated until he is thrown into savagery. In the end, Fahdlan returns home, reflecting on his experiences in a voice-over by saying "May Allah bless the pagan Northmen, who share their food and their blood, and helped Ibn Fahdlan become a Man."

The Viking of Archaeology and History

Each of these movies clearly benefited from "historical research" and the input of expert consultants. Each makes a laudable attempt to portray Viking material culture accurately, and although one can quibble over details, the care taken in the construction of the houses, weapons, costumes, and other artifacts is generally apparent. Ships, of course, are central to the Viking archetype, and academics and members of the public alike have long been enamored of Norse maritime technology. Viking ships were clinker-built and flexible and used oars, sails, and a shallow draft to allow the Norse to explore, settle, and raid across the Atlantic and the Mediterranean and down the river systems of Asia to the Black Sea (Noonan 1997; Christensen 2000).

The ships enshrined at the museums in Oslo and Roskilde rarely fail to impress. The aesthetic qualities of Norse ships, from the sleek design to the bow and stern-post carvings, reflect a sublime melding of form and function. The producers of these movies clearly enjoyed the opportunity to employ the strength of Hollywood cinematography to portray Viking ships, and each movie contains scenes of Viking ships and their crews "in action." Such scenes are a central part of *The Vikings* in particular, where cinematographer Jack Cardiff and director Richard Fleisher built three complete Viking ships based on plans derived from study of the Gokstad and Oseberg ships. The scenes of these ships sailing up the Norwegian fjord where the film was shot are spectacular indeed.

Unfortunately, this patina of authenticity masks and ultimately legitimates more problematic aspects of the archetype. The basic stereotype of a savage yet heroic Viking society remains unchallenged. For example, Hollywood Vikings are rarely shown actually doing any work, but academic research suggests that fishing and hunting, raising stock and growing wheat, spinning wool and baking bread, and other mundane tasks were the basic realities of daily Norse life rather than raiding England or questing after supernatural beasts (Kaland and Martens 2000). The gender roles portrayed in the movies are particularly problematic. In contrast to their Hollywood portrayal, Norse women enjoyed "independent authority and were respected members of their own social class," and the Icelandic saga literature portrays both men and women in positions of religious authority (Sørensen 1997; Roesdahl 1998:59; Jørgensen 2000:84). Although the Norse were indeed raiders, the films neglect the equally important point made by archaeologists and historians that the Viking Age was also characterized by the expanding trading networks that saw the Norse facilitating the movement of goods across much of the North Atlantic, European, and Mediterranean worlds (Roesdahl 1998:78–128).

Archaeological research also emphasizes the complex social, political, and ecological relationships maintained by Norse people and how these relationships were transplanted and changed with the settlement of new lands (Berglund 2000; Price 2000; Vésteinsson 2000a, 2000b; Arneborg 2003). Our own research in Iceland considers the ways that 10th-century Norse settlers impacted the ecology of the local environment and how, over subsequent generations, their manipulation of the landscape was part of their negotiation of local social and economic relationships (Figure 3.1). At the Hrísbrú site in Mosfellsveit, for example, a pagan cremation burial mound was found side by side with an 11th-century Christian chapel constructed on top of an earlier domestic structure (Byock et al. 2003, 2005). For the inhabitants of Mosfellsveit, the landscape was itself an ideological and ever-changing monument to their status and identity within a social landscape marked by dramatic change as they settled the land and converted to Christianity. Some of the most compelling recent archaeological scholarship emphasizes similar questions of identity, particularly within the dynamic interactions that took place with the Inuit, Sámi, Scottish, Irish, and other peoples the Norse encountered (Nordtrup-Madson 2000; Barrett 2003; Olsen 2003; Schledermann and McCullough 2003).

Still, academic research, like Hollywood movies, often plays a hand in celebrating and fostering more heroic, mythic, or problematic themes. The Norse expansion across the Atlantic to the British Isles, Iceland, Greenland, and ultimately to North

Shawna Rider and Jon Erlandson excavating a portion of the 11th-century Norse Christian chapel excavated at Hrísbrú, Mosfellsveit, Iceland, in 2003 as part of the Mosfell Archaeological Project.

Photo by Mark Tveskov.

America was an important and dramatic event, and documenting the causes and effects of this expansion and the successes and failures of Norse settlements in these far-flung places is a favored area of research (Wallace 1993; Lynnerup 2000; Peterson 2000; Arneborg 2003). The frequent use of the term "Viking" by academics is itself a bit of Hollywood showmanship. Although this term clearly resonates with the public and invokes the Viking archetype, *víkingr*, as originally used in the saga literature, was most commonly "reserved for brutal and unpleasant characters" such as "beserk thugs or heartless pirates" (Lönroth 1997:230; Price 2000:36–37).

Similarly, although famous figures and events portrayed in

the saga literature are understandably celebrated in popular culture and literary studies, using saga accounts to guide archaeological research is challenging as they offer wholly different kinds of insight into the past than archaeological sites, artifacts, and environmental reconstructions. Archaeologists frequently underestimate the literary and political nature of the sagas as well as the complexity of their transcription and translation from the Viking Age to the Middle Ages to the modern day and frame their work around celebrating famous events and figures from the sagas (Ólason 1998; Vésteinsson 2000a, 2000b; Friðriksson and Vésteinsson 2003).

Archaeologists often find themselves "chasing lore" by conducting studies that seek to confirm literary accounts of famous people and events (Friðriksson and Vésteinsson 2003:141). More problematically, the subtleties of the research is often lost as scholars attempt to present their work to a wider audience; all too often, it is the most sophomoric of images—famous figures, events, or the "oldest" of a phenomenon—that impress the public in press accounts of archaeological research.

Conclusion

Today's mythic image of the Vikings was recursively constructed through academic research and popular culture against a backdrop of developing nationalism, modernity, and now postmodernity. Such archetypes express, reinforce, and challenge notions of our collective identity, and their invocation is an ideological statement—sometimes tacit, sometimes overt—that is related in complex ways to North American and northern European society (Lönnroth 1997; Orrling 2000; Ward 2000). The Viking—a heroic, savage, and ancestral figure—constitutes a complex archetype that we hold up to provide a distorted mirror image of ourselves. The use of this image in academic research, literature, artwork, comic books, commercials, sports mascots, and movies reveals not only how Vikings are perceived but also provides a lens with which to view how we see ourselves (Ward

2000:368). Both academic and popular interests in the Norse thrive within various versions of North American and northern European nationalist sentiment. As an ancestral archetype, Vikings represent qualities that we like to think we embrace, qualities that contrast our perceived modern successes against our savage ancestry, and nostalgic images of what we think we have lost in becoming the society we are today—and sometimes each of these simultaneously.

Hollywood movies—a dramatic and powerful form of popular mythic expression—present this archetype in sharp relief and provide a clear window into how this image is portrayed. In the 1950s and 1960s, Vikings, Native Americans, and other similar archetypes were irrational and savage foils that celebrated the triumphs of the modern world and provided assurance that we were not, in fact, childlike, sexual, or emotional. At the turn of the millennium, however, as our society finds itself frequently dissatisfied with and alienated from our received culture, the same classic archetypes of the Other are invoked in our quest for authenticity and reassurance. In many ways, *The 13th Warrior* is the same movie as *Dances with Wolves* (1990) or the *Last Samurai* (2003). Each features a civilized but disillusioned man—whether it is Antonio Banderas, Kevin Kostner, or Tom Cruise—who finds refuge, truth, and satisfaction among the primitives, be they Vikings, American Indians, or Japanese Samurai.

Still, one can hardly fault Hollywood filmmakers for the nature of their historical depictions. The real strength and beauty of novels, theater, or movies is the presentation of the drama of individual emotions and interpersonal interactions; Shakespeare's Julius Caesar is not a history of the Roman Empire, but an exploration of human ambition, jealousy, and frailty. When Hollywood filmmakers invoke the "Viking" or similar archetypes in an uncritical way to tell dramatic stories, they are doing what people always do: utilizing the archetypes accepted at the time. That Hollywood movies and other forms of popular culture celebrate and reproduce easily accessible but clearly problematic themes is perhaps more the fault of the historians and archaeologists that lend their expertise to the reproduction of these themes—either as consultants or as they conduct their research. More than a hundred years of scholarly research has provided detailed, critical, and nuanced descriptions of Norse society and culture and has described their history and ecology in detail. This is a story worth hearing for its drama, heroism, literary and artistic quality, and the lessons it provides for the present day. Yet, given the success of Hollywood images of the Other, archaeologists and historians clearly have been less than successful in telling this story in a compelling way.

References

Arneborg, Jette

>2003   Norse Greenland: Reflections on Settlement and Depopulation. In *Contact, Continuity, and Collapse: The Norse Colonization of the North Atlantic,* James H. Barrett, editor, pp. 163–182. Prepols Publishers, Turnhout, Belgium.

Barrett, James H.

>2003   Culture Contact in Viking Age Scotland. *In Contact, Continuity, and Collapse. The Norse Colonization of the North Atlantic,* James H. Barrett, editor, pp. 73–112. Prepols Publishers, Turnhout, Belgium.

Berglund, Joel

>2000   The Farm beneath the Sand. In *Vikings: The North Atlantic Saga,* William W. Fitzhugh and Elizabeth I. Ward, editors, pp. 295–303. Smithsonian Institution Press, Washington, DC.

Byock, Jesse, Phillip Walker, Jon Erlandson, Per Holck, Jackie Eng, Mark Tveskov, Magnus Sigurgeirsson, Patricia Lambert, Madonna Moss, Kaethin Prizer, Melissa Reid, Davide Zori, Ashley Byock, and Hilde Fyllingen

>2003   A Viking Age Farm, Church, and Cemetery at Hríbrú, Mosfell Valley, Iceland. Antiquity 77:297. Available online at: http://antiquity.ac.uk/ProjGall/erlandson/erlandson.html.

Byock, Jesse, Phillip Walker, Jon Erlandson, Per Holck, Davide Zori, Magnús Guðmundsson, and Mark Tveskov

>2005   A Viking-age Valley in Iceland: The Mosfell Archaeological Project. *Medieval Archaeology* 49(1):195–218.

Christensen, Arne Emil

2000   Ships and Navigation. In *Vikings: The North Atlantic Saga,* William W. Fitzhugh and Elizabeth I. Ward, editors, pp. 86–98. Smithsonian Institution Press, Washington, DC.

Clinton, Hillary R.

2000   Preface. In *Vikings: The North Atlantic Saga,* William W. Fitzhugh and Elizabeth I. Ward, editors, pp. 8–9. Smithsonian Institution Press, Washington, DC.

Crichton, Michael

1988   *Eaters of the Dead.* Ballantine Books, New York.

Fitzhugh, William W. and Elisabeth I. Ward, editors

2000   *Vikings: The North Atlantic Saga.* Smithsonian Institution Press, Washington, DC.

Friðriksson, Adolf and Orri Vésteinsson

2003   A Historiography of the Settlement of Iceland. In *Contact, Continuity, and Collapse: The Norse Colonization of the North Atlantic,* James H. Barrett, editor, pp. 139–162. Prepols Publishers, Turnhout, Belgium.

Jones, Gwyn

1968   *A History of the Vikings.* Oxford University Press, New York.

Jørgensen, Lars

2000   Political Organization and Social Life. In *Vikings: The North Atlantic Saga,* William W. Fitzhugh and Elizabeth I. Ward, editors, pp. 72–85. Smithsonian Institution Press, Washington, DC.

Kaland, Sigrid H. H. and Irmelin Martens

2000   Farming and Daily Life. In *Vikings: The North Atlantic Saga,* William W. Fitzhugh and Elizabeth I. Ward, editors, pp. 42–54. Smithsonian Institution Press, Washington, DC.

Lönroth, Lars

1997   The Vikings in History and Legend. In *The Oxford Illustrated History of the Vikings,* Peter Sawyer, editor, pp. 225–249. Oxford University Press, Oxford.

Lynnerup, Niels

2000   Life and Death in Norse Greenland. In *Vikings: The North Atlantic Saga,* William W. Fitzhugh and Elizabeth I. Ward, editors, pp. 285–294. Smithsonian Institution Press, Washington, DC.

Marshall, Edison

1951   *The Viking.* Farrar, Straus, and Young, New York.

Meldgaard, Jørgen

1993   Preface: Vinland Research 1832–1992. In *Viking Voyages to North America,* Birthe L. Clausen, editor, pp. 5–12. The Viking Ship Museum, Roskilde, Denmark.

Noonan, Niels s

1997   Scandinavians in European Russia. In *The Oxford Illustrated History of the Vikings,* Peter Sawyer, editor, pp. 134–155. Oxford University Press, Oxford.

Nordtrup-Madson, M. A.

2000   The Cultural Identity of the Late Greenland Norse. In *Identities and Culture Contacts in the Arctic,* Martin Appelt, Joel Berglud, and Hans Christian Gulløv, editors, pp. 55–60. Danish National Museum and Danish Polar Center, Copenhagen.

Ólason, Vésteinn

1998   *Dialogues with the Viking Age: Narration and Representation in the Sagas of the Icelanders.* Heimskringla, Reykjavík, Iceland.

Olsen, Bjørnar

2003   Belligerent Chieftains and Oppressed Hunters? Changing Conceptions of Interethnic Relationships in Northern Norway during the Iron Age and Early Medieval Period. In *Contact, Continuity, and Collapse: The Norse Colonization of the North Atlantic,* James H. Barrett, editor, pp. 9–32. Prepols Publishers, Turnhout, Belgium.

Orrling, Carin

2000   The Old Norse Dream. In *Vikings: The North Atlantic Saga,* William W. Fitzhugh and Elizabeth I. Ward, editors, pp. 354–364. Smithsonian Institution Press, Washington, DC.

Peterson, Hans Christian

2000   The Norse Legacy in Greenland. In *Vikings: The North Atlantic Saga,* William W. Fitzhugh and Elizabeth I. Ward, editors, pp. 340–350. Smithsonian Institution Press, Washington, DC.

Price, Neil S.

2000   The Scandinavian Landscape. In *Vikings: The North Atlantic Saga,* William W. Fitzhugh and Elizabeth I. Ward, editors, pp. 31–41. Smithsonian Institution Press, Washington, DC.

Roesdahl, Else

    1998   *The Vikings.* Second Edition. Penguin Books, London.

Roesdahl, Else and Preben Meulengracht Sørensen, editors

    1996   *The Waking of Angantyr: The Scandinavian Past in European Culture.* Actua Jutlandica Humanities Series 70, Aarhus University Press, Aarhus, Denmark.

Schledermann, P. and K. M. McCullough

    2003   Inuit-Norse Contact in the Smith Sound Region. In *Contact, Continuity, and Collapse: The Norse Colonization of the North Atlantic,* James H. Barrett, editor, pp. 9–32. Prepols Publishers, Turnhout, Belgium.

Sørensen, Preben Meulengracht

    1997   Religions Old and New. In *The Oxford Illustrated History of the Vikings,* Peter Sawyer, editor, pp. 202–224. Oxford University Press, Oxford.

Vésteinsson, Orri

    2000a   *The Christianization of Iceland: Priests, Power, and Social Change 1000–1300.* Oxford University Press, Oxford.

    2000b   The Archaeology of Landnám: Early Settlement in Iceland. In *Vikings: The North Atlantic Saga,* William W. Fitzhugh and Elizabeth I. Ward, editors, pp. 164–174. Smithsonian Institution Press, Washington, DC.

Wallace, Birgitta Linderoth

    1993   L'anse aux Meadows, the Western Outpost. In *Viking Voyages to North America,* Birthe L. Clausen, editor, pp. 30–42. The Viking Ship Museum, Roskilde, Denmark.

    2000   The Viking Settlement at L'Anse aux Meadows. In *Vikings: The North Atlantic Saga,* William W. Fitzhugh and Elizabeth I. Ward, editors, pp. 208–216. Smithsonian Institution Press, Washington, DC.

Wallace, Birgitta Linderoth and William W. Fitzhugh

    2000   Stumbles and Pitfalls in the Search for Viking America. In *Vikings: The North Atlantic Saga,* William W. Fitzhugh and Elizabeth I. Ward, editors, pp. 374–384. Smithsonian Institution Press, Washington, DC.

Ward, Elisabeth I.

    2000   Reflections on an Icon: Vikings in American Culture. In *Vikings: The North Atlantic Saga,* William W. Fitzhugh and Elizabeth I. Ward, editors, pp. 365–373. Smithsonian Institution Press, Washington, DC.

A PIRATE'S LIFE FOR ME!

BUT WHAT DID THAT REALLY MEAN?

Charles R. Ewen and Russell K. Skowronek

● ●

A pirate's life for me! This phrase, repeated endlessly on Disney's Pirates of the Caribbean ride, evokes images that, for most of us, were formed during childhood, more often than not from films. Usually, this was an image of somewhat scary bad men. They were only somewhat scary, not real enough or scary enough to cause us to lose sleep at night. Modern writers agree that these images regarding "real" pirates do not portray the truth about them; but what is the truth about real pirates and can we handle it?

Most people in this country get their first exposure to piracy in children's literature such as *Peter Pan* and *Treasure Island*. Those first impressions of Jolly Rogers, peg legs, and eye patches never leave us, despite what we learn later. Perhaps this enduring image is so persistent because of the continual parade of pirate literature and movies that pass before us.

Pirates in Popular Culture

Most of the classics of pirate fiction were penned during the late 19th and early 20th centuries. These included Gilbert and Sullivan's *Pirates of Penzance* (1879), James Barrie's *Peter Pan* (1904), Rafael Sabatini's *The Sea Hawk* (1915), *Captain Blood* (1922), and the *Black Swan* (1932), and Howard Pyle's magnificently illustrated and written *The Book of Pirates* (1921). Perhaps it is fair to say that the all-time great source of pirate imagery is *Treasure Island* by Robert Louis Stevenson (1949 [1883]). The story is a perennial favorite that has never gone out of print and has even been abridged as a comic book in the *Classics Illustrated* series (Boyette 1991). More than ten versions of the story have been filmed since 1918, including such fanciful adaptations as *Muppet Treasure Island* (1996) from Jim Henson Productions and Disney's *Treasure Planet* (2002). Each version brings the trademark Stevenson pirates to the silver screen, from the scary Blind Pew, Black Dog, and Israel Hands to the rough-hewn pirates with a heart of gold such as the Captain or Billy Bones, and the legendary Long John Silver.

No fewer than a hundred movies and television programs were made on the topic of pirates in the first sixty years of the 20th century (Parish 1995). Their portrayal on the silver screen and on television followed the literary stereotypes of Stevenson and those that followed him. From these productions it is clear that Howard Pyle was a key source of inspiration for every costume designer. As far as box office receipts were concerned, it appears that the public became less enchanted with pirates after the 1950s. Nonetheless, Hollywood's love affair with pirate tales has continued, albeit less frequently.

New life was breathed into the genre with Johnny Depp's over-the-top performance as Captain Jack Sparrow in Disney's cleverly marketed *Pirates of the Caribbean: Curse of the Black Pearl*. On its opening day in July 2003, it showed simultaneously in more than 3,200 theaters and earned $13.5 million (Hernandez 2003). By the end of October that same year, it had grossed in excess of

$300 million. The sequel, *Dead Man's Chest*, eclipsed previous box office openings, taking in $258.4 million in the first ten days of its release. Based on these figures and the deluge of pirate-themed merchandise available in stores and on-line, the pirate genre is back en vogue with the public. We can expect similar Hollywood productions to follow Disney's success and capitalize on the public's rediscovered passion for pirates.

Pirates have fared consistently better on the small screen. One of the most popular cartoons of the 21st century, *Spongebob Squarepants,* often incorporates pirate themes into its episodes. Today "Who lives in a pineapple under the sea?" has replaced "Way hey blow the man down" as the most recognizable sea chantey; however, the piratical iconography in the show (the sinister Flying Dutchman and the pirate-talking, money-grubbing Mr. Krabs) has changed little from that found in the literature of the past century. Many of these images come directly from Barrie's *Peter Pan.* Whether it was Mary Martin or Sandy Duncan flying on stage, Robin Williams in Spielberg's *Hook* (1991), or Universal Studios' visually impressive *Peter Pan* (2003), these images have joined Disney's re-release of their 1953 animation of *Peter Pan* in theaters and home video to perpetuate a pervasive image of pirates. This image has given three generations a shared experience.

A third source for pirate stereotypes is theme parks. Both children and adults are exposed to living, or at least animatronic, effigies of the perceived pirate past. The successful first *Pirates of the Caribbean* movies are based on one of Disney World's most popular attractions. The synergy between the two media is such that the theme park ride was updated to mirror the original movie's sequel in the summer of 2006. As a special treat at the reopening of the ride, "Captain Jack Sparrow lead lighthearted 'pirate training' where kids were invited to join the fun with interactive hi-jinks" (Disney World 2006). The term *hi-jinks* is emblematic of the pirate stereotype. The popular image of pirates' behavior has been softened to hi-jinks rather than mayhem.

Off-setting this fictional realm is a more "authentic" museum in Key West, Florida, devoted to all things piratical. The Pirate Soul Museum boasts the journal from Captain Kidd's last voyage, a genuine Jolly Roger flag, and a treasure chest once owned by Captain Thomas Tew (Pirate Soul Museum 2006). Besides viewing these authentic pirate artifacts, visitors also tour a replica of Port Royal and are ushered into the hold of a ship by the animatronic talking head of Blackbeard.

On a more adult level, the Treasure Island Hotel & Casino in Las Vegas featured a live battle between a Spanish galleon and a pirate ship in the lagoon in front of the hotel. The pirates always won; however, like its Disney counterpart, this attraction has been updated.

> The Sirens of TI begins with a 17th-century clash between a group of beautiful, tempting sirens and a band of renegade pirates. With their mesmerizing and powerful song the Sirens lure the pirates to their cove, stir up a tempest strong enough to sink a ship, and transform Sirens' Cove into a 21st-century party; experience music, dance, excitement and seduction—nightly in Sirens' Cove at the front entrance of Treasure Island Hotel and Casino. [Treasure Island Hotel & Casino 2006]

This time the pirates lose, or perhaps they really win. It depends on your perspective.

Clearly, fictional works have had an addictive influence on our perception of the pirate past. Is there no antidote? Books purported to be nonfiction historical studies are perhaps the most enduring media that deal with the romantic notion of pirates. Dozens, perhaps hundreds, of books are touted as the source of information about "who the pirates really were" (Rediker 1987; Cordingly 1995; Konstam 1999). Even the fictional works about pirates often have addenda that discuss the "true" nature of piracy. The Disney DVD of *Treasure Planet* has a bonus feature that the viewer can use to learn about historical pirates and their ways.

With the distance of history and the softening through adult and children's literature, the atrocities committed by real pirates seem less terrible. These acts of terror become "hi-jinks" and are more the stuff of adventure stories than actual, horrific events.

No doubt, this is due to the imprinting in our minds of the stereotypical images promulgated during childhood. Such terms as scoundrel, scalawag, rogue, and even cutthroat do not accurately portray the criminal nature of pirates. Indeed, in modern romance literature, these are regarded as positive character traits in the leading male characters. One exception to this romanticism was a book written by Peter Benchley, the author of *Jaws*. His novel, *Island* (1980), captured the terror that genuine pirates must have inspired, because clearly the people of the 17th and 18th centuries *were* terrified. That is why an instant death sentence was pronounced on anyone who chose to pursue piracy. Not only were they hanged, but their bodies were often suspended at the entrance to harbors as a warning to others contemplating pursuing a life of piracy. Perhaps if the term *terrorist* was used to describe them, this might resonate more with the modern public who would then equate pirates with their reputation as murdering thieves.

Defining a Pirate

How would you identify a pirate, a pirate ship, a pirate hideout, or even evidence of piratical activity in the archaeological record? What are their hallmarks? Would you expect to find barrels filled with hooks or peg legs? Perhaps there would be a large number of parrot skeletons? To identify a pirate site, you must first know what items you expect to encounter during the excavation. To know what to look for, it is important to understand something about the people we expect to study. There are many terms for pirate, including *buccaneer, corsair,* and *privateer.* These words are often used interchangeably, although there are significant differences between them.

Webster's (Guralnik 1979:455) defines a pirate as one who commits robbery on the high seas or the unauthorized use of another's idea or invention. A more colorful definition comes from the 19th-century *Pirate's Own Book*, "Piracy is an offence against the universal law of society. As, therefore, he has renounced all the benefits of society and government, and has reduced himself to the savage state of nature, by declaring war against all mankind, all mankind must declare war against him" (Maritime Research Society 1924:x). In other words, pirates are bad men who robbed ships. Not all men, however, who robbed ships were bad; at least not in their country's eyes. Some were even accorded special honors.

A privateer is an individual licensed to attack enemy shipping. Such a mariner had a contract with a specific government. They carried what is known as a Letter of Marque. These letters made the privateer an auxiliary to the regular navy of the state. It permitted the bearer to prey upon the shipping of an enemy country and split the prize with the authorizing government (Cordingly 1995:xvii). This makes the difference between privateers and pirates a matter of perspective. Sir Francis Drake was knighted by his government, as a hero of the realm, while at the same time he was viewed as a dreaded pirate by the Spaniards living in the Caribbean upon whom he preyed. The term *corsair* refers to sea robbers and can apparently be applied to either pirate or privateer; a handy term when you are discussing the career of Sir Francis Drake and don't wish to offend your English or Spanish colleagues.

Buccaneer is a corruption of the French *boucanier* and should be seen as a sort of proto-pirate. When the Spanish abandoned the western third of Hispaniola in the latter half of the 16th century, French smugglers filled the vacuum by squatting in the uninhabited area. Their subsistence was largely based on the hunting of wild cattle that were plentiful in the region. The meat from these cattle was smoked over grills called *boucans* and sold to passing ships. It wasn't long before these *boucaniers* supplemented their income by preying on some of the passing ships (Konstam 1999:74). The word later becomes Anglicized into buccaneer. Tortuga Island, off the northern coast of Haiti, became one of the early pirate lairs in the Caribbean. When the British captured Jamaica, the buccaneers, or "Brethren of the Coast," made Port Royal their home, ushering in a new reign of terror.

The Golden Age of Piracy

Piracy may be the second-oldest profession among state-level societies. Once humans began to use the sea to transport valuable cargoes, others tried to steal those cargoes. Certainly, there is documentary evidence of piracy in antiquity, as Julius Caesar was captured and held for ransom by pirates (Plutarch 1999). Some have argued that the Kyrenia wreck (Katsev 1980, 1987) was sunk by pirates in the Mediterranean, but that is far from certain. What is lacking is material evidence for piracy in the most part because the archaeology of piracy is not as widespread as piracy itself. All of the sites associated with archaeological literature are primarily products of the "Golden Age of Piracy" and excavated by North American or European archaeologists. This is the time period that Hollywood chooses to portray in movies and television shows and therefore the focus of the historical context is the Caribbean, North America, and the Indian Ocean.

The riches the Spaniards hauled out of the New World proved irresistible to many other nations. The French buccaneers were among the first to systematically harass Spanish shipping such that by the early 17th century they had established a stronghold on Tortuga Island off the north coast of Haiti. By the middle of the 17th century, the ranks of these freebooters included many nationalities and numbered in the thousands.

In 1655, Jamaica was captured by the British. This prompted many of the pirates-*cum-* privateers to relocate their base of operations to the haven of Port Royal. Over the past fifty years, the excavation of this notorious port has been directed by Texas A&M archaeologist Donny Hamilton and others. His research reveals that piracy is less apparent in the archaeological record than it is in the historical record (Hamilton 2006).

It was during this time that Jean L'Olonnais and Sir Henry Morgan terrified the Spanish Main. The depredations by these pirates fell on both ships and ports. As a result, the Spanish were forced to fortify these ports with imposing stone "castles" and sail their treasure fleets in armed convoys. Even these measures, however, were not entirely successful, as evidenced by the sack of Panama Viejo by Henry Morgan in 1671 (Mendizábel 1999).

The so-called Golden Age of Piracy was born at the end of the 17th century. Though officially discouraged by the European powers, piracy actually increased in scope between 1690 and 1730. The infamous Edward Teach (Blackbeard) and Samuel Bellamy spread terror up the east coast of North America and beyond in the years following the conclusion of Queen Anne's War in 1714. This era finally drew to a close when powerful merchant interests arose and national navies became strong enough to deal with the policing of increased peacetime trade.

Piracy was not limited to the New World. At the same time that pirates were plundering the Americas, others discovered rich booty was to be had in the Indian Ocean. Captains William Kidd and Richard Condent preyed upon the treasure-laden ships of the Moghul Empire from their base off the coast of Madagascar. It was the pirates' toll on the shipping of the East India Company that brought down the wrath of corporate Britain and essentially ended this pirate reign. The scourge of piracy, however, has never really ended and continues to be the bane of honest seamen to this day.

The problem with trying to characterize historical pirates is that piracy has existed for as long as humans have sailed the seas and has been found wherever there were vessels to be robbed. How do you characterize piracy through time and space? Hollywood simply falls back on the popular literary stereotype. As archaeologists, we try to dispel popular misconceptions about the past by examining the material record that people have left behind, but is it even possible to recognize a pirate in the archaeological record?

The Archaeology of Piracy

In conducting research on piracy, two things become abundantly clear. First, there is no shortage of historical works about pirates; second, there is very little in the archaeological literature about piracy. This is surprising because the discovery of what has been touted as the wreck of Blackbeard's flagship dominated the archaeological discussions in North Carolina during the first decade of the 21st century; however, when looking beyond this site, only a couple of other pirate-related sites are known (Figure 4.1). How can this be if piracy has played such a pervasive role in maritime history?

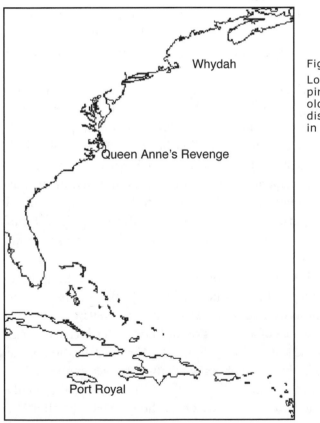

Figure 4.1. Location of pirate archaeological sites discussed in text.

Historical literature suggests that pirates most often stole commercial cargoes, which they then sold for gold and promptly spent as fast they could. Yet, history is replete with people trying to find pirate buried treasure, even though there is virtually no historical record of pirates burying their gold.

The Money Pit on Oak Island off of Nova Scotia is a good example of a great deal of effort being spent looking for pirate treasure that does not exist. Captain William Kidd, the only pirate who is actually recorded to have buried treasure on Gardiners' Island near his home in New York (Zacks 2002:241–243), allegedly careened his ship in Nova Scotia. Three hundred years later, the stories become conflated with Captain Flint's buried booty in *Treasure Island* and voila, a "mysterious," allegedly booby-trapped pit on the north end of Oak Island becomes the "Money Pit." Millions of dollars and at least ten deaths have been attributed to treasure seekers attempting to find the nonexistent pirate booty; however, legitimate pirate treasure *has* been discovered archaeologically.

Pirate booty aplenty was found at the wreck of the *Whydah* off Cape Cod. In the evening of April 26, 1717, the pirate ship *Whydah* ran aground and broke up during a violent gale. All but two of her crew perished, including her captain, Samuel "Black Sam" Bellamy. Just two months earlier, the English slaver *Whydah* had off-loaded its human cargo at Jamaica and was making its way back home. Bellamy captured the treasure-laden galley, outfitted it with thirty guns, and began plundering his way up the coast of North America until the nor'easter put an end to his depredations (Hamilton 2006:131–132).

Two hundred and sixty-one years after her wrecking, treasure salvor Barry Clifford found the *Whydah* off the coast of Cape Cod. Excavations were conducted from 1978 to 1989 by the salvors under the guidance of a succession of underwater archaeologists appointed by the state of Massachussetts. The identification of the wreck suggested by contemporary documents, was confirmed by the recovery of the ship's bell, inscribed "The + Whydah + Gally + 1716" during the 1985 field season. Although virtually all of the ship's hull structure was gone (contemporary records indicate recovered sections of the hull were burned to recover the iron fittings), more than 40,000 artifacts were found scattered across a 24,000-square-foot area (Hamilton 2006:133–135).

The identification of the vessel was never a mystery because documents regarding the salvage abound and the ship's bell was inscribed with the ship's name; however, the project was not without controversy. This was especially true in the archaeological community. Initially, the collaboration between the archaeologists and the salvors, although performed under legally mandated permit, was viewed as a blasphemy by most underwater archaeologists. Project participants were not permitted to present their findings at professional archaeological meetings at the time. This, in part, explains the rapid turnover of archaeological consultants who saw their careers damaged by their association with the treasure hunters.

Nevertheless, important information was recovered by the project and subsequently published, albeit in limited distribution (Hamilton et al. 1988, 1990). The archaeologists noted that although the ship had been broken up and scattered by the storm, the artifact distribution still reflected the general location of materials on the vessel and provided information on the stages of wrecking (Hamilton 2006:157). This information would later prove invaluable in the interpretation of another alleged pirate vessel, the *Queen Anne's Revenge.*

Hamilton also used the data recovered from the wreck to model pirate life and the general practice of piracy. According to Hamilton (2006:147), "the relationship of the Whydah pirate was egalitarian—or perhaps 'libertarian,' if one emphasizes political orientation—relative to the class-oriented society of early 18th century Europe and its colonies." Status was achieved through skill or brute force rather than being assigned by the navy or shipping company. Hamilton also noted that even the average pirate had the opportunity to acquire prestige items like "fine pistols" that would cost an ordinary seaman two year's pay (Hamilton 2006:149). On a larger scale, Hamilton (2006:157) suggests piracy played an important role in the dynamics of the world economic system as an expected hazard to shipping, which the various trading nations had to take into account.

Another pirate project concerns an 18th-century shipwreck found off Beaufort Inlet along the coast of North Carolina. This wreck was found in 1996 by treasure hunters who were looking for a Spanish treasure ship, *El Salvador*. Unlike the *Whydah*, which is spread over several acres, the Beaufort Inlet Wreck is confined to a relatively small area. The Beaufort Inlet Wreck, however, is similar to the *Whydah* in other respects.

If the identification of the Beaufort Inlet Wreck as the *Queen Anne's Revenge* is correct, the vessel started out as the slaver *La Concorde* when it was captured by the notorious pirate Blackbeard in the Caribbean toward the end of November 1717. Supposedly, Blackbeard upgraded the armament to around forty guns and began busily taking prizes in the Caribbean and up the Atlantic coast of North America. After blockading the harbor at Charleston, South Carolina, and holding the city for ransom, Blackbeard and his growing pirate flotilla proceeded up the coast. In a move viewed by some as an early example of corporate downsizing (Wilde-Ramsing 2006:162), the *Queen Anne's Revenge* and a smaller sloop, *Adventure,* were run aground in June 1718 off Beaufort Inlet and their crews marooned. Blackbeard commandeered one of the smaller vessels, only to be caught and killed off Ocracoke Island five months later.

The excavation of the Beaufort Inlet Wreck is controversial for two reasons (Figure 4.2). First, its association with treasure hunters sent up an immediate red flag with underwater archaeologists. Even though the salvors have little interest in the vessel (there is no treasure on it) and underwater archaeologists employed by the state of North Carolina have conducted virtually all the work on the site, some archaeologists still see an ethical dilemma. The second controversy surrounds the wreck's identification. Several archaeologists felt that the state of North Carolina acted hastily in declaring the wreck to be the *Queen Anne's Revenge*, saying there was not sufficient evidence to make such a claim (Rodgers et al. 2005; Lusardi 2006).

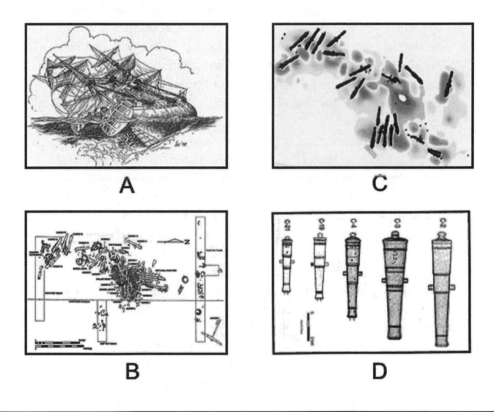

The Queen Anne's Revenge?

A

C

B

D

Figure 4.2. The wreck at Beaufort Inlet believed to be the *Queen Anne's Revenge.* A: artist's conception of wreck aground; B: map of the wreck site; C: magnetometry detection of cannons on the wreck; D: five of the cannons recovered from the wreck.

The identification of the vessel is somewhat ambiguous primarily because of the scant documentary evidence related to the wreck. When the history is sketchy, how does one distinguish a pirate ship from a heavily merchant vessel? It is here that the *Whydah* project provided assistance. Like the *Queen Anne's Revenge*, the *Whydah* was a converted slave ship. Both had off-loaded their human cargo when captured by pirates. They both operated in the same general region at the same time. When compared to each other, their archaeological assemblages are remarkably similar. A wide variety of cannon, many of them loaded and ready for action, were found on both sites (Wilde-Ramsing 2006:193). A preliminary assessment of the smaller artifacts recovered such as navigation instruments, utilitarian, and personal items show a concurrence as well. Pattern recognition in the artifact assemblage, using a site of known function to interpret a site whose function is not known, is a hallmark of historical archaeology (South 1977).

Pattern recognition is important even at sites with known pirate affiliation. Historically, Port Royal, Jamaica, was the major pirate lair of the Golden Age of Piracy. The "Wickedest City on Earth," as it came to be known, was heavily damaged by an earthquake in 1692 before being destroyed by a second quake in 1722. The pirates who are documented to have frequented this port town included the likes of Henry Morgan, Calico Jack Rackham, Anne Bonny, Mary Read, and Bartholomew Roberts. Yet, Donny Hamilton (2006:26), after decades of investigations, was hard pressed to find definitive evidence of their piratical activities, stating:

> Archaeologically speaking, little has been found that can be attributed exclusively to privateers or pirates. The best archaeological evidence comes from shipwrecks, and even here good historic documentation is essential to identify the ship. Without the written wills, inventories, deeds, and grantor's records that often record partial ownership of vessels used in privateering or trade, there would be little to equate Port Royal with its privateering citizenry.

Thus, more archaeology is necessary on pirate sites to help define this "pirate pattern" in the archaeological record.

The primary reason that more pirate sites have not been reported in the literature is that they are so hard to identify in the archaeological record. In fact, recent research has shown

(Skowronek and Ewen 2006) that without solid historical documentation, most of them would probably not be identified as associated with piracy by their investigators or at least their identity would be debated (Lusardi 2006; Wilde-Ramsing 2006). Indeed, because most pirate ships began as legitimate sailing vessels before they were captured, archaeologists must look to ship modifications and cargo to discern piracy in the past.

Who Were the Pirates—Really?

What did it mean to be a pirate and how does the popular perception of piracy as depicted today influence our interpretations of piracy in the past? How do we recognize a pirate site in the archaeological record? Are there any archaeological markers that give away a pirate site? If the archaeologist didn't have the documentary record to draw from, could a site be positively identified as a pirate shipwreck? In every site associated with pirates the identification was only successful when there was good historical documentation. If the documentation associated with a site is ambiguous or somewhat sketchy, as in the case of the *Queen Anne's Revenge*, then the identification is open to question. Does this rule out the possibility of identifying piracy in the archaeological record?

As professional archaeologists, we should not be dismayed. In fact, this is not an uncommon situation in historical archaeology. For example, archaeologists working on plantation sites have been searching for diagnostic artifacts that definitely denote the presence of African American slaves. A single blue bead or cowrie shell does not a slave site make; however, blue beads or cowrie shells in a historical context where slaves are historically recorded to have lived lends credence to such an association. Perhaps this will be the case with pirate sites.

Archaeologists are not as interested in individual artifacts as in patterns in the archaeological record. Each pirate site that is identified, explored, and published takes the archaeologist one step closer to defining such a pattern. Perhaps the pirate ship is characterized by a pattern of armaments, reconfigured mast placement, and a variety of cargo that differs from a merchant ship or naval vessel. Early work on pirate land sites suggests that one identifying trait may be the presence of high-status items such as ceramics, or clothing-related items in low-status contexts (Finamore 2006; Hatch 2006). If a pattern can be discerned, then it would be possible to identify a pirate ship for which no historical record exists. Unless we can be sure of our identifications we will not be able to recognize patterns nor address questions relating the "real" lives of pirates and their impact on the larger societies in which they lived.

Until archaeologists can identify the physical world in which pirates sailed, we are left with the Hollywood stereotype. This lack of evidence begs the question: is our image of pirates completely wrong, a scam perpetrated by the entertainment industry to whitewash past criminals and profit from our ignorance? Actually, some pirates during the late 17th and early 18th centuries probably *did* look like Long John Silver; however, many seamen of the period and even naval personnel probably looked just as sinister. The only harm, if there is any, is in overromanticizing these murdering thieves. In 2005, the town of Bath, North Carolina, resurrected an outdoor drama, *Blackbeard: Knight of the Black Flag*. In this bit of revisionist history, Blackbeard is portrayed as a basically decent man driven by circumstances and his own personal demons into a life he didn't choose. Does the audience believe this portrayal? Probably not completely, but the authors of bodice-ripping historical romances have been living off the stereotype for generations.

On September 19th, pirate fans around the world observed "Talk-Like-a-Pirate Day," and in Barnes & Noble bookstores across the country there were displays of "pirate" books with a green and cream sign boldly proclaiming, "Ahoy, Matey! September 19th is International "Talk-Like-a-Pirate Day." On that day, every e-mail or phone call we received sounded like it was from Blind Pew or Billy Bones. We responded in kind. Indeed, it seems that even serious pirate scholars cannot escape the hype of Hollywood.

References

Barrie, James Mathew

    1904   *Peter Pan* (play). London.

Benchley, Peter

    1980   *Island*. Doubleday, New York.

Boyette, Pat

    1991   Adaptation of Robert Louis Stevenson's Treasure Island (comic book). *Classics Illustrated*. No. 17, The Berkley Publishing Group and First Publishing, Inc., Chicago.

Cordingly, David

    1995   *Under the Black Flag: The Romance and the Reality of Life among the Pirates*. Random House, New York.

Disney World

    2006   Pirates of the Caribbean. Available online at http://disneyworld.disney.go.com/wdw/parks/attraction Detail?id=PiratesoftheCaribbeanAttractionPage. Accessed January 2, 2007.

Finamore, Daniel

    2006   A Mariner's Utopia: Pirates and Logwood in the Bay of Honduras. In *X Marks the Spot: The Archaeology of Piracy*, Russell K. Skowronek and Charles R. Ewen, editors, pp. 64–80. University Press of Florida, Gainesville.

Gilbert, W. S. and Arthur Sullivan

    1879   *Pirates of Penzance* (play). New York.

Guralnik, David, editor

    1979   *Webster's New World Dictionary of the American Language*. Popular Library, New York.

Hamilton, Christopher E., James R. Reedy, Jr., and Kenneth Kinkor

    1988   *Final Report of Archaeological Testing, the Whydah Shipwreck, Site WLF-HA-1*. Report submitted to the Massachusetts Board of Underwater Archaeological Resources, the U.S. Army Corps of Engineers, and the Advisory Council on Historic Preservation. South Chatham, MA.

    1990   The 1989 Annual Report of Archaeological Data Recovery, the Whydah Shipwreck, Site WLF-HA-1. Report submitted to the Massachusetts Board of Underwater Archaeological Resources, the U.S. Army Corps of Engineers, and the Advisory Council on Historic Preservation. South Chatham, MA.

Hamilton, Donny L.

> 2006   Pirates and Merchants: Port Royal, Jamaica. In *X Marks the Spot: The Archaeology of Piracy*, Russell K. Skowronek and Charles R. Ewen, editors, pp. 13–30. University Press of Florida, Gainesville.

Hatch, Heather

> 2006   Archaeology: Investigating Piracy in the Archaeological Record. Master's thesis, Department of History, East Carolina University, Greenville, NC.

Hernandez, Gred

> 2003   Disney's "Pirates" Hoists Victory Flag. *San Francisco Chronicle,* July 12.

Katsev, Michael

> 1980   A Cargo from the Age of Alexander the Great. In *Archaeology Uunder Water, An Atlas of the World's Submerged Sites,*. Keith Muckleroy, editor, pp. 42–43. McGraw-Hill, New York, NY.

> 1987   The Kyrenia Ship Restored. In T*he Sea Remembers, Shipwrecks and Archaeology.* Peter Throckmorton, editor, pp. 55–59. Weidenfield & Nicolson, New York.

Konstam, Angus

> 1999   *The History of Pirates.* The Lyons Press, New York.

Lusardi, Wayne

> 2006   The Beaufort Inlet Shipwreck. In *X Marks the Spot: The Archaeology of Piracy,* Russell K. Skowronek and Charles R. Ewen, editors, pp. 196–218. University Press of Florida, Gainesville.

Maritime Research Society

> 1924   *Pirate's Own Book.* Publication No. 4. Maritime Research Society, Salem, MA.

Mendizábel, Tomas

> 1999   Current Archaeological Research in Panama Viejo, Panama. *Papers for the Institute of Archaeology* 10:25–36.

Parish, James Robert

> 1995   *Pirates and Seafaring Swashbucklers on the Hollywood Screen.* McFarland & Company, Publishers, Jefferson, NC.

Pirate Soul Museum

> 2006   Available online at http://www.piratesoul.com/experi-ence_home.aspx. Accessed January 5, 2007.

Plutarch

   1999   *Roman Lives: A Selection of Eight Roman Lives,* Robin
   Waterfield, translator. Oxford University Press, Oxford.

Pyle, Howard

   1921   *The Book of Pirates.* Harper and Brothers, New York.

Rediker, Marcus

   1987   *Between the Devil and the Deep Blue Sea: Merchant
   Seamen, Pirates, and the Anglo-American World,* 1700–1750.
   Cambridge University Press, Cambridge.

Rodgers, Bradley A., Nathan Richards, and Wayne R. Lusardi

   2005   "Ruling Theories Linger": Questioning the Identity of the
   Beaufort Inlet Shipwreck. *The International Journal of Nautical
   Archaeology* 34(1):24–37.

Sabatini, Rafael

   1915   *The Sea Hawk.* Lippincott, Philadelphia.

   1922   *Captain Blood: His Odyssey.* Houghton Mifflin, New
   York.

   1932   *Black Swan.* Houghton Mifflin, New York.

Skowronek, Russell K. and Charles R. Ewen, editors

   2006   *X Marks the Spot: The Archaeology of Piracy.* University
   Press of Florida, Gainesville.

South, Stanley

   1977   *Method and Theory in Historical Archaeology.* Academic
   Press, New York.

Stevenson, Robert Louis

   1949   *Treasure Island.* Reprinted from the 1883 edition.
   Random House, New York.

Treasure Island Hotel & Casino

   2006   The Sirens of TI. Available online at http://www.treasure-
   island.com/pages/ent_sirens.asp#view. Accessed January 5, 2007.

Wilde-Ramsing, Mark U.

   2006   The Pirate Ship Queen Anne's Revenge. In *X Marks
   the Spot: The Archaeology of Piracy,* Russell K. Skowronek and
   Charles R. Ewen, editors, pp. 160–195. University Press of Florida,
   Gainesville.

Zacks, Richard

   2002   *The Pirate Hunter: The True Story of Captain Kidd.*
   Hyperion, New York.

TITANIC

James P. Delgado

• •

Intense moments of crisis, shipwrecks are ideal vehicles to explore the range of human emotions and responses. Cowardice, heroism, sacrifice, and selfishness have all played out on the decks of sinking ships; as such, wrecks have attracted the attention of storytellers since the days of Homer. Filmmakers have used the dramatic effect of a shipwreck since the earliest days of the genre. These films include a 1912 silent feature, *Saved from the Titanic*, featuring an actress who had been on board the ill-fated liner (Bottomore 2000), Hitchcock's *Lifeboat* (1944), *The Last Voyage* (1960), which capitalized on the 1956 sinking of the liner *Andrea Doria*, and the compelling human story culminating in the sinking of the fishing boat *Andrea Gail* in *The Perfect Storm* (2000).

Hollywood has enjoyed a vast range of dramatic opportunities that shipwrecks offer, but its depiction of physical wrecks on the bottom of the sea is a much narrower range. From cartoons to features, film has portrayed wrecks as entities on the seabed as underwater ghost towns—frightening places haunted by skeletons and monstrous sea creatures, usually acting as guardians of lost

treasures. For Hollywood, wrecks have been resources to be sal-
vaged or plundered, always with an element of romance and danger. These story lines range from the treasure retrieved by Captain
Nemo and his crew in Disney's *20,000 Leagues beneath the Sea*
(1954), the ancient wreck lying beneath the modern freighter lad-
en with morphine ampules in *The Deep* (1971), or the fictitious
Cold War–winning ore locked in the holds of the great liner in
Raise the Titanic! (1980).

Archaeology, whether practiced above or below the water,
works with the physical remains of the past to add to history, to
recover that which was lost to human memory, and to add details,
complexity, and life to our understanding of the past. Maritime
and nautical archaeologists, often working underwater, study the
history of humanity's interaction with the sea and its tributary
waters. This includes activities like trade, war, exploration, fishing
and whaling, and recreation. Seafaring is one of humanity's oldest activities, with seaborne colonization of Australia dating back
some 40,000 years before there were farms, domesticated animals,
pottery, or homes (Bass 2005:10).

Archaeologists have excavated and recovered an amazing
array of lost ships and through the study of their cargoes, fittings,
armament, provisions, and at times the remains of their crews
have added a considerable amount of detail to our understanding of seafaring. They have also contributed to our overall view
of history. Excavation of two ancient wrecks in Turkey at Cape
Gelidonya and Ulu Burun rewrote the history of Bronze Age trade
in the Mediterranean world, with proof that seafarers from the
east were engaged in an active and complex trade, with raw materials and manufactured goods flowing from at least ten different
cultures, all in the holds of the ships of peoples who linked the
ancient world by sea.

A Greek merchant vessel from Kyrenia, Cyprus, which sank
ca. 295–285 BC, illustrated not only how ancient shipwrights had
built their craft, but how this hard-worked vessel may have been
sunk in a pirate attack in the turbulent times following the death
of Alexander the Great. A wreck at Serce Limani, Turkey, dating

from ca. AD 1025 yielded the world's greatest collection of medieval Islamic glass, all of it painstakingly reconstructed from nearly a million fragments (Bass 2005:206).

Later-age wrecks have included two early cannon-armed warships, *Mary Rose* (1545) and *Vasa*, a completely intact Swedish warship of 1628, wrecks from the Spanish Armada, *La Belle*, a ship lost in 1686 during La Salle's abortive attempt to colonize the lower Mississippi, *Vrouw Maria*, the completely intact wreck of a Dutch trader lost in the Baltic in 1774 with a cargo of luxury goods for the Russian Court in St. Petersburg, including thirty-two paintings for Catherine the Great, British transports lost during the Siege of Yorktown in 1781, wrecks from the War of 1812 in the Great Lakes and on Lake Champlain, ships buried beneath landfill in downtown San Francisco from the California Gold Rush of 1849–1851, a host of Civil War wrecks including the ironclad USS *Monitor* and two early submarines, *H.L. Hunley* and *Explorer*, and two steamboats, *Arabia* (1856) and *Bertrand* (1865), both wrecked and discovered perfectly preserved with cargoes bound for the western river frontier.

More contemporary wrecks have yielded information on the development of modern warships, including those associated with some of the greatest naval battles of the modern age, from the USS *Arizona* at Pearl Harbor, the German battleship *Bismarck* and the British battle cruiser *Hood* and the Japanese super battleship *Yamato*. In the late 20th century, the extension of deep-sea technology into shipwreck research yielded some of the most exciting of these wrecks, lying at depths of two to three miles. It also rediscovered the most famous wreck of the century, *Titanic*.

Titanic on Film

The wreck of *Titanic* has received more cinematic attention than any other maritime disaster or sunken ship. From the beforementioned *Rescued from the Titanic* (1912), and a German film,

In Nacht Und Eis (1912), two other largely forgotten films included an adapted story, *Atlantic* (1929) and an anti-British Nazi propaganda film, *Titanic* (1943). The 1950s brought two classics, *Titanic* (1953), which featured Clifton Webb and Barbara Stanwyck, and then *A Night to Remember* (1958), based on the best-selling book by Walter Lord. A made-for-television drama, *SOS Titanic* (1979), *Raise the Titanic!* (1980), and a documentary, *Search for the Titanic* (1981) were the last films brought out before the rediscovery of the wreck in 1985. The sunken wreck, obsession with it, and dives to the hulk formed the focus of IMAX's *Titanica* (1992). The 1997 release of James Cameron's *Titanic* spurred an intense interest in the wreck. Cameron followed it with a documentary on diving to exploring the wreck, *Ghosts of the Abyss* (2003).

Titanic films made between 1912 and 1979 focused on the allegorical aspects of the wreck event, with the exception of *A Night to Remember* (1958). Considered "by many to be the definitive *Titanic* film" (Eaton and Haas 1999:239), this film has the feel of a dramatic documentary. Based on the research of author Walter Lord, whose investigation included interviews with numerous survivors, the British-made *A Night to Remember* faithfully followed events reconstructed from those interviews and the results of the official inquiries into the sinking. Dramatic license included reconstructions of the last moments of several characters in the film who did not survive, including a touching scene in which a crew member holds a young boy who has lost his mother as the water rushes up to claim them both. Another is the sacrifice of the engine room crew, who stayed at their posts knowing, as the line in the film states, there was "not much chance for us."

The shift in *Titanic* films came with the cinematic adaptation of Clive Cussler's *Raise the Titanic!* (1976). Cussler's bestseller focused on the ongoing fascination with locating and recovering all or part of the famous liner. Based on the contemporary understanding of the wreck event, Cussler's (and the film's) *Titanic* sank intact, with a few holes eventually patched by salvagers from the fictional National Underwater and Marine Agency. This allowed the ship to rise dramatically from the depths, water streaming from her rust-coated sides in a triumphant Hollywood reversal of the night to remember.

The thought of such a dramatic moment spurred a variety of searches, including a series funded by Texas oilman Jack Grimm and filmmaker Mike Harris, who collaborated on *Search for the Titanic*, which documented Grimm's obsession with finding *Titanic* and a 1980 expedition. The successful rediscovery of *Titanic* in 1985 ultimately sparked the next generation of *Titanic* films, in which the wreck on the seabed played as important a role as the events of April 14–15, 1912.

Rediscovering *Titanic*

The most recent films capitalize on the ongoing fascination with the lost liner and the desire to see and touch it. *Titanic*, one of three massive and luxurious transatlantic liners built for the White Star Line, gained international fame when lost on its maiden voyage in April 1912. Despite claims that it was "practically unsinkable," the 888-foot-long ship sank less than three hours after striking an iceberg on the evening of April 14. Watertight doors and bulkheads failed to stop the flooding because the builders did not contemplate the amount of damage and flooding caused by the collision. An insufficient number of lifeboats provided safety for less than half the passengers and crew; in all, only 705 lived and more than 1,520 died. The loss of a well-publicized ship, especially one with claims of technological superiority, tremendous loss of life, and the deaths of many prominent and influential passengers guaranteed that *Titanic* would go down in history as a wreck that no one would soon forget—as evidenced in the landmark 1955 book by Walter Lord and the 1958 film about the event, *A Night to Remember*.

Titanic remains a powerful icon. Seemingly lost forever, *Titanic* pulled and tugged at the Western world's consciousness. More than a thousand pieces of music were penned about the ship

Figure 5.1. Bow of *RMS Titanic,* on the bottom of the North Atlantic in 2000. Arguably one of the best-known contemporary images of an historic shipwreck, the bow gained even greater fame through its use in two iconic scenes in James Cameron's *Titanic.*

Photo by James P. Delgado©.

and its loss, numerous books and articles appeared, sermons and speeches were given, and various other forms of artistic expression, from paintings to poetry, examined the wreck's impact on the world (Biel 1997; Foster 2000).

The crews of passing ships, as well as the two vessels engaged in the recovery of bodies that bobbed in the sea-lanes of the North Atlantic, plucked poignant flotsam from the water in 1912. They included lifejackets, deck chairs, cushions, and broken pieces of ornate, carved panelling, banisters, and cabin fittings. Some of these, in the morbid late Victorian–early Edwardian custom of death souvenirs, were made into boxes, trays, picture frames, and furniture.

The sunken ship continued to fire the imagination of those who sought to find *Titanic*, and as the last decades of the 20th century approached, technology finally advanced to the stage where it was not only possible, but also probable that *Titanic*'s wreck would be relocated, despite the depth and the inherent challenges. When the news of the wreck's rediscovery by the joint French-U.S. team of Jean-Louis Michel and Robert Ballard reached the world in the early morning hours of September 1, 1985, the media provided images and information from the bottom of the Atlantic.

From a few simple views of the bow, the images that came back from the seabed made a distant, abstract event very real (Figure 5.1). As Robert Ballard commented, in the first hours after the discovery,

> It was one thing to have won—to have found the ship. It was another thing to be there. That was the spooky part. I could see the *Titanic* as she slipped nose first into the glassy water. Around me were the ghostly shapes of the lifeboats and the piercing shouts and screams of people freezing to death in the water. [Ballard 1987:84]

The rediscovery of *Titanic* reconnected modern society with the events of April 1912. The high level of preservation—despite the fact that surveys revealed it to be a broken, twisted, and rusting hulk—helped instill a sense of awe over the deep-sea discovery and the ability of the wreck to inspire imagination as well as memory. *Titanic*'s wreck is more than a physical link to the "night to remember." It is a time machine Ballard evoked when he found it. As the cameras panned across various spots mentioned in the history books, including the crow's nest where lookout Frederick Fleet had picked up the telephone and shouted, "Iceberg, right ahead!," the boat deck with empty lifeboat davits, and the remains of the bridge, where Captain Smith was last seen, observers were struck by the physical reality of *Titanic* (Figure 5.2).

This scene instantly connected them to distant events and

Figure 5.2. The bridge of the *Titanic* has largely vanished through the effects of the steamer's wreck and its long immersion in the North Atlantic. The variable effects of the wreck's deterioration are markedly demonstrated through the preservation of the bronze telemotor (steering gear) and the surrounding wood and steel of the bridge deck.

Photo by James P. Delgado©.

people, an emotional response shared with most archaeologists whose work first reveals a lost or forgotten aspect of the past. What ultimately transpired was not an archaeological look at the wreck, although a considerable amount of scientific research was undertaken. The nature of this wreck, both in its history, the relatively recent nature of the tragedy, and the preservation of the wreck—"a ghost town" as some termed it—also led to controversy. This controversy would ultimately play a role in Hollywood's late-century look at *Titanic*.

Demand to visit the wreck began immediately following the 1985 discovery. Beginning with Ballard's 1986 expedition in the submersible *Alvin*, over 150 known dives have been made on the wreck in the submersibles *Nautile*, *Mir 1*, and *Mir 2*. Controversy erupted with the first dives. Rumors that the 1985 discovery expedition was salvaging the wreck led to protests, and in 1986, as Ballard, in the submersible *Alvin*, dived to the wreck and flew the small robot, Jason, Jr. down the forward grand staircase, editorials against the dives appeared (Rubenstein 1986).

The controversy heated up in 1987. Following the 1985 discovery, a group of U.S. businessmen successfully negotiated a contract with IFREMER (Institute Français de Recherche pour l'Exploitation de la Mer) to recover artifacts from the *Titanic*. On August 5, 1987, they established a Connecticut-based "Titanic Ventures Limited Partnership." Working with IFREMER, they made their dives, recovered 1,800 artifacts, and sailed into a sea of controversy. A January 1988 editorial in *Discover* magazine, headlined "We All Loot in a Yellow Submarine," slammed IFREMER and their U.S. partners for the dives, and for a live television special, broadcast from Paris on October 28, 1987, that featured the expedition's recoveries and culminated in a "live" opening of a safe from the wreck (Kemp 1988).

"The *Titanic* Game Show," as one critic termed it, was a public relations disaster for the salvagers, and remains a strong memory to many preservationists who wish the wreck be left undisturbed. Among them is discoverer Ballard, who calls recovering objects from the wreck an act akin to removing watches and belt buckles from the sunken battleship *Arizona* or "personal effects from the site of the World Trade Center" (Ballard and Sweeney 2004:68). On the other side of the argument, worldwide exhibitions of the thousands of artifacts recovered from the wreck drew large crowds in St. Petersburg (Florida), Las Vegas, Memphis, Boston,

Seattle, Washington, Toronto, Greenwich (England), Hamburg (Germany) Paris, Oslo, Tokyo, Yokohama, and Sapporo, and Stockholm. Millions toured the exhibitions, with some 750,000 in Greenwich and 837,000 in Memphis alone (Eaton and Haas 1999:196, 203, 210). The argument will never be resolved. There are firmly entrenched opponents on either side of the issue, and each side has valid points to make.

The issue of *Titanic* and its artifacts remain a rallying point for preservationists, including Ballard, who see it as a bad precedent for other, older deep-ocean wrecks of historical or archaeological significance. For some, especially those related to victims or survivors (although opinion is divided), dives to *Titanic* are akin to disturbing the dead at best and grave robbing at the worst. For museums around the world, the salvage, and the ongoing exhibition of artifacts from *Titanic* highlights two major issues—the potential sale, and hence the trafficking of archaeological artifacts, and proper, scientific work on wreck sites through archaeological documentation and interpretation.

The controversy, particularly the question of recovery of artifacts from *Titanic*, and the powerful appeal of the sunken liner, all play a prominent role in the 1992, 1997, and 2003 films. Of particular significance is the detailed forensic knowledge gathered from the wreck because of the various dives—including those made by the filmmakers—that appear in the last two, Cameron-made films. Although this work was not undertaken by archaeologists, it is very much like that practiced as part of an archaeological project, seeking to gain as complete an understanding as possible about what happened, filling in lost or missing details, and also seeking to learn more about deep-ocean shipwrecks and their preservation as future searches and projects on other wrecks are planned.

The Wreck of *Titanic*

The wreck of *Titanic* and an associated scatter of artifacts from the vessel (sometimes referred to as the "debris field") rests in 12,434 feet to 12,451 feet of water in the North Atlantic off Newfoundland (Ballard and Sweeney 2004:61, 124–125). *Titanic* separated at the time of sinking into two major components, commonly referred to as the bow and stern. These sections of the hull are separated by 1,870 feet and are surrounded by broken sections of the midships hull and artifacts that spread out in discrete patterns that creates an overall site area approximately 5,000 feet by 3,000 feet (Ballard and Sweeney 2004:124–125).

Prior to the 1985 discovery, the commonly held assumption was that *Titanic* sank intact, with the forward funnel collapsing and a variety of material inside the wreck, including the boilers, tearing free inside the hull as the stern rose out of the water (Lord 1955:78–80; Garzke et al. 1995:1). The investigation of the wreck demonstrated that it had broken apart, and subsequent analysis provided a forensic overview of the probable sequence of events involved in the failure of the hull and its disintegration (Garzke et al. 1995:13–17).

Similar analysis of steel from the wreck and "rusticle" formations, as well as sonar imaging of the hull where *Titanic* struck the iceberg, has provided more details on the nature of the collision damage and the quality of *Titanic*'s steel. Analysis of the steel revealed that it was inferior to modern steel, although it was the best-quality steel in 1912 and that in the cold conditions on the evening of April 14, 1912, it most likely suffered from brittle fracture. Naval architects have also assessed theories of a forward coal compartment fire as a factor (Garzke et al. 1995:9–12).

Another line of inquiry has been the physical processes of preservation and deterioration on the wreck. This research has included analysis of bacteria that consume the ferric content of the steel, exuding the "rusticles" as a by-product as well as detailed analysis of other materials from the artifact scatter recovered by salvagers and subsequently treated in conservation laboratories. This work has provided insights into deep-ocean shipwrecks and how conditions on the seabed continue to transform the wreck. High levels of preservation of certain materials, such as treated leather, paper, fabric, and nonferric metals such as copper and bronze contrast with reports of accelerated deterioration of the steel hull. The rate of deterioration of the hull is controversial, although frequent observers report substantial changes in the hull since its 1985 discovery. Ballard and Sweeney (2004:73, 78–81) suggest this may due to human interaction with the wreck.

The level of preservation inside the wreck was a question first raised in 1985 and examined in 1986, 1991, 1997, and 2001. Documentation of the interior by James Cameron's 2001 expedition provided dramatic footage of preserved, painted wood, doors, glass, and furnishings in cabins that included clothing and in one stateroom, a bowler hat (Lynch and Marschall 2003:72–75, 97–105). This is as significant as the discovery that some of the baggage from the wreck, when recovered and opened, contained well-preserved items including personal correspondence, clothing, and in one container, perfume samples (Wels 1997).

These types of finds provide a human link to the sinking, giving voice, in a way, to the lost. They add to the sense of the wreck as a moment frozen in time, and speak to the power of artifacts to convey a broader and more profound sense of why wrecks and archaeological sites are excavated, studied and shared with the public. It is not the big ship or its loss that are at issue—it is the experience of individuals, involved in the larger context of crossing the Atlantic, for pleasure or to immigrate, who were caught up in a brief but intense disaster that killed most of them. Their luggage, preserved along with the ship, gives voice to their experiences, adding a more intimate layer of understanding to who was there on that ship and just what their loss meant. That premise, central to archaeology, would play out in the major Hollywood adaptation of the *Titanic* story—as would the controversies over who was on the wreck to recover its secrets and for what reason—profit or pursuit of knowledge?

James Cameron's *Titanic* (1997)

The filmmaker who interpreted the complexities and meanings of the wreck of *Titanic* was James Cameron, veteran director and producer of the highly successful *Terminator* (1984) and *Alien* (1979). Cameron also directed the deep-sea science fiction thriller *The Abyss* (1989), in which a salvage team seeking a lost nuclear submarine encounter an aquatic-based alien life form. While researching deep-sea technology, Cameron met with Robert Ballard. "Until then, I really had zero interest in the *Titanic*," said Cameron. "I knew it was a big ship that sank" (Shay 1997a:6). Much later, Cameron watched a videotape of *A Night to Remember*:

> As I sat there viewing it, I thought, you know, somebody should remake this. Then I started thinking that a pretty amazing film could be done by juxtaposing images of the wreck as it sits today with images of what happened on that night long ago, sort of collapsing time in a way that only cinema can do. [Shay 1997a:6]

Before scripting his film, Cameron made twelve dives on *Titanic* in 1995, gaining footage but also a personal perspective on the wreck. The power of the site, lit up briefly for his cameras on the dives, had a profound impact.

> The *Titanic* had been abstract for me. It had been a story. It had been a movie. But to actually be there, and to see the ship and to know from my research the people involved—the ones who survived and the ones who did not—and to have the curse of a vivid imagination, it was a pretty overwhelming feeling. I don't mind admitting that I cried. [Shay 1997a:8–9]

The film that Cameron made, although set within the parameters of a fictional love story, followed the events of April 14–15,

1912. This included a near full-scale re-creation of the ship's exterior and sections of the interior and a commitment to accuracy in costuming and props.

The film elicited criticism from some—the love story had its critics, historical nitpickers found a few small errors, and another historical reviewer found fault with what he termed Cameron's "preposterous class-consciousness overkill," with "every third-classer valorous and almost everyone on the top five decks scatter-brained, selfish, cowardly or malevolent" (Roquemore 1999:357). The same reviewer also took issue with the film's depiction of Captain Edward J. Smith as "indecisive and useless" and termed the film "great pyro-technics—mediocre history" (Roquemore 1999:357). *A Night to Remember* is summarized, in contrast, as "excellent history, super filmmaking, and top-notch entertainment" (Roquemore 1999:357).

Such reviews do an injustice to the film and to Cameron. In a larger scale, *Titanic* succeeds in a different way. It more accurately depicts what happened to the ship, based on Cameron's integration of the years of underwater survey and research and as a result of his own dives. The film also provides an accurate depiction of the forward section of the wreck as it rests on the seabed. Cameron achieved this through dive footage, models, and full-scale recreations based on the dives (Shay 1997b:34, 36, 46).

Given Cameron's reaction to his dives to the wreck, his emotional need to be technically accurate and yet infuse his film with a sense of humanity is understandable. The accuracy of the depiction of the wreck event and the physical remains of the ship provides filmgoers with access to the site, intermingled with Cameron's time-compression technique, in a way that humanizes the sunken wreckage and makes the story "real." A major premise of the film is how the saga of fictional survivor Rose DeWitt Bukater, played out in flashbacks as she views footage of the wreck, makes the salvagers in the film realize the true significance of *Titanic*. For viewers, the film allows them to participate in a dive exploration of *Titanic*, with the story interspersed for them—a theme Cameron returned to with *Ghosts of the Abyss*, in which the connection is made in a documentary style. In the long-standing tradition of cinematic depiction of shipwrecks, *Titanic*'s wreck is picture-perfect.

Finally, and most significantly, the story that plays out in James Cameron's *Titanic* is an implicit acknowledgment of the controversy surrounding the dives to and recoveries from the wreck. It is not a film about archaeology, but it is a film that addresses an archaeological controversy. *Titanic* opens with a dive to the wreck, starting with haunting music and cutting to salvager Brock (Bill Paxton) inside his submersible waxing eloquently into a video camera before stopping with "enough of that bullshit."

The salvagers then send remote operated vehicles inside the wreck to enter a stateroom and recover a safe they believe holds a priceless diamond. Their lights pass over a shoe, a pair of eyeglasses, the porcelain face of a child's doll. Their handling of the stateroom is rough—the ROV hits the doorframe, and a fallen door covering the safe is grabbed and flipped over. The safe, when raised, has its hinges cut off and Brock reaches inside, grabbing wet, muddy objects and tossing them on the deck looking for the diamond—which is not there. Ironically, when a television reporter interviews Brock about his controversial expedition, reminding him that some call him a grave robber, Brock answers with "I have museum-trained experts out here making sure these relics are preserved and catalogued properly." The recovered artifacts are undergoing conservation and treatment, but the larger question of why he is doing what he is, and what will happen to these artifacts remains open—with the diamond looming large as a target that will not end up in a museum.

Ultimately, the diamond loses its significance in the realization of the human stories—and the loss and sorrow. Salvager Brock abandons his quest, commenting that "for three years I thought of nothing but *Titanic*. But I never got it. I never let it in." The film ends with Rose dying in her sleep on the research ship moored above *Titanic*, and her spirit diving deep into the sunken wreck, which as she glides across the ruins, is transformed back into the gleaming vessel it was—and there, waiting inside for her, with all the other souls, is her lost love.

It is a message that speaks back to Cameron's initial response to the wreck—the response of most who have visited *Titanic*. It is a statement that the sunken wreck is more than a question of forensics, or of what valuables could be recovered from it. The imagery of the sunken *Titanic* at the end of Cameron's film was so powerful that the producers of *Pearl Harbor* (2001) ended their film about the December 7, 1941 attack with views of the sunken battleship *Arizona*. It remains powerful, as do the scenes from *A Night to Remember*. Visitors to the wreck cannot help but make comparisons between the films and the places they are visiting. That was the case for me on my visit to the wreck in 2000, and it was obviously behind Cameron's decision to make *Ghosts of the Abyss*.

Where does Hollywood's relationship with the wreck of *Titanic* leave us? What do these images of this ship, these things dredged up from the deep inspire as an emotional response? It seems, whether you agree with recovery or not, that the ship, its fittings and furnishings, its cargo, and the personal belongings of its passengers—both the dead and the survivors who lost "every-thing" in the sinking—are powerful, significant things that evoke, so much better than mere words alone, just what happened on that ship, on that night in particular. That is what archaeologists strive to do as we excavate, conserve, and interpret our finds.

The uniquely personal items are a connection to the human experience. In Cameron's *Titanic*, elderly Rose looks through the items recovered from her stateroom—a comb and a mirror—and emotion fills her face as they inspire recollection. In a nonfic-tional world, archaeology of the recent past can bring about such moments, especially working with survivors. In cases where there are no survivors, the preservation of artifacts in a deep-sea shipwreck like *Titanic* can fill in gaps, be they linked to a named individual or simply to an unnamed individual whose humanity comes to the forefront with a personal item. In the future, if more luggage is retrieved from the wreck, the possibility of preserved papers—whether love letters, diaries, family Bibles, or business correspondence—can give voice to both the lost and the saved whose baggage, and stories, remained behind.

Beyond the engineering and construction details, the forensics of the disaster, and the technological survey achievements of underwater archaeology is what untold stories archaeologists can offer about those on board. The most likely source of new and undocumented information about those who sailed on *Titanic* is the luggage that lies scattered around the broken hull. Family papers, books, correspondence, and personal items packed by those who sailed in *Titanic* can offer a fuller sense of who the victims were and possibly why they sailed.

Thanks to the magic of Hollywood, the story of *Titanic* and the power of the wreck remind us that archaeology is in the business of telling the story of people. Although the relationship between film, history, and archaeology is never perfect, Hollywood is also in the business of telling the story of people. They found a perfect match in *Titanic*, with a tragic tale played out masterfully and emotionally with the ghostly setting of the actual wreck to create the highest-grossing film of its time.

References

Ballard, Robert D.
    1987   *The Discovery of the Titanic*. Madison Press, New York and Toronto.

Ballard, Robert D. and Michael S. Sweeney
    2004   *Return to Titanic: A Look at the World's Most Famous Ship*. National Geographic Society, Washington, DC.

Bass, George F.
    2005   *Beneath the Seven Seas: Adventures with the Institute of Nautical Archaeology*. Thames and Hudson, New York and London.

Biel, Steven
    1997   *Down with the Old Canoe: A Cultural History of the Titanic Disaster*. W.W. Norton & Co., New York.

Bottomore, Stephen
    2000   *The Titanic and Silent Cinema*. The Projection Box, Uckfield, East Sussex, UK.

Cussler, Clive

1976   *Raise the Titanic!* Bantam Books, New York.

Eaton, John P. and Charles A. Haas

1999   *Titanic: A Journey through Time.* Patrick Stephens Ltd., Sparkford, Somerset, UK.

Foster, John Wilson, editor

2000   *The Titanic Reader.* Penguin Books, New York and Toronto.

Garzke, William H., David K. Brown, Arthur D. Sandiford, John Woodward, and Peter K. Hsu

1995   *The Titanic and Lusitania: A Final Forensic Analysis.* Society of Naval Architects & Marine Engineers, Chesapeake Section, Washington, D.C.

Kemp, Mark

1988   We All Loot in a Yellow Submarine. *Discover Magazine,* January: 62.

Lord, Walter

1955   *A Night to Remember.* Henry Holt and Company, New York.

Lynch, Don and Ken Marschall

2003   *Ghosts of the Abyss: A Journey into the Heart of the Titanic.* Madison Press Books, Toronto and New York.

Roquemore, Joseph

1999   *History Goes to the Movies: A Viewer's Guide to the Best (And Some of the Worst) Historical Films Ever Made.* Doubleday Main Street Books, New York.

Rubenstein, Steve

1986   Get Your Paws Off that Boat. *San Francisco Chronicle,* July 16, p. A16.

Shay, Don

1997a   Back to *Titanic. Cinefex: The Journal of Cinematic Illusions* 72:5–29.

1997b   Ship of Dreams. *Cinefex: The Journal of Cinematic Illusions* 72:30–82.

Wels, Susan

1997   *Titanic: Legacy of the World's Greatest Ocean Liner.* Time-Life Books, New York.

VOYAGE FROM MYTH

RETURN OF THE CONFEDERATE SUBMARINE H.L. HUNLEY

Robert S. Neyland

● ●

H.L. Hunley was a small experimental craft that destroyed and sank the 207-foot sloop of war USS *Housatonic* on the moonlit night of February 17, 1864. *Hunley*, the Confederacy's secret hope, was also lost that night with all hands. It had taken two crews previously to their deaths; ultimately, *Hunley* cost the South twenty-three sons. Its failure to return, the fate of the men, and the cause of its loss was a 136-year-old mystery for scientists to solve. As its history faded from memory, mythology and romance enveloped the sub, its commander and crew, and their demise. *Hunley* disappeared along with construction plans, personal accounts, and the identities of the sailors who died. Civil War veterans' collective memories about the submarine and its crew faded with the passing of time. Local lore filled the holes, burying the event in myth, and ultimately raising the story to legend.

Hunley's History

Hunley was the third in a production of submarines built by a group of inventors, investors, and Southern patriots. It was constructed in Mobile, Alabama, but never saw action in the broad shallow harbor of that city. The depth of the harbor and the distance to the Union blockaders made it impossible to reach enemy ships, where it could dive underneath with its towed torpedo. General P. G. T. Beauregard, commander of the military defense of Charleston, South Carolina, requested that the submarine be transferred there to strike at Union ships and lift the blockade of that port. The submarine arrived in Charleston in 1863 and was put through a series of trials. Tragically, it sank on two separate occasions with the collective loss of thirteen crewmembers. The second sinking claimed the lives of Captain Horace Hunley, the submarine's namesake, and crewmen enlisted from the design and engineering team from Mobile. General Beauregard, although discouraged, allowed the submarine to be raised and deployed again with a new volunteer crew. The submarine was put under the command of Lt. George E. Dixon, a Confederate Army engineer from Mobile, who had worked on a steamboat prior to the war and was reputed to exhibit great courage. Dixon was convinced that the submarine could successfully attack and destroy enemy ships. He solicited a third volunteer crew who he put through rigorous training in preparation for an assault on one of the Union blockade vessels (Ragan 1999:187–191).

On the evening of February 17, 1864, the submarine left Battery Marshall, a Confederate gun emplacement located at Breach Inlet on Sullivan's Island, Charleston. *Hunley's* commander steered a course for USS *Housatonic*, a 207-foot steam screw sloop-of-war stationed about four miles outside Charleston Harbor. At about 8:45 p.m., *Hunley's* crew planted a barbed torpedo in the starboard side of the *Housatonic's* hull, locating the explosive near the officer's quarters and the magazine. They backed their vessel away, and a member of the crew exploded the charge by pulling a lanyard attached to a trigger detonator. The torpedo stuck well beneath the *Housatonic's* waterline and the hole that resulted from the explosion caused the ship to sink in a matter of minutes. The ship's hull sank to the bottom, its masts and rigging protruding from the water, where the crew clung until rescued. From their position in the wreck's rigging, *Housatonic* survivors saw a blue light waved from the submarine. Confederate sentries ashore also reported seeing the blue signal light and in response lit a bonfire to help the submarine to navigate home. These are the last reported sightings of *Hunley*; the submarine never returned to Breach Inlet.

After a fifteen-year search, Clive Cussler, adventure novelist, discovered the confederate submarine *H.L. Hunley* 900 feet seaward of the *Housatonic* wreckage (Figure 6.1). The announcement of the submarine's discovery initiated discussion about ownership, protection, and responsibility for the wreck's remains. Eventually, the U.S. Navy and the State of South Carolina Hunley Commission were established as the principal entities that would oversee the submarine's recovery, excavation, and long-term preservation. In 1996, an underwater archaeological team revisited the site and confirmed the earlier claim of finding the *Hunley* and discovered that the sub appeared to be intact and well preserved.

In 2000, a diverse team of archaeologists, engineers, and divers raised the *Hunley*. A year later, the excavation began inside of a saturated tank in Charleston. Four iron hull plates were removed and the interior sediments were archaeologically excavated. Personal artifacts, along with eight crewmen, were exhumed from the silt-filled sub. International media coverage hailed this as a jewel of underwater archaeology encapsulating a wealth of information about the construction of the submarine, clues to its sinking, and stories of these almost forgotten men. Research and analysis on the project will likely continue for another decade.

Hunley Goes to the Movies

Hunley's recovery generated international news coverage, including *National Geographic* and *History Channel* specials, numerous popular books and articles, and even a musical. Her legacy is

Figure 6.1. *H.L. Hunley* in the conservation tank at the Warren Lasch Conservation Laboratory, North Charleston, South Carolina. The view is of the port side from the bow looking aft. Notice the hole in the forward conning tower, which was speculated to have been shot out by Union sailors firing on the *Hunley* during its attack. There is no archaeological evidence of small arms fire creating this hole. The presence of the hole is a mystery, but it may be the result of damage that occurred by an anchor or grapple hanging post sinking.

Photo courtesy of Friends of the *Hunley*.

extraordinary and when stories are larger than life, Hollywood embraces the romance and mysticism that accompanies such legends. Two television movies have been based on the sub, both unoriginally named *The Hunley*.

The earliest film was a 1963 CBS production produced as part of *The Great Adventure* historical series. This movie came out when television was still exploring its role as either entertainer or educator. CBS's *Hunley* movie had an outstanding cast of actors and was produced by John Houseman and directed by Paul Stanley. It is only available in black and white 16 mm film and runs fifty-four minutes. The production has several notable actors, including, Jackie Cooper as Lt. Dixon, James MacArthur as Lt. Alexander, Wayne Rodgers as Cdr. Tombs, and George Lindsey as Hampton, a fictitious sailor whose name never occurs on *Hunley*'s crew roster. If there is one thing movie productions do well, it is setting the stage. The 1963 movie, although performed in the early days of television, was no exception; building three full-sized versions of *Hunley*, a quarter-scale model of the sub, a full-size waterfront set, and a miniature-scaled version of the city of Charleston.

The movie opens with the narrator explaining the historical events leading up to *Hunley* and the desperate situation of Charleston, while the audience views the sub's recovery and opening of the hatch after the death of its second crew. Lt. Dixon dramatically reaches into the opened hatch and lifts Horace L. Hunley's dead hand, which still tightly clasps the unlit candle. Horace L. Hunley was financier and captain of the sub's second crew. It was his failure to light the candle in the sub and close the valve, allowing water to flow into the forward ballast tank, that resulted in the loss of the sub and its second crew.

Ted Turner was familiar with the story of *Hunley* from his boyhood in South Carolina and encouraged TNT Productions to tell the story on film. TNT's *The Hunley* (1999) was produced by John Gray, filmed in color, and is ninety-four minutes in length. It stars Armand Assante as Lt. Dixon and Donald Sutherland as General Beauregard. Advances in special effects and a larger budget resulted in a movie set with three full-scale *Hunley* replicas, full-sized mock-ups of Charleston, a temporary conversion of downtown Charleston into a Civil War street scene, and computer-generated special effects showing the submarine operating underwater. The movie was filmed on a steel barge in the water of Charleston, with sets mimicking the decks of USS *Housatonic* and CSS *Indian Chief*. Although the 1999 movie duplicates parts of the 1963 movie, the former uses the Hollywood ploy of starting the movie with a dramatic action scene with *Hunley* plummeting bow first into the mud of Charleston Harbor with Horace L. Hunley and his crew desperately struggling and failing to save themselves.

The primary historical source used by the directors of both movies is the account of *Hunley* veteran and survivor William Alexander (Alexander 1902a, 1902b, 1903). Other primary historical records such as the *Official Records of the Union and Confederate Navies* are readily available sources containing the correspondence of officers on the operation and loss of the submarine (Naval History Department 1894). The 1999 movie did use archaeological information from Clive Cussler's 1995 survey and the more intensive work conducted by federal and state archaeologists in 1996 (Murphy 1998). The archaeological information allowed the film director to improve the design of the sub. In addition, they interpreted the sub's demise based on the 1995 discovery of a broken viewing port in the forward conning tower and the speculation by archaeologists that it was shot out by Union fire, injuring or killing its commander, Lt. Dixon.

Archaeology to the Rescue

The last decade has given archaeology the chance to tell *Hunley*'s story. Historical records and oral histories, although meager, were formerly the only primary documents written about *Hunley*. As a result of the preliminary archaeology surveys in 1995 and 1996, TNT incorporated archaeological findings into their 1999 movie. Hollywood, if it chose, could use archaeological findings to tell a more accurate and interesting history of the submarine and its crew. Hollywood did use available archaeological information, but adapted it to the storytelling method of film. *Hunley* archaeology corrected many erroneous historical details about the submarine and the crew. For example, archaeology substantiated several historical documents of the sub. It also corrected many misconceptions about the submarine and its use. In addition, archaeology has revealed previously unknown features of the submarine, learned how it was operated, and identified the men who manned her. In sum, archaeology has opened up new depths to our understanding of *Hunley* and the early development of submarine warfare that Hollywood has failed to communicate.

Submarine Set and Special Effects

The *Hunley* producers attempted to build very accurate replicas of the submarine by researching historical records, and the TNT movie incorporated archaeological findings into their story. Budget and filming constraints did factor into the accuracy of replicas in both movies as they were built with much room for the actors than the incredibly tight constraints of the actual *Hunley*. In reality, the men were extremely cramped, with an interior height of slightly less than four feet and width of only three and one half feet. The CBS 1963 movie economized on the sets by using close-ups that did not require the orchestration of many actors, a miniature-scale Charleston, and painted backdrops of the coast rather than filming on location in the city itself.

The 1999 TNT movie had the larger budget and was able to take advantage of the growing numbers of Civil War reenactors (which did not exist as a cultural phenomenon and pastime in 1963) and advancements in computer technology. The budget allowed for filming on site, even adapting the modern city of Charleston by covering the streets with earth and lining them with extras dressed in period clothing. Charleston street scenes suggest sociopolitical complexity through filming not only enslaved African Americans but captured African American Union soldiers. Missing from the crowd scenes of Charleston are the children, particularly babies and infants, who would have been prevalent in Charleston's community.

The CBS production focused on educating the audience as well as entertaining, discussing in detail *Hunley*'s construction and the sub's operation, and highlighting key features of the sub—diving planes, keel weights, ballast tanks, hand crank, and depth gauge.

This early film does a good job of explaining why the sub's crew switched from an explosive mine towed behind the sub to a torpedo attached to a spar. In following William Alexander's (1903) account of *Hunley*, written forty years after the submarine's loss, the movie is true to Alexander's story to the point of incorporating mistakes probably resulting from his failing memory. A prominent example is his drawing of *Hunley* that details a blunt-end vessel instead of the sharp-ended, graceful submarine revealed by her recovery. Other errors adapted from William Alexander's history, which made their way into the movie, include a steering wheel for the rudder control rather than the joystick-like device discovered by archaeologists. Despite these erroneous details, it is clear that the earlier movie attempted to educate the public as well as entertain.

A notable filming error in the TNT movie is that it shows *Hunley*'s attack on the USS *Housatonic*'s port side instead of starboard, where it actually occurred. Getting the battle historically accurate is an important part of the story. Curiously, National Geographic Television also places the attack on the same incorrect side as TNT and, although informed of this by the archaeologists, they were unable to change the animation prior to the movie airing. National Geographic Television was able to reduce the view of the port side shown and thus dealt with the issue by making it more difficult for the untrained eyes in the audience to determine the side of the ship under attack. The TNT movie might have influenced the documentary or both could have made the same mistake in attempting to interpret historical records with the battle's location. When the torpedo explodes in both movies it is dramatic but does not follow historic accounts, which indicate the explosion occurred underwater and did not produce flames or a loud report.

Although script writers had access to the deck officer's drawing and description of the explosion, they either did not search for the data or chose not to include them in their films. Another observation on the early film is that to counter costs, the CBS movie uses footage from another movie. The 1963 movie's *Housatonic* more closely resembles an 18th- or 17th-century ship from a pirate movie rather than a Civil War–era sloop-of-war. This substitution was probably acceptable at a time when audiences were less sophisticated.

Hunley's Crew

As archaeologists had not yet revealed who manned the *Hunley*, Hollywood created the crew to mirror recognizable characters from earlier movies. One of the perpetuated misconceptions about *Hunley* was the number of crewmen. The two movies cast nine actors for the crew, and archaeologists also expected the recovery of nine men. There is ambiguity in the historical accounts, particularly in the secondary sources that lead to this number. Nine crewmen had been reported many times in the secondary sources therefore, nine bodies were fully expected to be found in the sub. Only when archaeologists counted pairs of shoes and craniums and compared this information with the number of places in the sub for crewman did we realize that there were only eight. Archaeology resolved this perpetuated error only after the release of the *Hunley* movies.

The movies' directors only had sparse historical details to work with on developing the crew's characters. In the case of the 1963 movie, they did not use the correct names of the crew. The TNT movie had more historical information to work with and accurately reported the crew's names. A more complete history of these men is being discovered from the work of genealogist Linda Abrams and forensic anthropologist Douglas Owsley.

Initially, the crewmen were thought to be southern, young, and small enough to fit into the tiny sub with its narrow hatches. Archaeology and forensic analysis revealed a crew who varied in age, stature, and origin. Only half the crew was born in the United States, the others were European immigrants, their origin identified from carbon 12 isotope analysis. Carbon 12 is more prevalent in the European wheat-based diet than in the American corn diet. Owsley used it as a marker to determine a wheat or corn diet and thus hypothesize the crew's regions of origin (Owsley 2006). Four men showed relative differences in the isotope that was correlated to their length of time in the United States. Miller, one of the older sailors aged between forty and forty-five, had only been in the country a short time as had Arnold Becker, estimated to be in his early twenties. Lumpkin, a seasoned sailor aged between thirty-seven and forty-four years, had immigrated many years before, as shown by the relatively less prevalent carbon 12 isotope.

The men varied in age as well as their origins. The average age of a Civil War soldier was 25.8 years (Gould 1869). Three of the men were in their forties, one was in his thirties, and the remaining men were in their early to mid-twenties. Lt. Dixon was twenty-six years old; Arnold Becker was the youngest crew member. Becker, although in his early twenties was a strong and hardy individual, however, his bones already showed a life of hard labor. Many of the men were taller than expected, with three crewmen five feet ten inches and one over six feet (Owsley 2006). These men would be considered much taller than the average Civil War soldier, who ranged in height between five feet six inches and five feet ten inches (Schablitsky 1996:39–40).

The men's bones exhibit a past of injuries reflective of working-class lives. *Hunley* sailors Lumpkins and Miller had the healed injuries indicative of a dangerous and strenuous life of seafaring. The vice of tobacco was obvious from Lumpkins's damaged teeth, which were heavily stained from tobacco use and were grooved from clenching his pipes. In addition, a previous foot injury gave him a permanent limp. Frank Collins had subtle injuries to his teeth. Tailor notches discovered in his front teeth were supported by research showing that his grandfather and uncle were both cobblers, suggesting he likely carried on the trade (Owsley 2006).

Romancing the Coin

Romance, even when there is no relevant love story, is common if not necessary to movies. The gold coin found with the remains of Lt. Dixon has been interpreted as the gift of his young sweetheart "Queenie" Bennett, who was sixteen years old in 1864 and ten years younger than Dixon. The coin had the following inscribed on it: Shiloh./April 6th 1862/My Life Preserver/G.E.D.

(Figure 6.2). The love story is derived from a newspaper article written well after the war and based on now missing letters from Dixon to Queen Bennett (*Mobile Daily Herald* 1904). The article relates that the $20 gold piece saving Dixon's life at the Battle of Shiloh was given to him by Queen, who at that time would have been only fourteen years old, a considerable sum for a young girl. Another newspaper article dating to a period during the Civil War relates a different story of Dixon's coin but there is no mention of Queen (Linda Abrams 2005, pers. comm.). The story might be accurate but it may also be that the newspaper reporter embellished the story. The romance would fit into the genre of romantic and nostalgic stories about the Civil War that were written and presented in many different art forms after the war, particularly in the South. Dixon typifies the heroic Southern

Figure 6.2. View of Lt. George Dixon's $20 gold coin, which stopped a bullet at the Battle of Shiloh. The coin has been identified as a romantic gift to Lt. Dixon from fourteen-year-old Queen Bennett of Mobile, Alabama. The romantic story of the coin has yet to be conclusively proven.

Photo courtesy of Friends of the *Hunley*.

soldier who sacrifices for his country, and Queen is the epitome of virtuous Southern womanhood, devoted to her man, family, and the Southern cause.

As Queen was viewed as Dixon's fiancée, it is not surprising that her records were searched for signs of Dixon. Despite contacting living relatives, no original Dixon letters turned up, but a photo found in her album contained a young man that no one recognized as family. The unidentified man was assumed to be Dixon until historical evidence and forensics proved the photo dated from a post–Civil War period and the image of the cranium overlaid with that of the photo did not match. Later, another one of Queen's personal artifacts—a locket—revealed another man's photograph, who was again thought to be Dixon. When his likeness was superimposed on the forensic information, his anatomy did not match Dixon. Romantic imagery can be dangerous when trying to interpret an archaeological record. Jewelry including a gold and diamond broach and ring found on Dixon has been interpreted to be gifts for Queen; however, when these finds are placed in context with the political and economic climate, their presence on Dixon make logical, and not romantic, sense. Paper and coinage were worth nothing during the Civil War, therefore, people kept their investment in property that held value, in this case, gold and diamonds.

The romantic story of Queen Bennett and Lt. Dixon was not published until 1995 (Ragan) therefore, it is missing from the 1963 movie. TNT, however, embraced the mythic love story and it played center stage in their movie, particularly in explaining Lt. Dixon's character. Inaccuracies exist within the story, for Queen is not portrayed as the sixteen-year-old southern belle from Mobile but is cast as a woman in her twenties who nurses Dixon after he is brought off the Shiloh battlefield. Tragically, she is killed in a steamboat explosion, ironically the result of a drifting explosive mine, explaining Dixon's disillusionment, alcoholism, and death wish. Whether the director intends it or not, Queen symbolizes the "lost cause" of the Confederacy. In reality, it is Dixon who dies and Queen who survives in Mobile, reaches adulthood, and marries.

Final Act: *Hunley* Death Scene

Theories about the sub's death are manifold. Early theories considered that the sub was destroyed by the initial explosion and flooded with burst steam or perhaps was sucked into the hole made in USS *Housatonic*. Another theory of the time was that *Hunley* was simply swept out to sea by the current. Contemporary theories include that *Hunley* slowly settled to the bottom without the crew's knowledge until it was too late, with the air depleted, the crew slipped into unconsciousness. It is possible *Hunley* went to the bottom in an attempt to hide and could not resurface. The recovery of a grapple anchor from the same geological layer as the keel of the sub resulted in another theory. This scenario suggests that when the sub anchored it became stuck on the bottom. Yet another theory suggests that small arms fire from defenders on *Housatonic* shot out the glass viewing port in the forward conning tower; although unlikely, this scenario is not easily vanquished, perhaps because it is a dramatic scene in the movie. The most probable theory to date is that the ship coming to the aid of the *Housatonic* crew, the USS *Canandaigua*, struck *Hunley* or swamped it. As speculations continue to be disproved, a careful study of the archaeological and historical data will lead to the eventual discovery of the real reason for the loss of the *H.L. Hunley*.

Conclusion

For archaeologists, the creative product is the written publication of the historic context, methods, findings, and interpretations of an archaeological site. The final report carries a payload of details, hypotheses, analysis, and conclusions. Movie directors cannot easily incorporate scientific method or expect their audience to be objective. A film is not produced to "evaluate sources, make logical arguments, or systematically weigh evidence in its allotted time and hold the audience's attention" (Rosenstone 1995:27). The two *Hunley* movies fit history into the common cinema structure of three acts: exposition, complication, and resolution. This structure makes a good story for the audience but leads to omitting historical facts that may be tangential to the three acts. Movies, to please their audiences and to get their message across, simplify and condense history into a limited number of frames dependent on film length. An archaeologist is director of his or her scientific analysis. Like the movie director's dramatic work, the archaeologist's field of inquiry carries interpretative license. Archaeologists can be selective in the way they choose and use facts to draw conclusions. At the end of the day, archaeologists and film directors both want to say something definitive and please their respective audiences.

In the case of the TNT *Hunley* film, archaeology was used to interpret details that were incorporated into the set, costumes, and special effects. The *Hunley* movies did use available histories to create relatively accurate replicas of the sub's construction, Civil War–period sets, and costumes. Film does what archaeology and history do not do well—express the visual and sensual experiences of another time and the thrill of dramatic historic events. The *Hunley* movies share emotions with the audience that evoke feelings and the physical strain of the men on *Hunley*, their fear, anger, determination, and courage. Archaeologists, as scientists viewing the past from the mountain-top, are much less engaging with their story.

Hollywood tells its story in its own format; movies engage their audience with familiar themes that moviegoers love to see played out. Audiences prefer movies that have identifiable heroes and villains, where there is distinct difference between good and evil, with the former winning out over the latter. Hollywood knows public tastes and that they prefer morally uplifting stories, which have underdogs and battles between David and Goliath. *Hunley* certainly fits into this formula. Directors simplify plots and use a limited number of characters to make the story understandable to the general public; therefore, their portrayal of historic events is focused and seen from an elementary and limited perspective. Archaeologists also sometimes take the narrow window view of history because of the nature of investigating one site at a time.

Whether movies intend it or not, they educate the public and both mirror and influence current culture. When film directors consider the broader interpretations of historic events, their art reflects popular culture and the era in which they were produced rather than the past culture in which they were set (Toplin 2002:41). This is clearly the difference between the early 1963 *Hunley* film in which the officers and crew are positive about their mission and the Southern cause. In contrast, the 1999 version is influenced by the post-Vietnam antiwar disillusionment with war. Dixon is portrayed in both movies as a man of vision, courage, and determination. Movies use the strong leader or "great man" figure to move history forward. Historians spurn the role of individuals and focus more on broader economic and political issues as the motive force behind change. In the case of the *Hunley*, archaeologists are interpreting the leadership of Lt. Dixon and the determination of *Hunley*'s crew to sink USS *Housatonic* and impact historical events by freeing the Confederacy of the Union blockade.

Film has become the public's ambassador of the past, providing the cliff notes for the audience. According to Rosenstone, "history is dead" movies make the history the public knows (1995:23). Film's mission primarily entertains and accidentally educates. In our increasingly multimedia world, we as archaeologists may take a lesson from Hollywood and learn how to incidentally entertain as well as teach.

References

Alexander, William A.

    1902a   The Confederate Submarine Torpedo Boat *Hunley. Gulf States Historical Magazine.*

    1902b   Thrilling Chapter in the History of the Confederate States Navy. *Southern Historical Society Papers.*

    1903   The Heroes of the *Hunley. Munsey Magazine.*

Gould, Benjamin Apthorp

    1869   *Investigations in the Military and Anthropological Statistics of American Soldiers.* Cambridge Riverside Press, New York.

Mobile Daily Herald

    1904   Dixon Builder of Submarine *Hunley,* Went to Death in the Deep. *Mobile Daily Herald,* November 15.

Murphy, L. E., editor

    1998   *H.L. Hunley* Site Assessment. National Park Service, Sante Fe, NM.

Naval History Department

    1894   *Official Records of the Union and Confederate Navies in the War of the Rebellion.* U.S. Government Printing Office series I, Vols. 1–27; series II Vols. 1–3 (1894–1922), Washington DC.

Owsley, Douglas

    2006   *H.L. Hunley,* Identifying the Crew. Paper presented at the 39th Historical and Underwater Archaeology Conference, Sacramento, CA.

Ragan, Mark K.

    1995   *H.L. Hunley: Submarines Sacrifice and Success in the Civil War.* Narwal Press, Charleston, SC.

    1999   *Union and Confederate Submarine Warfare in the Civil War.* Savas, Mason City, IA.

Rosenstone, Robert A.

    1995   *Visions of the Past: The Challenge of Film Tour Idea of History.* Harvard University Press, Cambridge, MA.

Schablitsky, Julie M.

    1996   Duty and Vice: The Daily Life of a Fort Hoskins Soldier. Masters thesis, Anthropology Department, Oregon State University, Corvallis.

Toplin, Robert Brent

    2002   *Reel History: In Defense of Hollywood.* University Press of Kansas, Lawrence.

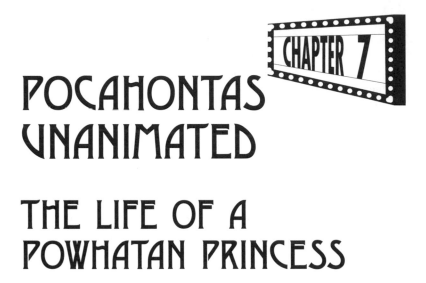

POCAHONTAS UNANIMATED

THE LIFE OF A POWHATAN PRINCESS

Randy Amici

● ●

Perhaps the most famous Indian woman in American history, Pocahontas, the young daughter of an Indian chief, has been portrayed and represented in historical writings and in Hollywood movies. Until now, her life has primarily been interpreted from ethnohistorical sources but, as archaeological excavations are undertaken and the findings published, the life of this Powhatan child is becoming clearer yet more complex than scholars have been led to believe.

Combining historical writings and archaeology, it is now possible to gain insight into the life of Pocahontas that has eluded Hollywood producers for years. Subsistence patterns within the Powhatan community varied little between higher- and lower-status individuals. Houses were of similar construction, and "royalty" tended fields alongside "commoners." Archaeology is demonstrating that this was also true of "Princess" Pocahontas.

She was treated as an average community member and lived a much different lifestyle than the myth has led us to believe. Ironically, it was her common upbringing that provided her with the domestic skills that would truly change American history.

Pocahontas and Hollywood: The Creation of a Legend

At the core of the Pocahontas myth is romance, a customary formula for many Hollywood productions. Physically, she is always depicted in her late teens or early twenties, with a thin build and an uncontrollable infatuation with Captain John Smith, an English colonist. The common theme in the Pocahontas legend is that Smith and the Indian princess meet and begin an ambiguous love affair. The legend maintains that Pocahontas's obsession with Smith was so great that she threw her body over his to prevent Smith's execution ordered by her father in December 1607. In truth, Pocahontas's life and contribution to history was far more complex life than alluded to in these films.

The legend of Pocahontas has evolved over the past four centuries to become a fictitious tale perpetuated by the U.S. film industry; this is evident in the paramount misconception that Pocahontas was romantically involved with John Smith. The mythical Pocahontas first appears in film in the 1924 silent movie, *Pocahontas and John Smith*. In 1953, the film *Captain John Smith and Pocahontas* went so far as to have the "Indian Princess" and Smith marry. The 1995 animated Disney film *Pocahontas* raked in $141 million at the box office and had one of the biggest premieres in movie history. The film is filled with historical inaccuracies and ethnocentric ambiguities. The cartoon movie portrays Pocahontas as a teen-aged "Barbie doll-like figure," a Powhatan princess who falls in love with the peaceful blond, blue-eyed Captain John Smith. In reality, Smith was a short, squatty twenty-seven-year-old redhead with a penchant for violence. Pocahontas was only nine or ten years old when the two first met in the spring of 1607 (Townsend 2004:13).

Perhaps the most realistic and most recent portrayal of Pocahontas and her environment was by filmmaker Terrence Mallick. He endeavored to guarantee historical accuracy in his 2006 movie *The New World*, hiring local craftsmen to weave mats and to replicate war clubs, leather bags, and belts. He also consulted with Chief Robert Two Eagles Green of the Patawomeck tribe of Virginia and Chief Steven Adkins of the Chickahominy tribe to ensure an accurate depiction of their culture. Researchers went to the Ashmolean Museum in Oxford, England, to examine Powhatan's opulent mantle, comprised of four deer skins and 30,000 hand-sewn beads, to create a design that would be as similar to the original as possible. Mallick had art director David Crank re-create a fort for the set using Jamestown archaeological data. Mallick's tenacious attempt to re-create an accurate Jamestown was augmented by planting the two-acre movie set with corn and tobacco species that would have been grown in early 17th-century Virginia. Yet, despite this detail to historical accuracy and despite being the first film to indicate that Pocahontas did not save Smith from death (Mallick suggests that Smith was ceremonially executed and brought back to life as a Powhatan warrior, allowing him to be adopted into tribe. It may be that this was motivated by Powhatan's interest in securing trade relations with the English), the fictitious love story survives. Mallick, as did his predecessors, kept the mythical romance alive in the movie. In this rendition, Pocahontas does marry John Rolfe, as she did in history; however, the movie hints that it was Smith who she truly loved (Vincent 2006).

The Hollywood Pocahontas is much different from the historical Pocahontas. The real Pocahontas was not a love-obsessed teenager or a carefree privileged child. She was a seminal figure in American history who was fundamental to the survival of the first permanent English colony that ultimately led to the formation of the United States of America (Figure 7.1). Considering all the evidence, Pocahontas was far from the besotted and innocent adolescent girl Hollywood has presented; instead, she was a Powhatan child and a political pawn. To date, there has been a tendency to look at the life of Pocahontas from a purely historical point of view. Yet, with the recent focus on colonial Virginia and the upsurge of archaeological excavations in Pocahontas's homelands there is an opportunity to challenge the legends and clarify the story. In other words, our understanding of the life and culture of Pocahontas and the Powhatan Indians can be enriched, clarified, and quantified by combining historical documents and archaeological evidence left behind 400 years ago.

Figure 7.1. Pocahontas engraving made by Simon Van de Passe in 1616. The engraving is considered to be an accurate depiction of the real-life Powhatan princess.

Pocahontas—
A Daughter of the Powhatan Confederacy

The majority of what we know about Pocahontas and her people comes from early observations by European colonists. Pocahontas was most likely born in 1597. Her given name at birth was Amonute; the Algonquian meaning of this name has been lost over the last four centuries (Townsend 2004:13). Her secret name, a name that she would use once married or on reaching puberty, was Matoaka. It was the nickname Pocahontas, given by her father, the world would immortalize. The name Pocahontas is thought to translate to *little wanton* or *playful one* (Rountree 2005:37–38). Later in life, she would convert to Christianity, marry an English colonist, and be given yet another name, Rebecca Rolfe.

Pocahontas was the daughter of the paramount chief of the Algonquian-speaking peoples who lived in what is now Tidewater, Virginia. Powahatan's given name was Whunsonacock (Freeman 1970:18), Whunsenacawh (Rountree 2005:17), or Wahunsenacaw (Townsend 2004:12), but he is better known in history as Chief Powhatan.

The tendency has been to portray Pocahontas as a princess associated with a class society rather than the egalitarian one in which she was raised. As a member of the Powhatan tribe, Pocahontas would have worked alongside the people of her village, with her father's other children and their mothers, toward a common goal of survival. Late Woodland subsistence in the latter 16th and early 17th centuries was an egalitarian system that required all individuals to contribute to societal welfare through farming, hunting, fishing, and gathering wild nuts and berries. Ironically, this survival strategy would take many months for the Jamestown settlers to understand and adopt, ensuring their own survival.

Pocahontas: The Powhatan

Virginia is one of the most archaeologically studied areas in North America. Thousands of prehistoric- and historic-period sites have been excavated; consequently, a vignette of early Virginia is emerging from the numerous research reports. As a girl growing up in the early 17th century, Pocahontas's life was quite dull and unlike Hollywood would have us believe. As a part of the Powhatan Confederacy, Pocahontas would have been raised in a community consisting of 200 small villages (Johansen 2005:118). Archaeological excavations lining the East Coast have shown that indigenous people of this region resided in small and relatively permanent villages made up of houses and other smaller structures. On the central Atlantic coastal plain, the usual house was about sixty feet long and about eighteen feet wide and high. The Powhatan princess would have eaten and slept in a structure constructed on a framework of poles covered by overlapping elm or cedar bark. A wide hallway would have split the interior with either individual people or families occupying sections along each side. These compartments were furnished with sleeping platforms, reed mats, shelves and communal fire hearths. Food and supplies were stored in pits at either end of the structure (Newcomb 1974). In Virginia, the houses in Powhatan settlements generally had rounded endings to make them more wind resistant (Rountree and Turner 2002:14). Pocahontas would have been raised in this type of bark-and-pole-constructed communal home.

Pocahontas's position as a princess would not have provided her with much status in her community. It is doubtful that she had hours of expendable time to frolic through the countryside as portrayed in Disney's adaptation of her life. The colonists at Jamestown were warned, "Those who do not work, do not eat"; this would have been no different for Pocahontas. Archaeology has shown that Powhatan people's primary subsistence was an agricultural-based community augmented by hunting and gathering. Ethnobotanical reports show that maize, hickory nuts, acorns, and fleshy fruits occur frequently on Late Woodland sites (Pearsall 1989:5). Slash-and-burn agriculture was pursued wherever it was productive, and corn, beans, squash, and tobacco were raised in carefully tended gardens. During the European contact period, the Powhatan peoples had hundreds of acres under cultivation around their villages (Newcomb 1974: 63). Pocahontas's life would have been very basic and painfully uneventful; however, all of this changed when the colonists from England landed on the shores of Powhatan territory in 1607. Almost instantaneously, Pocahontas was catapulted from a mere member of the Powhatan chiefdom to a political representative and bargaining tool.

Pocahontas: The Political Pawn

The Powhatan paramount chiefdom was a union of many Algonquian-speaking tribes in the Chesapeake Bay region and consequently immersed in a world of complicated politics. Pocahontas was raised within this culture, but where did she fit into this society? It is unlikely she was a holder of any political sway or that she would inherit the *throne* from her father. The Powhatans were like most other Algonquians in following a matrilineal system of inheritance, meaning that the chieftainship was inherited through the female line (Townsend 2004:15). It is unclear how Powhatan succeeded to the throne, but it is likely that he followed an older brother or his mother as leader of the Powhatan tribe (when he died, power was passed to his brother or possibly his cousin, Opechancanough). Captain John Smith states in his writings that none of Powhatan's children would ever hold power in the chiefdom, but Pocahontas proved to be a central political representative in other ways, specifically in her relationship with the newly arrived colonists (Freeman 1970:19).

The knowledge we have of the Powhatan society and Pocahontas's position within it is primarily based on the analysis and writings of the early ethnographic observations by

Europeans; it is from these sources that many of the misconceptions of Pocahontas were born. It is important to recognize that when John Smith and his cohorts arrived in Virginia in 1607, it took them years to write down their observations and experiences. Gathered from a nonnative perspective, the writings were intended for a European audience and perhaps simplified to make the Indian way of life comprehensible to the less well traveled. In addition, Smith's writing had to effectively satisfy the Virginia Company directive to not interfere with the "Naturals." The Virginia Company was fully aware that the Spanish could form an alliance with the Powhatans and easily gain control of the region. It was therefore in the company's best interest to maintain a good relationship with the aboriginal peoples.

Perhaps evidence of writing for the masses back in Europe is best demonstrated by John Smith and his contemporaries labeling Pocahontas a princess. Europeans understood the term *princess* and use of this title made it appear that the colonists had made contact with the royal family of the New World. It is at this juncture that we can use archaeology to lend credibility to the theory that there was a Powhatan confederacy and a stratified, complex society already in existence in Virginia in 1607. Until recently, colonial historians have relied on the subjective observations of a few early colonial English men through their writings to the Virginia Company to understand Powhatan culture at the time of contact.

Excavations at Late Woodland sites in Tidewater Virginia do support and, in some cases, clarify that the indigenous people had developed elaborate trade networks and advanced resource extraction methods. There is evidence in the form of structural remains and artifacts from the Powhatan chiefdom to augment the writings of Smith and his contemporaries. Some of the observations recorded by the European ethnographers detailed information on the housing in Powhatan settlements. They noted the houses for chiefs were bigger and better crafted than other houses in the community. Smith states, "The great King hath foure or five houses, each containing fourscore or a hundred foote in length" (Barbour 1986:51). Robert Beverly documented that the

Virginia natives palisaded their king's house (Wright 1947:177). The archaeological excavations at the Powhatan village of Jordan's Point, Virginia, illustrate that the society Pocahontas grew up in had a large degree of social organization. Forty Indian houses were located ranging in size from sixteen feet to twenty-seven feet, but most interestingly, one house was unique from the others. Structure 16 was an elaborate building that probably belonged to a chief. It was larger than the others at thirty and one-half feet long and eighteen feet wide. It was also an exceptionally well-constructed building, with double-spaced posts, internal divisions, and a built-in bench (Rountree and Turner 2002:65).

At the Late Woodland site of Great Neck, Virginia Beach, Virginia, another larger structure was found by archaeologists. This site showed structural remains in the form of longhouses and other smaller structures similar to what the Europeans described in the latter half of the 16th century. The site director stated, "The Late Woodland structural remains encountered at Great Neck are generally what would be expected given information on building practices among coastal Algonquian peoples in Virginia" (Hodges 1998:203).

Another tantalizing clue comes from the initial excavations at Werwowocomoco, the capitol of the Powhatan Confederacy and assumed birthplace of Pocahontas. Excavations at Powhatan's main settlement of Werwomocomoco show evidence of a palisade, and although excavations here only began in earnest in recent years, it is hoped that future seasons reveal more about the site structure and village lay out. In addition to structural remains, higher-status trade goods such as copper, freshwater pearls, shell beads, and chlorite pipes have been located at a number of Powhatan settlements (Rountree and Turner 2004:46). These artifacts show a level of social stratification visually separating the high-level indigenous leaders from the ordinary citizens. These recent archaeological discoveries and interpretations underscore the complexity of the Powhatan Confederacy.

If we can conclude that John Smith and his contemporaries were accurate in their observations and that the Powhatan chiefdom was well established, then we can accept that Pocahontas, as the daughter of the chief, had a certain degree of status in her society. Initially, Pocahontas was to have very little to do with the politics of the Powhatan chiefdom; however, this changed dramatically in 1607 when the colonists arrived from England and Pocahontas developed a relationship with John Smith and John Rolfe.

Pocahontas—The Relationships and Politics that Defined History

Pocahontas, John Smith, and John Rolfe are significant figures in U.S. history, but not for the reasons one would think. What Hollywood has overlooked in their creation of the Pocahontas love triangle is that her real interactions with the colonists helped shape history.

The prominent relationship between Pocahontas and Smith is characterized by their supposed love affair and the death-defying rescue. In reality, Pocahontas and Smith did have a significant relationship, just not a romantic one. Pocahontas was by all accounts a curious and confident child who did form a friendship with Smith; it was this friendship that saved the Jamestown colony in its early years. When the colony was failing, it was Pocahontas who brought food; probably a direct result of her friendship with Smith (Price 2003:5). This was the first act that distinguishes Pocahontas as a significant figure in American history. If she did not make this gesture, the colonists would surely have starved and the settlement of the "new world" would have failed.

Captain John Smith

At the forefront of the Captain John Smith legend is his rescue by Pocahontas. He mentions in his writings that Pocahontas saved him from execution in 1607 by Chief Powhatan. After examining other historical accounts, contemporary scholars have concluded she did not play an instrumental role in saving his life. The details of the event can be left to speculation;

Pocahontas may have been playing a role, possibly encouraged by Powhatan to gain Smith's trust by pretending to rescue him. It is just as possible that the event did not happen at all and was the concoction of a self-promoter. In his earlier writings of 1612, Smith omitted the story when Pocahontas and her husband were still alive. Years after Pocahontas and her husband had passed away, Smith published the account of his rescue in 1624, making it hard for the story to be refuted. Perhaps Smith created the story to favor himself with future investors in the New World by illustrating he had gained the trust of one of the most important natives.

Also entwined in the Smith and Pocahontas myth was their supposed love affair. Smith arrived in 1607 and left two years later when Pocahontas was just entering puberty. Smith and Pocahontas would never meet again. Smith never mentioned a romantic relationship with Pocahontas in any of his writing. Instead, this myth was created by storytellers swept up in the excitement of the colonization and intent in romanticizing events in a New World.

When Pocahontas was approximately twelve or thirteen, she married a man named Kocoom. He was a warrior of little political influence who she married by choice. The "princess" as stated, was not part of the noble line and was therefore not expected to bear the political burden of an arranged marriage. Kocoom was possibly an officer in Powhatan's personal guard where she would have come to know him (Price 2003:155; Townsend 2004:128). Pocahontas's marriage to Kocoom did not provide political gain; however, there is some speculation that this marriage provided a trust with a northern tribe that was not under Powhatan's thumb (Townsend 2004:87–88).

The New World brushed over this important event in Pocahontas's life, as did most other Hollywood productions. Disney did introduce Kocoom in the 1995 animation, *Pocahontas*. In the film, Powhatan selects Kocoom to marry Pocahontas. He is concerned that the young princess is spending too much time with John Smith and instructs Kocoom to find Pocahontas and bring her back to the Powhatan village of Werowocomoco. Kocoom finds Pocahontas and Smith frolicking through what appears to be a tropical paradise, a sharp contrast to the swampy environs of southeastern Virginia. Kocoom confronts Smith and a struggle ensues. A young colonist who has witnessed the struggle fires a musket at Kocoom, which mortally wounds him. With the exception of character names, the string of events that Disney represents is a complete fabrication. In truth, Pocahontas's Indian husband was not assassinated by the English. Pocahontas and Kocoom were married for approximately three years. It is unclear whether or not they had children or in which Powhatan village they took up residence (Townsend 2004:87). What is clear is their relationship did end under unexpected terms.

In March 1613, Samuel Argall, an English adventurer and naval officer, left Jamestown for the Potomac River, returning to the Patowomeck village of Pasptanzie to once again barter for corn. Once there, Argall learned from an informant that Pocahontas was in the village visiting relatives. Tensions between the paramount chiefdom and the English colonies had been high since the English attack on the Warrascoyaks. Argall was well aware of the Virginia Company's desire to take high-profile Powhatans hostage and knew that Pocahontas would be the ideal candidate to negotiate hostage and weapon exchange (Townsend 2007:101). While harbored at Pasptanzie, Argall sent for the village *werowance* (tribal chief) and demanded that Pocahontas be brought to him. It is uncertain what happened at this point. The *werowance*, Yapassus, may have been intimidated by threats of violence if he did not comply with Argall's demands (Townsend 2004:102; Rountree 2005:156). Another possibility is that Yapassus may have seized the opportunity to exchange Pocahontas for desired trade items. The *werowance* and his wife escorted a reluctant Pocahontas to the English vessel where she was tricked into boarding (Barbour 1969:107–108; Hume 1994:324; Rountree 2005:157). Argall returned to Jamestown with the captured Pocahontas.

Powhatan's reaction to the capture of his daughter was not what the colonists anticipated. After three months, Powhatan sent seven captured colonists and several damaged muskets to be exchanged for his daughter. Sir Thomas Gates, the colony's governor, declared that the gesture was inadequate and refused to release Pocahontas (Townsend 2004:108). Gates turned the matter over to Jamestown marshall Sir Thomas Dale, who subsequently made the decision to send Pocahontas north to the town of Henrico where she could be "educated" in proper English fashion by a young minister named Alexander Whitaker (Barbour 1969:110–111; Townsend 2004:108–109). It was at this place and with these people that Pocahontas would become a leading figure in U.S. history. It was here she met her future husband John Rolfe and it is here that she determined the future of her people.

All things considered, it is Pocahontas's upbringing in an egalitarian society that would have prepared her to become an integral figure in American history. When John Rolfe came upriver from Jamestown to make his tobacco experiments in the fertile lands being cleared and fenced by Sir Thomas Dale around Henrico in 1613, he had no idea that he was embarking on a journey that would change history forever. Rolfe was an Englishman, little accustomed to the ways of agriculture that Virginia was based on, yet he had a vision of making a profit. English merchants knew there was a demand for tobacco, as Spanish-grown tobacco was dominating their market. Rolfe was one of the first to realize Virginia was the perfect place to grow it and to make a profit by supplying British tobacco to England. Virginia was a perfect location, as many generations of Indians had grown tobacco there long before the colonists ever arrived.

The Powhatan Indians knew how to raise and smoke tobacco, although not in the same quantities or manner as the Europeans. The earliest tobacco in eastern North America dates to the Middle Woodland contexts—as early as the first century BC to the second century AD (Wagner 2000:185), but based on archaeological evidence tobacco did not reach the east coast until the Late Woodland period. Excavations at a Powhatan settlement of the Patawomeke tribe found eighteen complete and 264 fragments of clay smoking pipes, the majority of which are attributed to pre-contact contexts (Stewart1992:54). This is augmented by finds of similar artifacts at sites such as the Hatch site in Prince George County (Gregory1980), the Crab Orchard site in Tazewell County (MacCord and Buchanan 1980), and the Jamestown settlement

(Harrington 1951). Ethnobotanical reports from Woodland sites in the Tidewater area also illustrate tobacco's presence (Hodges 1998). The Indian variety cultivated in North America was slightly different than the western variety, and for this reason Rolfe experimented with a Spanish variety (Price 2003:154).

His exposure to Pocahontas is considered one of the most important events of his life. Because of her upbringing in an agricultural society, Pocahontas may have suggested techniques that would help Rolfe's tobacco crop grow. Although this is mere conjecture, certainly interactions with her would have proved invaluable in Rolfe's quest to cultivate tobacco. For example, Pocahontas had knowledge of slash-and-burn horticulture, a practice that would help the crop thrive in recently burned woodlands. Twentieth-

Figure 7.2. Site of the John and Rebecca Rolfe tobacco plantation. The site is located on a promontory adjacent to a tributary of the James River.

Photo by Randy Amici.

century anthropological studies of surviving indigenous tribes showed that the Havasupai in Arizona cut down mesquite trees and burned them before throwing the tobacco seeds in the ashes (Spier 1928:105). Groups in California cultivated tobacco on newly burned ground (Setchell 1912:411), and a number of Northern Paiute groups burned prior to planting (Stewart 1941:376).

In addition, Pocahontas recognized the best type of soil to plant in. Powhatan/Late Woodland sites that have been identified in Virginia have been found to cluster in areas where the soils are deep and well drained and the land is practically level and free from erosion problems (Turner1976).

Pocahontas may have suggested to Rolfe that he pick an area with a southern or southwestern aspect to maximize the exposure of the crop leaves to the sun. She also may have passed on the knowledge that removing the flowers as they form encourages more leaf growth. Collectively, these tips would have been obvious to a girl raised tending crops in Virginia, but not to a man raised in the English countryside.

It is not possible to determine if Pocahontas told Rolfe all she knew about New World agricultural practices, but it is recorded through his letters that she worked alongside him and all its residents, colonists or Indians, to grow food on the plantation. Her knowledge of general horticulture and tobacco likely contributed to the success of the first crops Rolfe produced and exported (Figure 7.2).

Pocahontas lived side by side with her husband and enjoyed all the benefits that his success offered. Ironically, it was the success of the tobacco trade in the early years of the colony that lead to the demise of the Powhatan peoples. As the profits and demand for tobacco grew in Europe, so did the demand for land in Virginia. The Powhatan people's main settlements were on the best land in the Tidewater region, and the lust for land led to the subsequent massacres and forced evictions of Pocahontas's people.

Conclusion

Pocahontas died at Gravesend, England, on March 21, 1617, with her husband John and son Thomas Rolfe by her side. She had achieved celebrity status in London prior to her death because of her Indian ethnicity, cross-cultural diplomacy, and role in making the Virginia Company profitable. This was her true legacy in colonial history, contrary to the Hollywood depiction. As more and more data are recovered, our understanding of the interrelationship between the Powhatan paramount chiefdom and the early Virginia colony will be augmented. As the archaeological record is slowly exposed, it is hoped that Pocahontas's factual role in our nation's beginnings will begin to overshadow the mythological persona most Americans know and lead to more accurate Hollywood productions.

References

Barbour, Philip

　1969　*Pocahontas and Her World: A Chronicle of America's First Settlement in Which Is Related the Story of the Indians and the Englishmen, Particularly Captain John Smith, Captain Samuel Argall, and Master John Rolfe.* Houghton Mifflin, Boston

Barbour, P. L., editor

　1986　*The Complete Works of John Smith (1580–1631), Vol. I.* The University of North Carolina Press, Chapel Hill.

Freeman, David

　1970　*Captain John Smith's History of Virigina; A Selection.* Bobbs Merrill, New York.

Gregory, L. B.

    1980   The Hatch Site (Prince George County, VA). A Preliminary Report. *Quarterly Bulletin of the Archaeological Society of Virginia* 34(4):33.

Harrington, J. C.

    1951   Tobacco Pipes from Jamestown. *Quarterly Bulletin of the Archaeological Society of Virginia* 5(4):7.

Hodges, M. E.

    1998   *Native American Settlement at Great Neck: Report on VDHR Archaeological Investigations of Woodland Components at Site 44VB7, Virginia Beach, Virginia, 1981–1987.* Virginia Department of Historic Resources, Research Report Series No. 9, Richmond.

Hume, Noel

    1994   *The Virginia Adventure. Roanoke to James: An Archaeological an Historical Odyssey.* Alfred A Knoff, Inc. New York.

Johansen, B. E.

    2005   *The Native Peoples of North America—A History, Vol. I.* Praeger, London.

MacCord, H. A. and W. T. Buchanan

    1980   The Crab Orchard Site, Tazewell County, Virginia. *Special Publication of the Archaeological Society of Virginia* 21(1):113.

Newcomb, W. W.

    1974   *North American Indians: An Archaeological Perspective.* Goodyear Publishing, Pacific Palisades, CA.

Pearsall, Deborah M.

    1989   *Paleoethnobotany: A Handbook of Procedures.* Academic Press, New York.

Price, D. A.

    2003   *Love and Hate in Jamestown: John Smith, Pocahontas and the Heart of a New Nation.* Alfred A. Knopf, New York.

Rountree, Helen

    2005   *Pocahontas, Powhatan and Opechancanough: Three Indian Lives Changed by Jamestown.* University of Virginia Press, Charlottesville.

Rountree, Helen and E. Randolph Turner, III

2002   *Before and after Jamestown: Virginia's Powhatans and Their Predecessors.* University Press of Florida, Gainesville.

Setchell, W. A.

1912   Studies in Nicotania, part 1. *University of California Publications in Botany* 5(1):1–86.

Speir, L.

1928   *Hauasupai Ethnography. Anthropological Papers of the American Museum of Natural History 29, part 3.* American Museum of Natural History, New York.

Stewart, O. C.

1941   *Cultural Element Distributions, 14: Northern Paiuate.* University of California Anthropological Records 4, no. 3, Berkeley.

Stewart, T. Dale

1992   *Archaeological Exploration of Patawomeke: The Indian Town Site (44St2), Ancestral to the One (44St1), Visited in 1608 by Captain John Smith.* Smithsonian Institution Press, Washington, DC.

Townsend, C.

2004   *Pocahontas and the Powhatan Dilemma.* Hill and Wang, New York.

Turner, E. R.

1976   An Archaeological and Ethnohistorical Study on the Evolution of Rank Societies in the Virginia Coastal Plain. Ph.D. dissertation, Department of Anthropology, Pennsylvania State University, College Station.

Vincent, Mal.

2006 New World Buys into Old Legend. *The Virginia Pilot,* January 15, Section E, Norfolk, VA

Wagner, G.

2000   Tobacco Use in Prehistoric Eastern North America. In *Tobacco Use by Native North Americans: Sacred Smoke and Silent Killer,* Joseph C. Winter, editor, p. 3. University of Oklahoma Press, Norman.

Wright, L. B., editor

1947   *The History and Present State of Virginia by Robert Beverley.* Dominion Books, Charlottesville, VA.

CHAPTER 8

THE LIFE AND TIMES OF THE EVER-CHANGING HOLLYWOOD INDIAN

Charles M. Haecker

● ●

Just a few decades ago, patrons of movie theaters and television shows found entertainment by regularly viewing that Hollywood staple, the Western. Silver-screen reenactments of those golden days of yesteryear portrayed cowboys, gamblers, gunslingers, soldiers, hurdy-gurdy gals, and Indians—lots of Indians. Cinema warriors instantly commanded one's attention, especially when they were on the warpath. Usually on horseback, they sported feathered bonnets; clad themselves in buckskin; and gripped bows, knives, and firearms. They charged with reckless abandon against well-armed troopers; fired flaming arrows at covered wagons and log forts; and scalped and tortured their White enemies. Indians of the old West, many movie-goers would have concluded, were dangerous indeed.

Dangerous, drunken, deceitful, lazy, and lustful. Over a hundred years of filmmaking has produced incredible distortions of

Native Americans and their traditional life ways. Film reviewers of their day decried the gullibility of viewers who accepted these distortions as accurate re-creations of historical events, but this criticism is a bit off target. In large measure, the film industry simply reflects centuries-old misperceptions about Indians. Our mental image of the classic horse-mounted Plains warrior has its roots in romantic images of 19th-century popular culture; however, ideas that shaped this familiar figure were created in imaginations of late medieval Europeans. Early Spanish explorers saw native inhabitants of the New World as monstrous races, and philosophers wondered if they were even human (Hanke 1959:3–4).

Sensational tales of tortures and killings by Indians dominated news throughout the 18th century. Chronic bloody encounters between British colonists and French allied Iroquois culminated during the French and Indian War of 1754–1763. In one notorious incident, over a hundred captive British soldiers were massacred by Iroquois warriors after the surrender of Fort William Henry to the French in 1757. Written and oral accounts of this event were memorialized in 1826 by the publication of James Fennimore Cooper's *The Last of the Mohicans*, an exciting story about courage, slaughter, deceit, and dishonor.

Cooper's work influenced 19th-century U.S. outrage directed at western tribes that dared to hinder the U.S.'s expansion to the Pacific; however, period newspapers and dime novels were primary disseminators of virulent attacks on Indians. Printed media also entertained their readers with accounts about Indian cultural values that confirmed the correctness of America's own values and goals. Newspapers printed brief reports from the frontier, which described Indians purportedly maiming, capturing, and killing emigrants crossing the continent. "Extermination of the Indian … is the most effective method for life and security," wrote William N. Byers, editor of the *Daily Rocky Mountain News* (1864:2), "and the only way to secure it is to fight [Indians] their own way." Months later, Byers's demand for genocide was realized when, on November 29, 1864, Colorado Volunteer troops attacked and destroyed a southern Cheyenne and Arapaho village along Sand Creek in southeastern Colorado.

Another source for shaping misconceptions was the illustrated press, whose drawings regarding the Indian Wars provided apparent realism. The Fetterman massacre was a sensational event worthy of meticulous illustration. On December 21, 1866, Captain William Fetterman led his eighty-man command out of Fort Phil Kearney, Wyoming Territory, and into a trap that was executed by over 1,000 Cheyenne and Arapaho warriors. No soldiers survived to describe the resulting massacre but this did not stop the artist for *Harper's Weekly* (1867:1), who drew what he believed had occurred. Annihilation of the Seventh Cavalry at Little Bighorn ten years later was represented in similar manner: Sioux and Cheyenne warriors are shown engaged in desperate combat with troopers, the ground littered with bodies, horses, equipage, and so forth (Coward 1999:142–144). All was bogus speculation.

The military debacle at the Little Bighorn made Colonel George Armstrong Custer an instant martyred hero. It also caused a wave of anti-Indian news, with special vitriol reserved for America's new Public Enemy Number One: Sitting Bull. Although this Sioux chief did not participate in the main part of the battle—he remained in the Indian village that day to help defend women and children against possible cavalry attacks—Sitting Bull became the focus of hatred for all things Indian. James W. Howard, one of many newspaper reporters who tried to explain this unbelievable defeat, knowingly stated in the *Chicago Tribune* that a Jesuit priest taught French to Sitting Bull, who then read French history regarding the Napoleonic wars, "and modeled his generalship after the little Corsican Corporal" (*Chicago Tribune* 1876:6). How else could "that red demon" defeat our military?

Sitting Bull's notoriety as Custer's supposed killer was both exploited and softened when, in 1885, he joined William "Buffalo Bill" Cody's Wild West Show, which reenacted historical scenes interspersed with feats of rodeo-style events and sharp-shooting. Audiences especially enjoyed seeing "live Indians" chase a stagecoach, attack a homestead and, once again, massacre Custer's command. Regardless of their various tribal affiliations, all the Indians in the troupe were bedecked in either Sioux or Cheyenne regalia, rode horses, "dwelled" in High Plains–style tipis, and "hunted" buffalo (Moses 1996:169). Cody's show, along with contemporaneous dime novels, newspaper articles, and illustrated magazines, fixed the concept of Plains warriors as dangerous, albeit dashing adversaries. Apache warriors of the desert Southwest, however, were quite another matter. Their lack of colorful regalia and unchivalric methods of waging war—the latter including ambush and calculated use of torture as a psychological weapon—did not endear them as honorable adversaries. Consequently, portrayals of Apaches were unsuitable for entertainment in Cody's Western-themed revues, save for one major exception: Geronimo, who joined the act in 1894.

The murder of Sitting Bull on December 15, 1890, and the related massacre of Sioux men, women and children two weeks later at Wounded Knee forever ended "the Indian problem" as far as mainstream America was concerned. Indians were no longer feared but became symbols of an exciting, bygone era and a source for public entertainment. It was just in time for the debut of motion pictures.

Cody's show was one of several variety acts filmed in 1894 by the earliest kinetoscope motion pictures. Cody's Indian troupe in this film ensured America's romantic notions regarding various 19th-century Plains tribes would carry over into the next century. Western-themed silent movies developed allegorical histories of the western frontier. We see settlers displaying virtues of rugged individualism, pragmatism, agrarianism, and equality as well as an exciting roughness. Silent-movie Indians, however, adhered to different stereotypes. Lack of sound, of course, ensured they were taciturn. They also grimaced a lot, their actions narrowly defined between wooden stoicism and sudden irrational violence. The latter emotion they directed toward Whites, as seen, for example, in D. W. Griffith's *Massacre* (1912). Plots of several silent movies did allow a few warriors to demonstrate marked interest toward attractive White women. The suggestion of an Indian man and White woman having a sexual relationship threatened societal norms, at the very least providing plot tension for movie audiences.

The sound era began in 1927, and almost immediately Hollywood brought Westerns alive with thundering hooves, gun shots, and Indian war whoops. Sound also permitted greater character development. Instead of exaggerated facial expressions to show emotions, actors who portrayed White settlers, miners, cavalry officers, and others conveyed subtle feelings through spoken words. In contrast, when Hollywood Indians spoke at all, it was usually a Hollywood-invented Pidgin English, or else they emitted the all-purpose "Ugh" or "How." From 1927 to 1940 alone, Hollywood Indians attacked, pillaged, burned, and scalped their way through over 300 Westerns with an Indians versus Whites theme (Friar and Friar 1972:290–294).

Director John Ford's *Stagecoach* (1939) is a Western classic. There is plenty of excitement, character development, and Apaches. The plot revolves around perilous situations that tested the mettle of various colorful personalities cooped inside a stagecoach. A persistent hazard is none other than Geronimo and his warriors. One dramatic scene occurs when the stagecoach passes through a defile, where warriors have prepared an ambush. They are positioned on precipices overlooking the defile, and shoot down on the rapidly passing stagecoach. Their attack, however, only perforates luggage on the roof of the stagecoach, which continues its mad pace down the trail. The underlying lesson conveyed by the director is that Apaches were incapable of setting a workable ambush.

Hollywood produced at least nine films about the Battle of Little Bighorn; *They Died with Their Boots O n* (1941) is perhaps the most memorable. In one of the last scenes, Colonel Custer (Errol Flynn) is at the center of the surrounded and outnumbered remnants of his command. Custer keeps firing his pistol until bullets finish him off. In this scene, we are taught the real Custer lost his final battle only because his command was hopelessly outnumbered by a horde of wild Indians.

John Ford received deserved acclaim for directing Westerns. Several of these films revolve around the exploits and hardships experienced by the cavalry in its efforts to subdue various Indian tribes. Ford even inserts some sympathy for the Indians' loss of life ways. Battle scenes are abundant: mounted Apaches attack cavalry columns, Apaches attempt varieties of ambush (they fail yet again), and there is hand-to-hand combat. A Western of lesser pedigree is *The Battle of Apache Pass* (1952), which features in its climactic scene hordes of mounted Apaches clashing with mounted troopers. This movie tells us Apaches primarily fought on horseback, homogenizing all Indian tribes and linking them to horse-and-buffalo life ways of Plains Indian tribes.

The 1950s and 1960s witnessed more sympathetic scripting for Hollywood Indians, and television also became a significant source of popular entertainment. One could now stay at home and watch installments of *The Lone Ranger* and *The Cisco Kid* instead of going to a theater to see a Western. Due to budget constraints rather than a desire to downplay Indian-White conflict, battle scenes of Indians versus Whites on made-for-TV Westerns were less ambitious in scope when compared with scenes depicted in the movies.

By 1970, the Vietnam War was coming to a close. This unpopular war had become shameful when United States soldiers massacred hundreds of unarmed Vietnamese civilians, mostly women and children, in the hamlet of My Lai in 1968. Director Ralph Nelson wanted to make a statement about the political events of the day and he chose the American Indian as a symbol for the oppressed Vietnamese (Kilpatrick 1999:77). *Soldier Blue* (1970) received much criticism for its graphic depiction of the 1864 Sand Creek massacre. Although film critics disapproved of Nelson's realism, historical documents and corroborative archaeological data suggests a filmmaker would find it difficult to match the obscenities that actually occurred at this place. Oral histories regarding the Sand Creek massacre describe soldiers taking certain body parts as trophies, and archaeologists have discovered at the massacre site cannonball shrapnel intermixed with domestic possessions.

The Battle of Apache Pass: The Written Accounts

Lieutenant De Bruin (Bruce Davidson):
  "Where will he fight us?"

McIntosh (Burt Lancaster):
  "He don't mean to fight you, Lieutenant, he just means to kill you."

—*Ulzana's Raid (1972)*

The above exchange succinctly defines two principles of the Apache Wars. First, Apache warriors attacked only when certain they could inflict maximum damage with minimum loss to themselves. Apaches were known to abruptly terminate an attack if pressing on to victory might require too high a price of losing irreplaceable warriors. Second, West Point–trained officers of the period were taught to fight conventional wars that included well-defined battle lines. Apaches, however, knew their only strategy lay in guerilla warfare rather than direct confrontations with a numerous and well-armed adversary. Only after decades of costly trial and error did the U.S. military finally adopt strategies and corresponding tactics appropriate for guerilla warfare. Furthermore, the military's ultimate victory in the southwest was due in large part to its use of Apache scouts, who guided soldiers to hideouts of hostile Apaches (Watt 2002).

The actual battle of Apache Pass in southeastern Arizona exemplifies how Apaches set an ambush. Around noon on July 15, 1862 a ninety-six-man company of New Mexico–bound California Volunteers entered the western approach into Apache Pass. After marching for twelve hours, the exhausted soldiers needed water from a spring located deep within this pass. Lying in wait were scores of Apaches led by Chiefs Mangas Coloradas and Cochise. The chiefs placed their men in two advantageous positions. One group hid on both sides of the western approach, in an area of rugged terrain: here the soldiers would be forced to proceed slowly, making them easy targets. A larger group was on high ground overlooking the spring, hidden behind rock-stacked breastworks, boulder outcrops, and thick underbrush. Once the soldiers reached this location, they would be exposed to withering fire from both sides. If the ambush went according to plan, all the soldiers would die either by gunfire or from thirst.

Their plan went awry when some warriors fired their weapons at the company's rear guard before it entered the pass. This group of twenty men was escorting wagons and two, 12-pounder howitzers. Although the Apaches' premature volley killed one soldier and wounded two others, the rear guard fended off this attack and hastened to catch up with their comrades. Distant gunfire alerted company commander Captain Thomas Roberts, and it also signaled Apaches positioned within the pass to open fire. Roberts immediately ordered half his men to advance toward the spring in skirmish formation. The others, led by Roberts, slowly fought their way upslope and drove back the Apaches. By then the rear guard arrived and immediately wheeled the two howitzers into action, firing several rounds of spherical case shot in the general direction of warriors who had not experienced cannon fire until then.

By late afternoon, the soldiers commanded the spring and quenched their thirst, but Roberts believed his outnumbered men could not hold both the spring and surrounding high ground, so he regrouped and retreated onto relatively less constricted and thus more defensible terrain west of the spring. The Apaches soon returned and reclaimed their previously abandoned positions. Any soldiers who tried to gain access to the spring were driven back by sharpshooters. The grim situation of Roberts's command improved the next morning when reinforcements arrived. Daylight once again permitted use of howitzers, which advanced down the pass and periodically fired shrapnel-scattering case shot at various elevated positions believed held by the Apaches. Finally, soldiers charged up the slopes—to discover the Apaches had melted away (Fountain 1962:33). The two chiefs presumably realized success was now impossible and that no value remained in continuing the fight.

The soldiers retelling of the battle turned the event into a struggle of epic proportions. Newspapers picked up the story and interviewed several soldiers, who believed there had been as many as 800 Apaches, all of them armed with state-of-the-art Sharps carbines, rifled muskets, and revolvers. Captain Roberts reported two soldiers killed and nine wounded; he could verify six dead Apaches but believed his men killed many more. Albert Fountain, a veteran of the battle, decades later recalled that "For hours, the air was constantly filled with lead," and "the shells burst splendidly" (Fountain 1962:32). Conversely, Apache versions understate the incident, claiming the soldiers killed few warriors (Ball 1970:46). Were these accounts true? The actual location of the battle was not in question; rather, battle intensity and complexity were open for testable questions: What varieties of firearms did the Apaches use? Did the Apaches construct breastworks as described by the soldiers? Approximately how many Apaches participated in the battle? Was artillery fire as intense and accurate as described by the soldiers?

The Battle of Apache Pass: The Archaeology

Using metal detectors, archaeologists swept high ground over-looking the spring, the bottom of the pass where soldiers held defensive positions, and the western approach to Apache Pass where the Apaches attacked the rear guard (Figure 8.1). The location of each artifact was determined via laser transit. Resultant data produced an artifact distribution map that resurrected the battle of Apache Pass.

Of the 362 artifacts recovered, 84% were found on high ground overlooking the spring. In addition to shrapnel, this artifact grouping included fired .58 caliber Minié balls, .52 caliber Sharps carbine bullets, and .36 caliber pistol balls, which reflect all known types of firearms issued to the California Volunteers. Additionally, these bullets tended to cluster around three rock-stacked breastworks that overlook the spring, indicating the soldiers' attempts to neutralize these Apache positions. Within areas

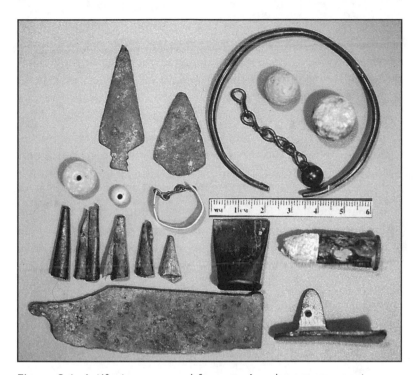

Figure 8.1. Artifacts recovered from an Apache encampment that was attacked by the U.S. cavalry, November 1869. Artifacts include metal arrow points made from a piece of barrel hoop, a brass bracelet, a pocket watch chain, rifle balls, silver earring, beads, cone jingles made from a tin can, an unfired Spencer cartridge and a cartridge case, a metal fitting from an 18th-century British musket, and a skinning knife blade.

Photo by Christopher D. Adams.

where soldiers once held their positions, archaeologists discovered Apache-fired bullets, which derived from a mix of military issue and nonmilitary firearms. Furthermore, Apache-fired bullets represent only 4% of the total artifact count. Fragments of exploded cannonball shell and lead-ball shrapnel were scattered primarily on high ground overlooking the spring; however, evidence of exploded cannonballs were found almost a mile from Apache Pass. Survey of the vicinity where the rear guard was attacked produced 12% of the total artifact count.

Together, these findings indicate that most of the battle took place in the vicinity of the spring. The firepower of the soldiers was superior to that of the Apaches, suggesting the Apaches neither significantly outnumbered the soldiers nor were they uniformly armed with quality weapons. There is only limited protective cover within the few acres of high ground that confines the spring, making it unlikely that much more than a hundred warriors could safely obscure themselves here. In fact, the Apaches did not require superiority in numbers. All they had to do was expend just enough ammunition to keep the soldiers both pinned down and away from the spring. The amount of shrapnel recovered on high ground was surprisingly sparse—just two spherical case shots could have accounted for all recovered shrapnel balls found there. This discovery, combined with widespread dispersion of shrapnel well beyond the confines of Apache Pass, suggests the howitzers were fired less often and with less accuracy than what was later recalled by the soldiers. Finally, contrary to the 1952 film version regarding this battle, only a relative few Apaches were mounted. Instead, their duty was to chase down any soldiers who tried to escape (Haecker 2001; McChristian 2005:48–61).

The Army Versus the High Plains Indians

Westerns were out of vogue by the 1970s. Since then, Hollywood has occasionally produced films having an Indian versus Whites theme; one of the more remarkable achievements is *Dances with Wolves* (1990). This film, which won eight Academy Awards, was highly acclaimed because it made a serious attempt to treat American Indians as multidimensional human beings, even going as far as speaking their own language. The Lakota Sioux of the mid 1860s are presented as individuals possessing various foibles and virtues recognizable in all of us.

In one particular scene, Lieutenant Dunbar (Kevin Costner) is a guest in the tipi of his host, Kicking Bird (Graham Greene), who tries to make his guest feel at ease. They interact through the passing of a communal pipe, a bonding ritual that communicates peace between strangers. What if Kicking Bird had instead offered Dunbar a tin cup full of freshly brewed coffee laced with condensed milk and sugar, topped off with a snack of canned peaches and crackers? Moviegoers would see this gesture as a jarring anachronism, yet it is within the realm of possibility that such vignettes took place in circa 1864 tipis. By the mid-19th century, the Plains Indians had become dependent on U.S.-manufactured items, especially firearms and ammunition, as well as metal tools, containers, and utensils. These objects helped ease the burdens of a strenuous way of life. Obtaining them, however,

Figure 8.2. Members of the Cheyenne tribe excavating artifacts from the Sand Creek massacre site. Dr. Douglas Scott, project field director (extreme left), is observing the excavation.
Photo by Charles M. Haecker.

required interaction with White men or through Indian intermediaries, which sometimes led to conflict. Also, it became essential that a tribal band acquire firearms and ammunition for hunting and protection, otherwise their enemies who had firearms would destroy them. The scene in *Dances with Wolves* in which a Pawnee war party is foiled in its surprise attack on Kicking Bird's village underscores this point (Figure 8.2).

A later scene shows Lieutenant Dunbar held captive as a deserter and being transported under guard to a military prison.

To save him, Sioux warriors execute an ambush that virtually wipes out the guard detail. Plains warriors, as the Apaches, used surprise attacks as a tactic that could defeat a numerous and well-armed foe. The military likewise employed the element of surprise when its units attacked Indian villages. This tactic worked best during the winter season, when bands of one or more tribes gathered together into large villages; otherwise, each hostile band had to be laboriously hunted down and destroyed. It was considered regrettable if noncombatants were inadvertently killed when an Indian village was attacked. As acts of war were defined during this period, such actions would not be considered an atrocity. But what happened at Sand Creek, many Americans agreed at the time, went beyond the pale of human decency.

Sand Creek

At dawn on November 29, 1864, Colonel John M. Chivington led approximately 700 volunteer troops to an Indian village along Sand Creek, in southeastern Colorado Territory. Approximately 500 Cheyenne and Arapaho occupied this village, supposedly under U.S. Army protection. As troops maneuvered to surround the village, Cheyenne chief Black Kettle waved a white flag to forestall attack, but he barely escaped with his life. A mass of his people fled in all directions for safety; however, cavalrymen followed in pursuit and indiscriminately killed many of them. Numerous tribesmen sought shelter in hastily dug pits and trenches at the base of the dry stream's banks. They fought back with what few weapons they had grabbed in flight but were no match against the cavalrymen's firepower. Then four, 12-pounder howitzers joined in the uneven match, lobbing spherical case shot into the Indians' positions. By 2:00 P.M., the job was done. Over the course of seven hours, the soldiers killed at least 150 men, women, and children.

Chivington then ordered all Indian belongings destroyed so those who had escaped slaughter could not recover anything useful if they later returned. The next day, soldiers finished taking scalps and various other body parts, then continued the campaign.

On their return to Denver, they were feted as heroes who, boasted Chivington, vanquished as many as 600 warriors who defended well-built earthworks. Reports of what actually occurred spread beyond Colorado Territory, and in time Sand Creek became known as one of the most controversial and disturbing events in American history.

Until the early 20th century, it was still possible to identify the site of the destroyed Indian village, indicated by concentrations of artifacts and occasional fragments of human bone. Eventually wind- and water-borne soil hid these remains and, by the 1940s, its exact location became a matter of speculation. In 1998, the National Park Service, under congressional direction, began a research program to identify where the massacre took place. The search was a multicultural and multidisciplinary effort. It brought together members of the Cheyenne and Arapaho people with historians, ethnographers, geomorphologists, and archaeologists. The first phase of research involved assembly and examination of all known historical documents including period maps, diaries, and first-hand accounts by Indians and soldiers. Multiple lines of evidence converged on a locale approximately one mile north of Sand Creek's "South Bend" area, which is the traditionally embraced site of the massacre.

With this information, archaeologists systematically metal detected various designated areas along Sand Creek, beginning at South Bend. During the first few days, their discoveries consisted primarily of 20th-century ranch-related items. When archaeologists came within 0.3 miles of the targeted locale and on the southern side of the creek they began to discover quantities of Civil War–era military bullets. It was theorized these were overshot projectiles that fell to the ground at the end of their respective trajectories. This distribution suggested their intended targets were on the northern side of Sand Creek. Metal detection proceeded onto that location and soon hundreds of circa 1864 artifacts were discovered: remains of tin cups, coffee pots, varieties of utensils and horse tack, iron arrowheads, hide scrapers made from strap iron, and other personal accoutrements. Significantly, few items are in usable condition. Tin cups are flattened, eating utensils

135

twisted, kettles fragmented, and food cans bayoneted. Intermixed with these purposely mangled items are fired bullets and cannonball fragments. These artifacts, scattered over a twelve-acre area, indicate the site of the Indian village.

Archaeologists additionally discovered Indian possessions and military bullets as far as 2.5 miles north of the village site, and tentatively identified the location where the Indians excavated defensive positions. The overall artifact pattern confirms Chivington's report that his command attacked the village in crossfire and killed numerous Indians who fled the carnage. It also refutes his later defense that hundreds of well-armed warriors defended the village; only a few Indian-shot projectiles were recovered from the site (Greene and Scott 2004).

This multidisciplinary team approach, supplemented with tribal knowledge, led archaeologists to the village location. Identification of the massacre site, however, is more than an exercise in academic curiosity; it is an intensely personal and spiritual experience for the Cheyenne and Arapaho peoples. One year after its discovery, legislation established the Sand Creek Massacre National Historic Site, ensuring that what happened there will never be forgotten.

The Battle of Little Bighorn

News of Sand Creek spread rapidly among the Plains tribes, producing a pervasive fear the U.S. government planned the same fate for all Indians. In response, many tribal leaders advocated armed resistance. Although large-scale battles occasionally took place, it was primarily characterized by ambush, massacres, raids, calculated terror, and punitive campaigns. Tenuous treaties were designed to place Plains tribes onto reservations and away from principal emigrant trails and tillable lands; however, peace was not achievable until around 1890. Euro American accounts of the late 19th-century Plains war are prolific. These accounts typically misrepresent the Sioux and Cheyenne as lacking a sophisticated military system and incapable of adapting and evolving their tactics. In fact, both tribes possessed a long military tradition based on organization, discipline, and a propensity for close combat (Panzeri 1996). By 1876, they had mastered close combat tactics using modern firearms of the era—much to the chagrin of Custer's Seventh Cavalry at Little Bighorn.

Archaeologists investigating the Little Bighorn battlefield have recovered over 5,000 artifacts. Their overriding research approach is to treat the battlefield as a crime scene, utilizing law enforcement forensic techniques. Studies of firing pin marks on cartridge cases and rifling marks on bullets were combined with precise artifact location data, permitting one to track positions and movements of various firearms. Analysis of cartridge cases, fired bullets, and firearm parts indicate the combatants used forty-five firearm types. The Indians possessed all forty-five firearm types, ranging from obsolete muskets to repeating rifles, and included military issue carbines and revolvers they obtained from the bodies of killed troopers.

The ability to determine markings that are unique to each fired cartridge case and bullet permitted archaeologists to re-create the chronology of battle events and corresponding tactics used by the opposing forces. It appears that Custer initially deployed his four companies in skirmish formation to check the Indians' probing attacks. The greater range, hitting power, and accuracy of their military issue firearms gave the troopers an advantage, but the Indians countered by utilizing the landscape. They crept sufficiently close to where their superiority in firepower volume overwhelmed the troopers. Once cohesion of one company was destroyed, the Indians maneuvered onto the next two companies and destroyed them in similar fashion. Those few troopers who survived the collapse of their companies fled, or tried to flee, to the last remaining company now under Custer's personal command. This remnant was quickly and efficiently snuffed out under the full brunt of over 2,000 warriors (Fox and Scott 1991). It was a grisly ending that the cast of *They Died with Their Boots On* would not have recognized.

In summary, archaeologists are presently utilizing innovative approaches in their investigation of historic battlefields, including those of the Indian Wars. Their data-based, impartial conclusions regarding how soldiers and Indians actually fought is a reality check for official accounts suspected as biased, for color-ful but often inaccurate recollections of battle participants, and for mythic popular beliefs codified by Hollywood storytellers. Yet it is not enough for a battlefield archaeologist to function sim-ply as gatherer and arbiter of esoteric facts. Good archaeologists become great ones when they also tell a story, deploying techni-cally precise evidence in a manner that reconstructs past events as tales both intriguing *and* plausible. So, Kicking Bird, please pass the canned peaches. ...

References

Ball, Eve

    1970   *In the Days of Victorio: Recollections of a Warm Springs Apache*. University of Arizona Press, Tucson.

Chicago Tribune

    1876   *Chicago Tribune*, July 15, p. 6.

Coward, John M.

    1999   The *Newspaper Indian, Native American Identity in the Press, 1820–90*. University of Illinois Press, Urbana and Chicago.

Daily Rocky Mountain News

    1864   Exterminate Them. *Daily Rocky Mountain News*, April 1, p. 2.

Fountain, Albert J.

    1962   The Battle of Apache Pass. In *Arizona Cavalcade: The Turbulent Times*, Joseph Miller, editor, pp. 31–35, Hastings House, New York.

Fox, Richard A. and Douglas D. Scott

    1991   The Post-Civil War Battlefield Pattern. *Historical Archaeology* 25(2):90–103.

Friar, Ralph E. and Natasha A. Friar

    1972   *The Only Good Indian ...The Hollywood Gospel*. Drama Book Specialists/Publishers, New York.

Greene, Jerome A. and Douglas D. Scott

2004   *Finding Sand Creek, History, Archeology, and the 1864 Massacre Site.* University of Oklahoma Press, Norman.

Haecker, Charles M.

2001   A Well-Laid Trap: Artifact Pattern Analysis of an Apache Ambush Site, Apache Pass, Arizona. Paper presented at the 34th Conference on Historical and Underwater Archaeology, Long Beach, CA.

Hanke, Lewis

1959   *Aristotle and the American Indian.* Indiana University Press, Bloomington.

Harper's Weekly

1867   The Indian Battle and Massacre near Fort Philip Kearney, Dakotah Territory. *Harper's Weekly*, March 23, p. 1.

Kilpatrick, Jacquelyn

1999   *Celluloid Indians, Native Americans and Film.* University of Nebraska Press, Lincoln.

McChristian, Douglas C.

2005   *Fort Bowie, Arizona, Combat Post of the Southwest, 1858–1894.* University of Oklahoma Press, Norman.

Moses, L. G.

1996   *Wild West Shows and the Images of American Indians.* University of New Mexico Press, Albuquerque.

Panzeri, Peter F.

1996   *Little Big Horn 1876: Custer's Last Stand.* Praeger Publishers, Westport, CT.

Watt, Robert N.

2002   Raiders of a Lost Art? Apache War and Society. *Small Wars & Insurgencies* 13(3):1–28.

IMAGINING BLACKNESS

ARCHAEOLOGICAL AND CINEMATIC VISIONS OF AFRICAN AMERICAN LIFE

Paul R. Mullins

● ●

African American archaeology and Hollywood visions of African American experience are each rooted in a White imagination that has long contemplated itself by constructing Black identities. Cinematic Black subjectivity has offered a host of simplistic or racist misrepresentations including happy slaves in films like *Gone with the Wind*, the oversentimentalized White heroics in *Amistad*, or Jar-Jar Binks's overdone buffoonery. In 1914, African American journalist Lester Walton already saw that films were White racist imagination "representing the race at its worst," and he called for Hollywood to "emancipate the white American from his peculiar ideas" about African American life (Leab 1973:53). In 1942, Langston Hughes (2002a:219) bemoaned racist movie stereotypes, arguing that "A great many white people still accept the false grinning caricatures of the movies as being true of colored people—Negroes are happy-go-lucky, they always smile, they always sing, they don't care what happens to them, they're not sensitive about persecution or segregation." Hughes aspired to use literature to repudiate cinematic stereotypes, and many diasporan historians have long championed a similar "vindicationist" perspective that uses rigorous scholarship to repudiate stereotypes. African American archaeologists often use archaeological data in much the same way to repudiate many of the exact same racist stereotypes (Epperson 1990; Franklin 1997; Perry and Paynter 1999; Singleton 1999; Orser and Funari 2001; Blakey 2004).

Refuting racist characterizations in archaeology and popular discourse is an essential mechanism to more reflectively interpret identity. Nevertheless, archaeology that takes racist stereotypes as its primary framework for identity risks replacing stale racial stereotypes with equally essentialist racialized identities. African American scholars have long wrestled with this challenge of how to define the African diaspora in opposition to racist representations of Blackness; simultaneously, those definitions have aspired to provide diasporic identity with some substantial cultural or experiential roots (Harris 1982; Kelley 1999:28). African American historians have long confronted the construction of Black identity in a nation that denied citizen privileges to Black subjects. This African American intellectual tradition sometimes has included essentialist appeals to African cultural heritage; however, African American historiography underscores the bankruptcy of democratic American mythologies and an easily defined Black experience (Harrison and Harrison 1999).

Richard Wright (1995:74) argued that "The Negro is America's metaphor," insisting that African American heritage and experience was American history told in its most "vivid and bloody terms." Black subjectivity from this perspective is constructed as being outside an American mainstream, while it also constitutes that same mainstream. Consequently, it is infeasible to simply reduce racial representation to either a genuine experience (and its ostensibly objective material record) or an artificial cinematic stereotype rooted in racist caricatures. Rather than think of archaeological analysis as a mechanism to refute false racist subjectivities, archaeology should acknowledge the concrete reality of racial experience as it illuminates the social processes that construct racialized difference. An archaeology that destabilizes racial subjects should examine how and why scholars examine the African American material world, just as we critique the fascination White film audiences have with movies that examine race and African American experience.

An archaeology of life *along* the color line (as opposed to one simply *across* lines of difference) should produce a complicated picture of American experience that is not simply reduced to Black exoticism and an undefined White normality. This approach provides a complicated interpretive landscape characterized by ambiguous identities, shifting relationships between collectives, profoundly consequential politics, and unclear definitions of what even defines a collective (Meskell 2002). Embracing a radically multivalent notion of identity requires archaeologists to rethink how we define identity in material culture and how we can interpret the ways in which consumers projected distinctive contextual symbolism onto the world of things (Perry and Paynter 1999).

Untroubled by the challenge to paint a persuasive picture of social complexity across time, popular culture and films routinely distill complex experiences to essentialism that reduces African Americans to stereotypical Others. In movies, complicated differences are commonly reduced to overblown and familiar caricatures. Eric Lott (1993) argues the same case for black-face minstrelsy, indicating 19th-century White northeastern audiences came to understand and believe Black racial stereotypes based on their repetition. Yet Lott's critical insight extending vindicationist politics is that black-face belied an enduring White fascination with African America that continues to loom within mainstream cinema and a vast range of discourses including archaeology. Lott views black-face as a White effort to construct Black subjectivity in a form that simultaneously reflected an attraction to African American culture even as black-face appropriated and distorted that very culture. If archaeologists do not wrestle with how the discipline represents Black subjectivity, we risk reproducing the poverty of mainstream Black film images: movies are filled with people of color, but they are typically stock character types that reproduce persistent racial subjectivities. Historical archaeology also risks lapsing into its own stereotypical characterizations of Blackness and thieving from diasporan culture if we do not confront the complexity of racial subjectivity.

Archaeology's "Moral Mission": Stereotype and Resistance

Archaeologists often explicitly or implicitly underscore that archaeological narratives are based in concrete material data that are substantive correctives to incomplete or biased histories. James Deetz (1993:12) voiced what may be one of the discipline's most fundamental assumptions when he noted that "historical archaeology's prime value to history lies in its promise to take into account large numbers of people who either were not included in the written record or, if they were, were included in a biased or minimal way." Theresa Singleton (1999:1) recognizes the same trend in 1960s and 1970s African American archaeologies that were part of archaeology's "moral mission: to tell the story of Americans—poor, powerless, and 'inarticulate'—who had been forgotten in the written record" (compare Armstrong 1985:262). Hollywood has embraced the comparable idea that movies can correct racist stereotypes by presenting a "truth" that was once hidden by racist ideology. In 1924, pioneer "race film" director Oscar Micheaux championed this perspective, indicating that "I have always tried to make my photoplays present the truth, to lay before the race a cross section of its own life, to view the colored heart from close range" so that film created "a racial image of which they could be proud" (Smith 2001:278–279). Micheaux was not necessarily focused on representing all African Americans, though, as much as he aimed to portray a genteel Black model that broke from stereotypes even as it reproduced many ostensibly White American values.

Micheaux's vindicationist cinema never became common in Hollywood's representations of Black identity, but many contemporary filmmakers have aspired to tell uplifting stories about African American experience that comfort White audiences even as they appear to probe the complications of Black life. Like archaeologists, moviemakers often argue that their moral tales are supported by the objectivity of historical facts, staking a claim to authenticity that shields films from a critique of how they inevitably streamline reality to provide an engaging cinematic narrative. *Amistad*, for instance, tells the story of an 1839 mutiny among enslaved Africans, wielding what co-producer Steven Spielberg celebrated as "the truth" about the mutiny. A trailer for the film boldly opens by proclaiming that the film recounts "A True Story," and when an *Amistad* novelist sued Spielberg's company, his lawyers testified that the movie "is entirely based upon history" (Jeffrey 2001:77–78). The trailer for the African American–themed Civil War film *Glory* also trumpets that it is "A True Story. They Joined for Freedom. They Fought for Honor," and the *Ghosts of Mississippi*'s trailer heralds that "This Story Is True." Much of the explicit claim to *Amistad*'s historical veracity was made on the basis of scholarly consultation (Jeffrey 2001), but the movie's sensory richness painted in speech, sets, and visual detail are perhaps the most critical building blocks for that sense of realism. For instance, the mostly African actors and actresses playing the *Amistad*'s captives spoke Mende, wore genuine metal chains, and played out the movie on lavish period sets. *Glory* likewise presents African American subjects in compelling battlefield sets with small but critical touches, such as shoes that do not come in a left and right pair and relentlessly moving music heightening battlefield combat scenes.

Amistad's visual presentation of brutality weaves a compelling story that any historical archaeologist can understand. The most powerful stories museums and archaeologists tell about enslavement often use commonplace things to underscore the inhumanity of life in enslavement. For instance, one New Jersey home with a reputed structure for enslaved Africans bore shackles as well as caches attributed to West African spirituality, providing an interesting material contrast between domination and cultural persistence (Bankoff and Winter 2005:305). A Texas quarters contained a similar juxtaposition, including a conjurer's kit reflecting African spirituality as well as leg manacles bolted into the cabin's wall (Samford 1996:94). Patricia Samford (1996:94) details the archaeology of Chesapeake quarters architecture and paints a brutal picture with finely documented archaeological evidence, demonstrating that "keeping out cold drafts and insects was virtually impossible." Roughly eighty ankle and wrist shackles were recovered from the slave ship *Henrietta Marie*, which sank in 1700 off the Florida coast (Malcom 1998). The shackles' testimony to enslavement's brutality moved Daniel Jerome Wideman (1998) to lament that the "African leg bones formerly attached to the chains will not be found. They have long since dissolved, become fish meal, black bone and flesh passing back into the food chain, absorbed into the continuous cycle of the sea."

The bioarchaeological evidence from the African burial ground bears exceptionally powerful testimony to the lives Africans led in enslavement (Perry et al. 2006). The evidence that Africans led much shorter lives than their White neighbors and had numerous examples of traumatic or mortal injuries is a significant scholarly contribution, but the literal bodies of captive Africans may be the most critical dimension of the burial ground's unprecedented public response. Project director Michael Blakey (2001:414) recognizes that "the vivid contrasting of a human face of slavery with its dehumanizing conditions I believe accounts for much of the strong public feeling regarding this work," which has produced extensive popular press coverage. Blakey (2004:113) consciously places the burial ground's scholarship within a tradition of vindicationist African American histories. He positions the burial ground's ancestors as refutations of persistent stereotypes of "benign" northern servitude, arguing that "the most primary of evidence of northern slavery, the bones of the people themselves, has overturned the mythology of the free north." The burial ground is indeed a rich discourse about captivity because it is told through individuals' bodily testimony contextualized within a rigorous scientific methodology. The effort to examine emotionally charged experiences with scholarly rigor—avoiding charges that scholarship is being corrupted by political positioning—is common in vindicationist scholarship.

Vindicationist cinema has often targeted the simplistic racist stereotypes dating to films' primordial moments: the brutish Black male, tragic mulatto, shiftless thief, and ever-happy slave appeared in some the earliest short silent films (Leab 1973; Berger 2005:123–134). For instance, *Amistad* co-producer Debbie Allen considered the film a racist rebuttal, declaring "that no one had dared to make a movie of the *Amistad* because the story dispelled the image of blacks as 'Sambos' who were quietly acquiescent to slavery" (Jones 1997). The dilemma with *Amistad*, in particular, and many racially themed films, in general, is that they pose transparent solutions to racist inequalities. *Amistad* ends with a compelling Supreme Court oration by John Quincy Adams that urges the justices to have "the courage to do what is right," an apparently fitting prelude to a final scene that finds the newly freed Cinque on board a ship heading back to his African home (Dalzell 1998:132). Adams's impassioned courtroom defense of freedom and the implication that his experience moved him to rethink racial boundaries intimate a rather wishful antiracist justice that is not especially well supported. The reality was that freedom came because of a legal technicality instead of the Court's recognition of servitude's injustice, and Cinque returned to a region permanently torn asunder by the slave trade.

What *Amistad* does quite well is frame the fundamental contradiction in American life, the ever-present tensions within freedom across the color line. *Amistad* screenwriter David Franzoni indicated that the film was intended to portray "timeless black American rage" (Jeffrey 2001:81), aiming to capture the resistance at the heart of diaspora culture. Yet, ultimately many Hollywood visions of racial inequality confront racism only to resolve it in some comforting way. In *Glory*, for example, the 54th Regiment's story revolves around an African American Civil War unit under the command of White officer Robert Gould Shaw. As the African American soldiers soberly assess how their service will impact racism, the film sounds a compelling and tragic tone that is shaped by our contemporary acknowledgment that racism has never disappeared. *Glory* leans heavily on the African American soldiers' intense desire to be seen as full citizens through their military service. When the African American soldier Trip laments that the war cannot be "won," Shaw declares that there must be a victorious army. Trip, though, casts "victory" in broader terms of color line equality when he responds that "I mean, you get to go on back to Boston, big house and all that. What about us? What do we get?" Heroic wartime service has never yielded clear shifts in racism, so *Glory* uses that reality to underscore the tragic nature of these soldiers' desires. For instance, Trip questions whether any measure of service can secure citizen rights for African Americans, warning a fellow soldier that "You can march like the white man, you can talk like him. You can sing his songs, you can even wear his suits. But, you ain't never gonna be nothing more to him than an ugly ass chimp ... in a blue suit."

Glory joins *Amistad* by rather optimistically depicting the war as a cause for justice bonding people across the color line. For instance, a wise older African American soldier criticizes Trip's deep-seated contempt for Whites, concluding that "Dying's been what these white boys have been doing for going on three years now, dying by the thousands, dying for you, fool." Contemporary movie audiences' identification with the African American soldiers is heightened by the overt racism they confront within their own ranks, and the 1863 death of Shaw alongside 281 of his soldiers underscores the profoundly consequential potential of cross-racial alliances. *Glory* captures a deep-seated White desire to see the regiment's heroism as an indication that Americans have long desired interracial cooperativeness as Shaw bonds with his Black soldiers and eventually joins them in an undifferentiated mass grave.

Joanne Sarah Barclay's (2005) analysis of civil rights movies like *Ghosts of Mississippi* and *Mississippi Burning* sounds similar suspicion of historical films that romanticize Whites' sense of racial justice. In *Mississippi Burning*, for instance, the FBI is depicted as a diligent champion for justice in the case of three murdered civil rights workers, leaving the substantial African American civil rights movement invisible. The most unsettling dimension of the film is that it portrays the 1964 civil rights movement completely through White characters, pitting the FBI against overweight drawling White southerners and reducing racism to its caricature as Klan-directed brutality limited to the nation's backwaters (Sitkoff 1989). Like *Amistad*'s examination of John Quincy Adams's embrace of racial justice, *Ghosts of Mississippi* revolves around a White lawyer's growing consciousness of racist injustice and his crusade to convict the man who murdered civil rights worker Medgar Evers in 1963. These movies paint African American struggles as White fantasies of redemption, though *Ghosts of Mississippi* does at least imply that White liberals have failed to back up antiracist rhetoric with genuine structural activism (Barlowe 1998:36).

In 1961, James Baldwin delivered a scathing attack on the 1958 film *The Defiant Ones*, which painted a similarly romanticized and easy racial justice. The film told the tale of a Black and a White convict who escape a chain gang bound together, compelling them to cooperate and confront their commonalities. An exasperated Baldwin (1961:164) concluded that the idea

> that Negroes and whites can learn to love each other if they are only chained together long enough runs so madly counter to the facts that it must be dismissed as one of the latest, and sickest, of the liberal fantasies. … These movies are designed not to trouble, but to reassure; they do not reflect reality, they merely rearrange its elements into something we can bear.

Although Baldwin considered this a bankrupt idea, the movie

was remade three times: It appeared on television in 1972 (starring women and renamed *Black Mama, White Mama*); it again was made for the small screen in 1986; and in 1996 it returned in a feature-length film called *Fled*. This ever-resurfacing plot reflects the persistent attraction of the idea that people can bridge racial difference when compelled to do so.

Precisely what constitutes cooperation and archaeological engagement across the color line is ambiguous and burdened by the same well-intended but shallow politics of movies like *Glory*. Virtually every archaeologist now considers their work "public archaeology," but this can range across everything from speaking to visitors on an excavation site to embracing a long-term stakeholder-based project. Interchanges across the color and power lines have been featured in several films that raise familiar archaeological issues of how African American heritage is appropriated. Spike Lee's *Bamboozled* questions White expropriations of African American culture, especially the media stereotyping of African America to serve profit and reproduce Black subordination (Godfrey 2005). At the heart of *Bamboozled* is the question of precisely what defines Black identity, and Lee outlines an authentic Black identity that is being pilfered by Whites, although many African Americans have become alienated to it and broader Black social collectives (Barlowe 2003; Black 2003; Epp 2003). *Bamboozled*'s premise is that African American television executive Pierre Delacroix is assailed for proposing a string of Black-themed shows that aspire to an African American middle-class identity (e.g., *The Cosby Show*). Delacroix's proposals, however, do not fit executives' sense of Black culture and are deemed "too white." The exasperated Delacroix resolves to launch an outrageously racist show that will get him fired, hatching the idea for a minstrel show set on an Alabama plantation; the minstrel show, though, becomes a hit, confirming his boss's argument that the minstrels will "make us feel good to be Americans" and unleashing a White desire to embrace black-face stereotypes.

Lee's black-face racial masquerade is a precarious satirical venture that uses racialist symbols to critique those very symbols and the social assumptions that reproduce them along the color line. Some film critics like Roger Ebert (2000) have argued that those symbols are not viable launching pads for an antiracist critique, and many newspapers were reluctant to run advertisements for the film that featured stock Black stereotypes. *Bamboozled*, though, argues that the mechanisms of minstrelsy still structure popular cultural representations of Black subjects, and Lee responds that "I don't think these images should be swept under a rug just because they are offensive. The *New York Times* shouldn't not run them because they're offensive. They're real" (Fuchs 2002:187–188). *Bamboozled*'s closing credits likewise target concrete, if unpleasant, reflections of racism as they roll over images of Hollywood royalty in black-face (including Bing Crosby and Judy Garland) and racist Black toys, which Delacroix himself collects in the film. Lee argues that "A lot of people don't want to deal with the images in this montage. But we're showing them. And we're showing that these images ... reflected accepted behavior" (Fuchs 2002:196).

There are interesting implications for African American archaeology that revolve around how race and racism should be positioned in scholarship. In 1994, for instance, Colonial Williamsburg held a slave auction reenactment, and before the reenactment had even been staged, an article in the Richmond newspaper sparked criticism throughout the region (Krutko 2003:14). Representatives from the National Association for the Advancement of Colored People (NAACP) and the Southern Christian Leadership Conference were among the community members who met with individuals involved with Colonial Williamsburg prior to the reenactment. The NAACP bemoaned the reenactment as a nightmarish reminder of enslavement that masqueraded as entertainment and evaded the dehumanizing effects of portraying bondage in a fifteen-minute public presentation.

Erin Krutko's (2003:22) thesis on the auction reports that a Virginia NAACP official protesting the sale argued that "Colonial Williamsburg does not deal with real black history. ... Everything about Colonial Williamsburg is about the oppression of my people." When the sale reenactment began, he yelled out that "you cannot portray our history in 21-minutes ... and make it some kind of sideshow" (Krutko 2003:23). In an especially influential venue that is visited primarily by Whites, enslavement was long ignored and sanitized, so there was suspicion that Colonial Williamsburg was politically unable to paint a sufficiently dramatic picture of bondage.

In 1978, an administrator found that African American employees were "extremely skeptical that the present interpretative core could be trusted ... to develop a story of black colonial life. ... They could not really conceive that the institution they knew as Colonial Williamsburg could possibly interpret their history the way it needed to be done" (Krutko 2003:48). Such mistrust of scholars long dedicated to ignoring enslavement and African American life led an auction protestor to argue that "we are always concerned when the African holocaust is going to be portrayed ... there have been so many myths and lies and distortions in the past" (Krutko 2003:49). Nevertheless, the presentation aspired to present African American heritage as integral to the Williamsburg experience, even as it posed a jarring challenge to untroubled stereotypes of African American life. *Bamboozled* champions a similar confrontation of racism and the inequalities it has rationalized.

Colonial Williamsburg found that African American stakeholders were uneasy over the appropriation of African American heritage by White scholars, and *Bamboozled* points to similar tensions over White society's appropriation of African American culture: Lee launches an attack on the commodified forms such appropriation takes, ranging across Tommy Hilfiger, gangsta rap, and sitcoms. *Bamboozled* illuminates the question of how African American heritage is constructed, appropriated, employed, and even commodified, underscoring how and why White archaeologists can make a claim to being stakeholders in African American history. Many archaeologists examining African America aspire to community partnerships between White archaeologists and

Black communities, but this scholarship is compelled to explore how such authority is structured by participants' positions along the color line. Maria Franklin (1997:36) argues that "we seldom question our intentions in 'giving a voice' to people of the past. Is it simply so that people of the present can better understand and appreciate their cultural heritage and national identity?" Franklin presses African American archaeologies to clearly articulate their concrete reasons for conducting such research, or this scholarship hazards being defined as White appropriation despite "good intentions."

Historical archaeology has painted an especially sophisticated picture of the material details of enslaved plantation life, but Parker Potter (1991) argues that much of this literature fails to clearly wrestle with the structures of oppression. The dilemma is that plantation symbolism and enslavement are laden with contentious racial imagery, and enslavement's heritage remains bitterly disputed in contemporary discourse (Franklin 1997:41–42). Archaeologists are compelled to become part of this discourse, but since the 1940s the movies have overwhelmingly avoided plantation settings that were once commonplace in Hollywood films. The 1903 *Uncle Tom's Cabin* was perhaps the first of many early movies focused on antebellum plantations, and in the years leading up to World War II, African Americans on southern plantations were staples of both musicals (*Dixie* in 1929) and drama (*Gone with the Wind* in 1939). During World War II, though, the federal government pressed Hollywood to present the nation as a "melting pot" and ensure African Americans' commitment to the war (Campbell 1993:2). Disney's 1946 *Song of the South* was among the last films to romanticize an idyllic southern life, and plantations rarely appeared on film again until Blaxploitation movies in the 1970s (*Mandingo*, in which an enslaved African played by boxer Ken Norton is seduced by the plantation owner's wife, or *Quadroon*—"¼ black, ¾ white, all woman") (Guerrero 1993:31–35). Consequently, many of the contemporary popular stereotypes associated with plantation life are most clearly rooted in distant movies, rather than recent ones.

Representing Race

Langston Hughes (2002b:226) lamented in 1943 that

> for a generation now, the Negro has been maligned, caricatured, and lied about on the American screen, and pictured to the whole world in theatres from Los Angeles to Bombay, Montreal to Cape Town as being nothing more than a funny-looking, dull-witted but comic servant. Even Hollywood knows that is not a true picture of American Negro life.

Confronting such stereotypes is certainly the first step toward an antiracist cinema, but a vindicationist cinema or scholarship is not inherently antiracial if they do not pose representations that can potentially step outside conventional racial subjectivity. Rather than simply conclude that movies "lie," we might instead ask how and why they represent identity and lived experience in specific ways. Movies, like all popular culture, caricature commonplace dimensions of everyday life, presenting something familiar yet portraying it in an exaggerated form: we all understand the theoretical distinction between good and bad, but it is far less clear in our everyday lives than it is on the Death Star as a horde of teddy bear Ewoks confront the coldly inhuman Darth Vader. We embrace popular culture because it provides these clearly defined experiences and resolute settlements we rarely have in our real lives.

Because race and inequality are embedded in American society, movies constantly revisit color line issues of power and racism that reflect our widespread uneasiness with these issues, but they simultaneously paint a simplistic picture. Movies capture widespread social fascination with race and Black experience, but mainstream cinema rarely frames those processes especially well or offers concrete strategies to confront and change those conditions. Historical archaeology does not necessarily move us closer to the "truth" as much as it provides an exceptionally complicated vision of everyday life that interrogates how we define those truths and why they are socially constructed in particular forms. Whether historical archaeology can construct newly challenging subjectivities is not settled, but archaeology has produced a complex vision of African American life and the color line that has the potential to significantly destabilize simplistic archaeological representations and probe how such academic representations are rooted in broader popular culture.

References

Armstrong, Douglas V.

> 1985   An Afro-Jamaican Slave Settlement: Archaeological Investigations at Drax Hall. In *The Archaeology of Slavery and Plantation Life*, Theresa A. Singleton, editor, pp. 261–287. Academic Press, New York.

Baldwin, James

> 1961   *Mass Culture and the Creative Artist: Some Personal Notes, Excerpt from Mass Media in Modern Society*. Black Thought and Culture. Available online at http://www.alexanderstreet4.com/ cgi-bin/asp/bltc/getobject_?c.3742:1./projects/artfla/databases/asp/ bltc/fulltext/IMAGE/.5274. Accessed February 11, 2006.

Bankoff, H. Arthur and Frederick A. Winter

> 2005   The Archaeology of Slavery at the Van Cortland Plantation in the Bronx, New York. *International Journal of Historical Archaeology* 9(4):291–318.

Barclay, Joanne Sarah

> 2005   UnCivil War—Memory and Identity in the Reconstruction of the Civil Rights Movement. Masters of Arts thesis submitted to the Department of History, East Tennessee State University, Johnson City, Tennessee.

Barlowe, Jamie

  1998   The "Not-Free" and "Not-Me": Constructions of
  Whiteness in *Rosewood* and *Ghosts of Mississippi*. *Canadian
  Review of American Studies* 28(3):31–46.

  2003   "You Must Never Be a Misrepresented People": Spike
  Lee's *Bamboozled*. *Canadian Review of American Studies*
  33(1):1–15

Berger, Martin A.

  2005   *Sight Unseen: Whiteness and American Visual Culture*.
  University of California Press, Berkeley.

Black, Ray

  2003   Satire's Cruelest Cut: Exorcising Blackness in Spike Lee's
  Bamboozled. *The Black Scholar* 33(1):19–24.

Blakey, Michael L.

  2001   Bioarchaeology of the African Diaspora in the Americas:
  Its Origin and Scope. *Annual Reviews of Anthropology* 30:387–422.

  2004   Theory: An Ethical Epistemology of Publicly Engaged
  Biocultural Research. In *The New York African Burial Ground
  Skeletal Biology Final Report, Vol. I*, Michael L. Blakey and
  Lesley M. Rankin-Hill, editors, pp. 98–115. Howard University,
  Washington, DC.

Campbell, Edward D. C., Jr.

  1993   Film as Politics/Film as Business: The Blaxpolitation
  of the Plantation. In *Hollywood as Mirror: Changing Views of
  "Outsiders" and "Enemies" in American Movies*, Robert Brent
  Toplin, editor, pp. 1–18. Greenwood Press, Westport, CT.

Dalzell, Frederick

  1998   Dreamworking *Amistad*: Representing Slavery, Revolt,
  and Freedom in America, 1839 and 1997. *The New England
  Quarterly* 71(1):127–133.

Deetz, James

  1993   *Flowerdew Hundred: The Archaeology of a Virginia
  Plantation, 1619–1864*. University of Virginia Press,
  Charlottesville.

Ebert, Roger

  2000   Review, *Bamboozled*. Rogerebert.com. Available
  online at http://rogerebert.suntimes.com/apps/pbcs.dll/
  article?AID=/20001006/REVIEWS/10060301/1023. Accessed
  March 12, 2006.

Epp, Michael H.

2003   Raising Minstrelsy: Humour, Satire and the Stereotype in *The Birth of a Nation* and *Bamboozled*. *Canadian Review of American Studies* 33(1):17–35.

Epperson, Terrence W.

1990   Race and the Disciplines of the Plantation. *Historical Archaeology* 24(4):29–36.

Franklin, Maria

1997   "Power to the People": Sociopolitics and the Archaeology of Black Americans. *Historical Archaeology* 31(3):36–50.

Fuchs, Cynthia, editor

2002   *Spike Lee Interviews*. University Press of Mississippi, Jackson.

Godfrey, Esther

2005   "To Be Real": Drag, Minstrelsy and Identity in the New Millennium. *Genders*. Available online at http://www.genders. org/g41/g41_godfrey.html. Accessed March 12, 2006.

Guerrero, Ed

1993   *Framing Blackness: The African American Image in Film*. Temple University Press, Philadelphia.

Harris, Robert L.

1982   Coming of Age: The Transformation of Afro-American Historiography. *Journal of Negro History* 67(2):107–121.

Harrison, Ira E. and Faye V. Harrison, editors

1999   *African American Pioneers in Anthropology*. University of Illinois Press, Urbana.

Hughes, Langston

2002a   Negro Writers and the War. In *The Collected Works of Langston Hughes, Vol. IX: Essays on Art, Race, Politics, and World Affairs*, Christopher De Santis, editor, pp. 215–219. University of Missouri Press, Columbia.

2002b   Is Hollywood Fair to Negroes? In *The Collected Works of Langston Hughes, Vol. IX: Essays on Art, Race, Politics, and World Affairs*, Christopher De Santis, editor, pp. 226–228. University of Missouri Press, Columbia.

Jeffrey, Julie Roy

2001   Amistad (1997): Steven Spielberg's "True Story." *Historical Journal of Film, Radio and Television* 21(1):77–96.

Jones, Howard

    1997   A Historian Goes to Hollywood: The Spielberg Touch. *Perspectives.* Available online at http://www.historians.org/perspectives/issues/1997/9712/9712FIL.CFM. Accessed January 24, 2006.

Kelley, Robin D. G.

    1999   "But a Local Phase of a World Problem": Black History's Global Vision, 1883–1950. *Journal of American History* 86(3):1–54.

Krutko, Erin Marie

    2003   Colonial Williamsburg's Slave Auction Re-Enactment: Controversy, African American History and Public Memory. Master of Arts thesis submitted to the Department of American Studies, College of William and Mary, Williamsburg, VA.

Leab, Daniel J.

    1973   The Gamut from A to B: The Image of the Black in Pre-1915 Movies. *Political Science Quarterly* 88(1):53–70.

Lott, Eric

    1993   *Love and Theft: Blackface Minstrelsy and the American Working Class.* Oxford University Press, New York.

Malcom, Corey

    1998   The Iron Bilboes of the *Henrietta Marie. The Navigator: Newsletter of the Mel Fisher Maritime Heritage Society.* Available online at http://www.melfisher.org/research%20pdf/Iron%20Bilboes%20Article.pdf. Accessed January 26, 2006.

Meskell, Lynn

    2002   The Intersections of Identity and Politics in Archaeology. *Annual Review of Anthropology* 31:279–301.

Orser, Charles E., Jr. and Pedro P. A. Funari

    2001   Archaeology and Slave Resistance and Rebellion. *World Archaeology* 33(1):61–72.

Perry, Warren, Jean Howson, and Barbara A. Bianco, editors

    2006   *New York African Burial Ground Archaeology Final Report, Vol. I.* Report prepared by Howard University for the United States General Services Administration Northeastern and Caribbean Region, Howard University, Washington DC.

Perry, Warren and Robert Paynter

　1999　　Artifacts, Ethnicity, and the Archaeology of African Americans. In *"I, Too, Am America": Archaeological Studies of African American Life*, Theresa A. Singleton, editor, pp. 299–310. University of Virginia Press, Charlottesville.

Potter, Parker B., Jr.

　1991　　What Is the Use of Plantation Archaeology? *Historical Archaeology* 25(3):94–107.

Samford, Patricia

　1996　　The Archaeology of African-American Slavery and Material Culture. *The William and Mary Quarterly* 53(1):87–114.

Singleton, Theresa A.

　1999　　An Introduction to African-American Archaeology. In *"I, Too, Am America": Archaeological Studies of African-America Life*, Theresa A. Singleton, editor, pp. 1–17. University Press of Virginia, Charlottesville.

Sitkoff, Harvard

　1989　　Review, *Mississippi Burning. The Journal of American History* 76(3):1019–1020.

Smith, J. Douglas

　2001　　Patrolling the Boundaries of Race: Motion Picture Censorship and Jim Crow in Virginia, 1922–1932. *Historical Journal of Film, Radio and Television* 21(3):273–291.

Wideman, Daniel Jerome

　1998　　The Door of No Return? A Journey through the Legacy of the African Slave Forts, An Excerpt. *Callaloo* 2(1)1–11.

Wright, Richard

　1995　　*White Man, Listen! Lectures in Europe, 1950–56.* Harper Perennial, New York.

FIVE POINTS ON FILM

MYTH, URBAN ARCHAEOLOGY, AND GANGS OF NEW YORK

Rebecca Yamin and Lauren J. Cook[1]

• •

Unlike Rome, New York has never learned the art of growing old by playing on all its pasts. Its present invents itself, from hour to hour, in the act of throwing away its previous accomplishments, and challenging the future.

—*de Certeau (1984)*

The Urban Context

While Martin Scorsese was building a piece of "old" New York on a set in Rome, eighteen archaeologists were working on the analysis of approximately 850,000 artifacts recovered from the very place Scorsese was trying to recreate; a block that was once part of the notorious Five Points neighborhood. In 1991, the site was a parking lot, the only undeveloped land left for the construction of a new federal courthouse at Foley Square. Archaeologists exposed the tightly packed foundations of the tenements that stood there in the late 19th century and uncovered the yards behind buildings that preceded them. This once vibrant, working-class neighborhood was transformed in the early 20th century as courthouses and other civic buildings replaced the tenements, forcing the people to move elsewhere.

Cities are perpetually remaking themselves, and archaeologists, along with everyone else who works underground, get to examine the process. That is the challenge, and the fascination, of urban archaeology. In North America, urban archaeology is subject to particular conditions and site formation processes that do not apply to rural areas or to prehistoric sites. In the preindustrial city, these processes were small in scale despite the density of the built environment and population. Buildings were wood or brick, reaching, at most, several stories in height. Areas behind and between the buildings were crowded with activities, from hanging out the laundry to the disposal of human waste.

Density of settlement meant that cities, metaphorically at least, eventually consumed themselves. After fifty to a hundred years, the structures, whether unsound, unsightly, or merely outmoded, were usually destroyed and replaced. The remains, where feasible, were recycled into other structures, burned in fireplaces, or joined the archaeological record alongside items discarded or lost in smaller, less visible depositional episodes. In the small-scale world of the preindustrial city, cellars and privies were often filled with structural remains; what didn't fit was carted off to one of the landfill operations that generally operated on the waterfront. After another fifty years or so, the process was repeated, a cellar dug atop or adjacent to the old one, and another building constructed atop the newly vacant lot. The process was generally accretive, resulting in the progressive building up of a rich and complex stratigraphic record.

Over time, cities grew both in size and scale. Fueled by a rapidly expanding economy, builders in cities such as Boston, New York, Philadelphia, and Chicago built larger and taller buildings from the mid-19th century on. Changes in construction technology, including the structural steel frame, both enabled and fed the demand for large-scale office buildings and commercial structures (Jordan 1969:307–310). Taller buildings needed deeper foundations to contain essential mechanical systems and other infrastructure (Condit 1973:91–93), which had a devastating cumulative effect on the archaeological record in many central urban districts. In other areas, the record was simply buried beneath layers of fill, creating a complex layer cake of strata representing multiple occupations and activities.

This complex layered record of the past was not what Scorsese was shooting for in *Gangs of New York* (2002). What he wanted, and in great part achieved, was the "feel" of Five Points, as it had been portrayed in the yellow journalism of the day and in the book, *Gangs of New York*, by Herbert Asbury (1927), from which he took his title. The Five Points archaeological project achieved something quite different. It provided a rare opportunity to study the evolution of an urban neighborhood from its beginnings as an industrial district on the banks of a fresh-water pond in the 18th century to a haven for one immigrant group after another during the 19th and early 20th centuries, and finally into a depopulated civic center.

The Five Points Excavation

Historic Conservation and Interpretation, Inc., a New Jersey consulting company, conducted the excavation at the Five Points site. The late industrial archaeologist Ed Rutsch managed the project, and Len Bianchi directed the fieldwork. The preliminary documentary work (done by Marjorie Ingle and Jean Howson) identified the site as part of a neighborhood characterized as "America's first and foremost slum," where "poverty and depravity, ignorance and all uncleanliness walk hand and hand" (Ingle et al. 1990:47). Ingle and Howson recognized that some descriptions were more forgiving, which raised the possibility that archaeology might be used to sort fact from fiction, reality from myth. Fourteen historic properties fell within the project area, some facing Pearl Street, others facing Chatham Row, and still others facing a portion of Baxter Street that had been removed when Foley Square was created in the nineteen teens. Although the surfaces of the backyards behind the mid-19th-century tenements had been destroyed by the deep basements of later tenements, the artifact-filled bottoms of brick-lined privies and cisterns produced evidence of domestic life dating from the turn of the 19th century up to the last quarter of the century. Fifty of these features were identified; twenty-two were excavated.

The artifacts were mundane. There were things that had to do with tailoring—papers of pins, folding rules, bias tape, and buttons. One side of the project block had been lined with tailor shops and second-hand clothing dealers—New York's first garment district—the other side of the block held Irish tenements. From the Irish, there were tea sets made in Staffordshire, England (Figure 10.1), probably very much like the tea sets the newly arrived immigrants had used at home. There were matching edge-decorated dinner plates and even a few serving dishes; there were also sets of paneled tumblers, an occasional wine glass, and plenty of beer and wine bottles. The Irish workers who lived in the tenements used a variety of potions to treat aching muscles, but they also consumed a good deal of soda water, a cheaper alternative than patent medicines and also thought to counter the effects of alcohol (or even substitute for it).

The quantity of food remains found—particularly butchered animal bones—indicated that the working-class residents of Five Points ate lots of meat, a luxury they wouldn't have had in their countries of origin but could afford in America. Among the Irish, pork was favored even though fish would have been less expensive. At least one German household preferred lamb, and an orthodox Jewish family ate beef, but only from the front part of the animal as the rear parts were not considered kosher. Ornamental items found—figurines for the mantle, clay pots for flowers, and a teacup painted with the image of Father Mathew, a Catholic temperance leader preaching to his flock—suggest a concern for aesthetics. No matter how small the living spaces, efforts were made to decorate them. The artifacts recovered do not suggest the kind of dire poverty generally assumed for Five Points.[2] The reality was clearly more complicated.

Figure 10.1. Staffordshire teaware found in a large cesspool associated with an Irish tenement on Pearl Street.
Photo by Paul Reckner.

New York on Film

Even armed with material evidence, it is not easy to dislodge the mythic images of New York that live in peoples' imaginations. As already mentioned, these images come from yellow journalism, but they also come in more persistent form from the movies. The motion picture industry and New York City are perfect matches, and in the century or so since the technology was introduced, their histories have been closely intertwined.[3]

Early film production was centered in Manhattan, with images of New York "entering the movies at their birth" (Sanders 2001:25). Most early films of the city were "actualities," so called because they showed actual events filmed on location as they were occurring (the term survives in broadcast industry parlance for the snippets of tape that ground TV and radio news segments). Even if they were as prosaic as street scenes, or people at work, these glimpses of New York were popular with audiences across the nation. In 1901, Edison began staging "stories" and by 1906, his competition, the Biograph Company, was combining actuality with melodramatic storylines, to create a new genre, the "fiction film," or "acted film."

The development of talkies in the late 1920s dealt a blow to New York's film industry. Early microphones were too sensitive for an urban environment, and before long, most sound sequences were relegated to sound stages and back lots in Hollywood and Burbank, California. Although many films continued to be *set* in New York, very few were actually *filmed* there between 1930 and the filming of *Naked City* in 1948. The only parts of most films actually shot in the city were "establishing shots," brief, silent exterior shots, usually of the skyline, waterfront, or other easily recognizable New York images that served to situate the action that followed in the city.

Despite the exodus of the industry from the city, Hollywood produced what amounted to a mythic vision of New York in the 1930s, facilitated by several convenient factors. First, the novelty of talkies was that characters actually spoke. They needed something to say, and Hollywood needed people—a lot of them—to write dialog. Although there were few with the necessary skills in California, New York in the 1920s had been the mecca of literary life in America. In addition to magazine and book publishing, the city was the center for theatrical production, and who better than playwrights to produce credible dialog?

The Depression had hit New York's literary community hard, and many of its members moved to California to write for films. They were well paid, but felt unappreciated by their employers. Most of all, they felt they had lost the sense of community they had enjoyed in New York. Not surprisingly, given the popularity of the city in film, and the demand on the part of studios for New York stories, they were frequently called on to write about New York. They missed the city they had left behind and many of them wrote it the way they remembered it, or, perhaps, more the way they wished it had been:

> Los Angeles's sleepy boulevards would be retaliated against with an imaginary New York street life that surpassed almost anything the real city could offer. The lowliest sidestreet would have scores of pedestrians rushing purposefully across the frame; dozens more sat on stoops and played on the sidewalk ... the Italian hurdy-gurdy man, the Irish cop, the Jewish pushcart vendor, as if packing, by scripted instruction, all of New York's human diversity onto a single block. And on these streets, leading men and women would constantly bump into one another, chance encounters that not only served the needs of the plot but worked to demonstrate how a real city worked. [Sanders 2001:58]

That streetscape was the most technically accurate that the studios could buy, or more accurately, make from scratch. Each studio's art department kept a vast reference collection of photographs of buildings, street pavements, manhole covers, fire hydrants, lamp posts, and other furnishings that were used to build "the New York street," an elaborate outdoor backlot stage set with the look and feel of the real thing, but none of the problems. Once the studios had these sets, economics dictated that they use them, which, in turn, fed the demand for films set in New York.[4]

Several important films of the 1940s evoked nostalgia for a New York that had, or would soon pass out of existence. *Life with Father* (1947) and *The Heiress* (1949) both looked back longingly at bourgeois life during the second half of the 19th century in brownstones and single-family dwellings. At the other end of the spectrum, tenement houses were a part of the mythical New York. Often, their inhabitants were portrayed sympathetically, as working people beaten down by their environment, or as in *Dead*

End (1937), warped by it and seduced into a life of crime. In *On the Waterfront* (1954), set across the Hudson in Hoboken, New Jersey, with at least some exteriors filmed on location, the working folk are heroic when they resist the lure of easy money and take the workplace back from organized crime.[5]

After the tenement house, the culprit was "the streets." The very same polyglot locus of frenzied activity was reinterpreted as a threat precisely because it brought people with different concepts of morality in contact with one another, away from the supervision and moral certainties associated with the home. Ironically, a late entry in that genre was Scorsese's *Mean Streets* (1973), whose characters are unable to escape the pull of the streets (crime). All of these approaches to working-class problems held that altering the environment could solve them. Although films alluded to the poverty that kept people in those environments, until the effects of the civil rights movement and the Great Society began to be felt, they never went as far as examining the systemic inequalities that led to that poverty.

Scorsese's *Gangs of New York* falls solidly within this tradition, albeit with the added influence of Herbert Asbury's colorful book. The release of the movie, however, raised the expectation—created as much by the intellectual climate in the present as by the film's promotional materials—that it was meant to be about a real, rather than an imagined, past.

Gangs of New York: Asbury's Book and Scorsese's Movie

The book, *Gangs of New York*, by Herbert Asbury (1927), was a popular history of the "underside" of the city. Written in the late 1920s when the quintessential New York slums were in the vicinity of the Five Points and neighboring areas along the Bowery, these areas and their inhabitants formed the basis for his book. Although *Gangs* superficially resembles a history, in that it is organized roughly chronologically, it is not a work of history by any recognized standard. As a journalist, Asbury knew that consensus could emerge from varying accounts of the same phenomena and was versed in the critical techniques necessary to arrive at a version of past events. *Gangs*, however, is based largely on accounts from newspapers, and the quality of their information varies highly and is difficult to assess because they are sparsely cited. Where his sources are nativist, Asbury appears to be nativist. Where his sources are from the immigrant community, he is accordingly sympathetic to immigrants. Where the sources are in languages that he apparently did not read, such as German, Hebrew, or Chinese, his treatment relies more on external depictions of those communities, or, where available, English-language sources written by immigrants.

Asbury's work draws heavily on a second stream of sources, which, for lack of a better term, we can call the "sunshine and shadow" school of guidebooks to New York. These works, often written by journalists, reformers, or policemen, appeared every few decades in the second half of the 19th century, to "warn" and titillate readers with glimpses of hell, always at a safe distance (examples that specifically discuss Five Points include *The Old Brewery and the New Mission House at the Five Points* by Ladies of the Mission [1854] and *Darkness and Daylight or Lights and Shadows of New York Life* by Mrs. Helen Campbell [1896]). Like others working in this genre, Asbury made working-class neighborhoods into interchangeable scenes of drama and debauchery (see Mayne [1993] for an analysis of this tradition). Besides *Gangs of New York*, he wrote books about New Orleans, Chicago, and San Francisco, all with the common theme of criminality as an American tradition. Although this may have served as an anodyne to the elitist histories that were being written in the same period, it also generalized the condition of the immigrant working class into a class of criminals who learned to be Americans in the streets.

Scorsese's movie, *Gangs of New York*, begins with the violent murder of Priest Vallon (played by Liam Neeson), a Catholic priest associated with the Irish in the neighborhood who are defended by a distinctively dressed gang, colorfully called the Dead Rabbits.

The bloody battle in which Vallon is killed pits the Rabbits against the Bowery Boys, a nativist gang who claim superiority by virtue of being born on native soil. The murder is observed by Vallon's young son, and the not very plausible plot for the remainder of the movie hinges on the return of the son, played by Leonardo DiCaprio, grown to manhood, to avenge his father's death.

Although the movie includes an outstanding performance from Daniel Day Lewis as Bill the Butcher, the nativist leader, the real star is the set. Built at Cinecetta Studios in Rome, where Federico Fellini worked, the set draws its inspiration from several well-known historic images, and the Five Points portrayed in these images comes to life on the screen, a no less than stunning feat. There is the Old Brewery, an industrial building that was converted into a tenement in 1837 and, according to Asbury (1927:14), housed "more than 1000 men, women, and children, almost equally divided between Irish and Negroes." In the movie, the building has a multi-story courtyard (suspiciously similar to a building in Fellini's *Satyricon*), an unlikely waste of space in a district where overcrowding was a major problem. It is also unlikely that the rooms would have looked like caves (perhaps inspired by Roman catacombs) or that skulls would have rolled around on the floors. These images come from Charles Dickens's (1985) memorable description of Five Points in *American Notes* and from other contemporary descriptions rehashed by Asbury and intended to suggest that people who lived in such circumstances were less than human.

The famous George Catlin painting of the Five Points intersection, reproduced as a lithograph in *Valentine's Manual* (Valentine 1855) (Figure 10.2), provided the general look of the movie, which not incidentally conformed to the street scenes in Hollywood's mythical New York. The painting graphically portrays the prejudices of middle-class outsiders who saw the immigrant neighborhood as a notorious and dangerous slum. The streets are lined with establishments dispensing alcohol, couples romance in public, prostitutes hang out of upstairs windows, and as many as seven fights are underway.

Figure 10.2. Lithograph version of George Catlin painting showing the Five Points intersection (Valentine 1855).

The real place may well have looked much as it is portrayed to a bourgeois outsider, though other images show fewer people and considerably less frenzied activity (Cook 2000). Even on the archaeological project block, which was adjacent to the inter-section, there were saloons and brothels, but they were tucked between tenements, many with shops on the ground floor (Fitts 2000; Milne 2000; Pitts 2000). The immigrant residents were not just drunks and prostitutes; they were workers struggling to get a foothold in their new homes. The story of their private lives is less dramatic than the public life suggested in the Catlin image (and in Scorsese's movie), and it is this lack of drama that makes the mythical Five Points so difficult to counter.

The Historical Perspective

The archaeological project was not the first time an alternative perspective was suggested for Five Points. Carol Groneman's doctoral dissertation (Pernicone 1973) drew a picture of the neighborhood based on the 1855 New York State Census. From the census, Groneman concluded that in terms of age and marital status, Irish household composition did not differ from the rest of the city except for overcrowding, that the majority of Irish emigrated in family groups and continued to live with kin (often in addition to boarders), and that grown children remained in their parents' households rather than living in boarding houses. A higher percentage of Irish were married than other adults in the city, but there were also more female-headed households (Pernicone 1973:53–89). The archaeological analysis added physical authenticity to Groneman's picture of domestic life, which was based on statistics. Tyler Anbinder's more recent book, *Five Points, The 19th-Century New York City Neighborhood that Invented Tap Dance, Stole Elections, and Became the World's Most Notorious Slum* (2001), also presents a more complicated view of Five Points. This book, however, focuses on public life and politics rather than the more intimate perspective achieved by Groneman and the archaeological project.

Scorsese was clearly not interested in this inside view of everyday life, although he sent two production assistants to look at the Five Points artifacts. They, however, only wanted to know what the artifacts looked like, not what they might mean, and none of what they saw appeared in the movie. Scorsese considered Anbinder as a consultant for the movie, but rejected him in favor of Luc Sante who had published a best selling elaboration of Asbury's New York book in 1992. Historical authenticity was not what Scorsese sought. He knew better and says so in the walkthrough the set that accompanies the DVD. In the words of Jay Cocks (2002), Scorsese's screen writer, "*Satyricon, The Wild Bunch*, and *A Clockwork Orange* were their inspiration as much as fact. Probably more."

What is unfortunate is that the working-class nature of the neighborhood never becomes evident in the movie. Five Points is portrayed as a down-and-out slum where subhuman Irish immigrants struggle to hold their own against the pugnacious (and politically powerful) nativists who were there first. The Irish appear as a stereotype, fighting for survival rather than taking advantage of the opportunities for work, which brought them to America in the first place and which allowed them to support families under difficult conditions (both physical *and* psychological) not of their own making and maintain respectability in spite of them.

In fact, there is very little depiction of people actually at work, an activity that occupied a disproportionate amount of time in the lives of the neighborhood's historical residents. People in the film certainly have occupations—barber, butcher, policeman, politician, and thief—but the focus is on the web of graft surrounding the latter occupations. An exception is a scene where Bill the Butcher cuts meat (an occupation traditionally associated with the nativist gang members and firemen of the Bowery) to make telling points about violence and the role of the gang leader as distributor of the spoils.

Curiously, it was authenticity that obsessed the press when the movie came out. Following their lead, the public also appeared to want to know whether the movie was true or not. The archaeological project web site (http://r2.gsa/fivept/fphome.htm) received a flurry of hits from people who were interested in finding out more about the *real* Five Points. We took advantage of this interest, and a member of the project team (Paul Reckner) developed a questionnaire that asked people to compare their reactions to the movie with their reactions to the web site. Only eight people completed the survey, but their responses shed unexpected light on some of the assumptions we had made about the distortions in the movie.

Two-thirds of survey respondents who saw the movie did not expect it to be a historically accurate representation of New York City's past. On a scale of 1 to 5, respondents rated the overall accuracy of the film a 3, but most interesting of all was the fact that moviegoers did not accept or reject the accuracy of the film as a whole. Rather, they were willing and able to discriminate between elements of the film that they felt were more or less reliable. People found the film's overall "look" and "feel" quite convincing and successful in capturing the period and neighborhood. The impoverished and unsanitary conditions of life in the Five Points also struck viewers as accurate. Several respondents noted the near-universal criminality of the film's neighborhood residents as a problem, but it was the film's portrayal of major historical events, the draft riots in particular, that suffered the harshest criticism. The majority of survey respondents also felt that the film left out important elements of New York history. People wished to see more attention to the daily struggles and working lives of Five Points residents, the abuses of the neighborhood's renters by the city's landlords, and a greater focus on the African American population of the Points.

In light of viewers' opinions regarding the historical accuracy of the film, what was perhaps most interesting about the survey responses was the number of people who felt that the film conveyed a social/political message. Although one respondent characterized the movie's message as "a contrived message about the melting pot," others listed issues of class conflict, political corruption, racism, and cultural/religious intolerance, as major themes that emerged from the film. Recent social histories of New York City and Five Points, in particular (including the Five Points web site), address precisely these themes (Wilentz 1984; Stansell 1987; Stott 1990).

It is comforting to know that at least some members of the public did not swallow Scorsese's version of the past hook, line, and sinker, but the more the project team examined his allegorical tale the more sense it made, not as a true story of the past, but as a dramatic way to show the passing of old ways and the arrival of a new order. The movie ends with the Draft Riots of 1863, a plot twist somewhat unrelated to the previous story lines (although the riots are also described by Asbury). The violence of the Draft Riots was a reaction to the passage of the Conscription Law, which made all men between the ages of twenty and forty-

five eligible for service in the Union Army unless they could pay
$300. The Irish, among others, were not interested in fighting for
African American emancipation, nor could they afford the $300
it would cost to get out of it, and the movie depicts poor White
New Yorkers coming together in this violent, but common cause.
Although the inclusion of the Draft Riots is historically confusing,
it has a function within the larger myth and narrative. Rivalries
that had been settled in *old ways*, with ritualized combat between
working-class groups defined along lines of ethnicity, were rendered irrelevant when confronted with state power. Bill's cleaver
in the newly elected sheriff's back is the last act in the old way.
The federal troops interrupt further gang warfare and the world
is changed. Although Scorsese's version of the Draft Riots has the
navy bombarding the mobs from the sea (which simply did *not*
happen), it emphasizes the rise of federal power. It also reminds
us that Scorsese was not telling history, he was trying to dramatically capture the conflicts that are part of his beloved city's past.
As such, the film is well within the Hollywood tradition of the
mythical city, intended to resonate with us here, in the present.

Presenting the Complexity

Archaeologists cannot compete with the drama of the screen, nor
can we correct what isn't supposed to be literal truth in the first
place. What we do have is the ability to communicate the complexity of the past that we derive from archaeology. Post-movie
visits to the Five Points web site underscore the importance of
the Internet as a vehicle for alternative historical narratives,
particularly for those aimed at addressing problems in highly
publicized popular histories. Archaeology and history may not
be able to compete with the big-budget productions (and huge
advertising budgets) of the film industry, but we may be able to
use the Internet to position our ideas in the public realm so as to
take advantage of the media hype generated by cultural events
such as Hollywood films.

When all is said and done, Scorsese's movie could have been more noteworthy if it had included some of the textures of everyday life at Five Points. The filmmakers were interested in retelling the American myth of the melting pot, but they didn't want to know how it really worked. They reduced the process to a battle in the streets and "Irishness" to something that had to be shed to succeed. In fact, America was born, and reborn, in a lot of places along the surfaces of daily life. It was born in the political process, despite its flaws. It was born in the home, where plentiful goods were available. And it was born in the streets, which most often served as a means and facilitator of commerce and employment, as a circulatory system enabling communal social life, and only very rarely as a stage for riots, gang warfare, and similar ritual spectacles.

The impoverished culture of the Points, as shown in the movie and contrasted with bourgeois opulence uptown, suggests that inhabitants were somehow morally lacking. They spent their time at illegal pursuits like prostitution and theft, and disrupted society with old-fashioned rivalries and gang violence. Hard work is next to invisible in Scorsese's Five Points, and its material rewards, which we know were there from the multitudes of artifacts and food remains that were recovered by archaeologists, are completely absent. Scorsese's misrepresentation in this area, in particular, is troubling because it suggests that in the past, and in the present by extension, poor people didn't (and don't) have the right values. If they failed it was (and is) their own fault, not the fault of a society dependent on economic and social inequalities. Unfortunately, this view is not unique to *Gangs of New York*.

Notes

1. An earlier version of this paper was given at the 2004 annual meeting of the Society for Historical Archaeology in St. Louis. Entitled "Five Points and the Movies: The Archaeologists Respond" (Yamin et al. 2004), the paper was coauthored by seven members of the Five Points project team including, in addition to the present authors, Claudia Milne, Paul Reckner, Stephen Brighton, Tom Naughton, and Diane Dallal. Several ideas originally developed for that paper are discussed here and we wish to express our gratitude to the group effort that first developed them. Particular thanks are due to Paul Reckner, who designed and implemented the web survey discussed in this chapter. We are also grateful to Julie Schablitsky for inviting us to contribute to this volume.

2. The artifact analysis is fully reported in Yamin 2000. Most of the artifacts from the project are now a part of New York history. With the exception of eighteen items on loan to the Archdiocese of New York for an exhibit that never happened, the materials were stored in the project's laboratory in the sub-basement of Building 6 at the World Trade Center and were lost on September 11, 2001. The laboratory was fortunately unoccupied at the time.

3. The discussion in this section draws heavily on two sources, both of which treat the relationship between the city and film at length. Stern et al. (1995:1174–1199) focus on the way the city is portrayed, and James Sanders (2001) is particularly concerned with the impact of the city on the cinematic arts. Film titles are italicized and the date is added parenthetically the first time a film is mentioned. Films are not listed in the bibliography.

4. When necessary, movie magic could produce the city in miniature. For an excellent example, one need go no further than *King Kong* (1933), which used a miniature posable ape, stop-action photography, rear projection, mattes, and miniature sets to create a very believable New York … if, that is, one ignores the rampaging Kong swatting at airplanes while clinging to the mooring mast of the Empire State Building. The most recent remake (2005) uses computer animation to return Kong to the Midtown of the 1930s and to the Empire State Building. The effects are superb, but they make one appreciate the technical achievement of the original all the more.

5. Although *On the Waterfront* is based on Malcolm Johnson's Pulitzer Prize–winning articles in the *New York Sun*, which detailed the complicity of large shipping companies in the abusive system that ruled the lives of harbor workers, those companies are conspicuously absent from the Hollywood version (Johnson 2005).

References

Anbinder, Tyler

    2001   Five *Points, The 19th-Century New York City Neighborhood that Invented Tap Dance, Stole Elections, and Became the World's Most Notorious Slum.* The Free Press, New York.

Asbury, Herbert

    1927   *Gangs of New York, An Informal History of the Underworld.* Garden City Publishing Co., Garden City, NY.

Campbell, Helen

    1896   *Darkness and Daylight or Lights and Shadows of New York Life.* A. D. Worthington and Co., Hartford, CT.

Cocks, Jay

    2002   Is *Gangs of New York* Historically Accurate? Gotham Gazette NYC Book Club live chat with Tyler Anbinder, author of *Five Points,* and Jay Cocks, screenwriter of "Gangs of New York." Available online at www.gothamgazette.com/article/feature-commentary/20021223/202/162. Accessed November 23, 2003.

Condit, Carl W.

    1973   *Chicago, 1910–29: Building, Planning, and Urban Technology.* University of Chicago Press, Chicago.

Cook, Lauren J.

    2000   The Construction of a Slum: A Visual Archaeology of Five Points. In *Tales of Five Points: Working-Class Life in Nineteenth-Century New York, Vol. II,* Rebecca Yamin, editor, pp. 460–499. John Milner Associates, Inc., West Chester, PA.

de Certeau, Michel

    1984   *The Practice of Everyday Life.* University of California Press, Berkeley.

Dickens, Charles

    1985   *American Notes, A Journey.* Originally published in 1842. Fromm International, New York.

Fitts, Robert K.

2000 The Five Points Reformed, 1865–1900. In *Tales of Five Points: Working-Class Life in Nineteenth-Century New York, Vol. II*, Rebecca Yamin, editor, pp. 67–89. John Milner Associates, Inc., West Chester, PA.

Ingle, Marjorie, Jean Howson, and Edward S. Rutsch

1990 A Stage IA Cultural Resource Survey of the Proposed Foley Square Project in the Borough of Manhattan, New York, New York. Prepared for Edwards & Kelcey Engineers, Inc., New York. On file, John Milner Associates, Inc., Philadelphia.

Johnson, Malcolm

2005 *On the Waterfront*. Chamberlain Brothers, New York.

Jordan, R. Furneaux

1969 *A Concise History of Western Architecture*. Thames & Hudson, London.

Ladies of the Mission

1854 *The Old Brewery and the New Mission House at the Five Points*. Stringer and Townsend, New York.

Mayne, Alan

1993 *The Imagined Slum*. Leicester University Press, Leicester, UK.

Milne, Claudia

2000 "The Slaughterhouses in which I Labored": Industry, Labor and the Land from Colonial Times to 1830. In *Tales of Five Points: Working-Class Life in Nineteenth-Century New York, Vol. II*, Rebecca Yamin, editor, pp. 15–36. John Milner Associates, Inc., West Chester, PA.

Pernicone, Carol Groneman

1973 The "Bloody Ould Sixth": A Social Analysis of a New York City Working-Class Community in the Mid-Nineteenth Century. Unpublished Ph.D. dissertation, Department of History, University of Rochester, Rochester, NY.

Pitts, Reginald H.

2000 "A Teeming Nation of Nations": Heyday of Five Points, 1830 to 1865. In *Tales of Five Points: Working-Class Life in Nineteenth-Century New York, Vol. I*, Rebecca Yamin, editor, pp. 37–66. John Milner Associates, Inc., West Chester, PA.

Sanders, James

2001 *Celluloid Skyline: New York and the Movies*. Alfred A. Knopf, New York.

Sante, Luc

 1992   *Low Life, Lures and Snares of Old New York*. Farrar Giroux Strauss, New York.

Stansell, Christine

 1987   *City of Women, Sex and Class in New York, 1789–1860*. University of Illinois Press, Urbana.

Stern, Robert A. M., Thomas Mellins, and David Fishman

 1995   *New York 1960: Architecture and Urbanism between the Second World War and the Bicentennial*. Monacelli Press, New York.

Stott, Richard B.

 1990   *Workers in the Metropolis, Class, Ethnicity, and Youth in Antebellum New York City*. Cornell University Press, Ithaca, NY.

Valentine, David T.

 1855   *Valentine's Manual of the Municipal Government of the City of New York*. David T. Valentine, New York.

Wilentz, Sean

 1984   *Chants Democratic, New York City and the Rise of the American Working Class, 1788–1850*. Oxford University Press, New York.

Yamin, Rebecca, editor

 2000   Tales of Five Points: Working-Class Life in Nineteenth-Century New York. John Milner Associates, Inc. Report submitted to Edwards and Kelcey Engineers, Inc., and General Services Administration, Region 2, West Chester, PA.

Yamin, Rebecca, Lauren Cook, Claudia Milne, Paul Reckner, Steve Brighton, Tom Naughton, and Diane Dallal

 2004   Five Points and the Movies: The Archaeologists Respond. Paper presented at the 37th Annual Meeting of the Society for Historical Archaeology, St. Louis.

WESTERN BOOMTOWNS
THE LOST EPISODES

Julie M. Schablitsky

● ●

Over fifty years ago, families sat down in front of their black-and-white televisions and faithfully tuned into Western shows such as the *Lone Ranger*, *Bonanza*, and *Gunsmoke*. Between 1958 and 1959, America had access to thirty-one different Western-style television shows that set heroes against the backdrop of the untamed and rugged Wild West (Peterson 1996:54). Popular culture historians have studied the Western genre *ad infinitum* (Cawelti 1968; West 1987; Walker 2001; Simmon 2003). Many of their earlier analyses took issue with Hollywood's lack of attention to historical accuracy (Sarf 1983; Tuska 1985). Today, scholars have moved past the fact that movies and television shows will never be able to teach history effectively, tell the entire story, or get every detail correct. When asked, Hollywood producers have responded to historians' reprimands regarding their complacency with historical facts and myth perpetuation. Many explain that they are in the business of making us feel, not think (Carnes 1995:11–28; Toplin 2002). In their defense, production companies should not be crucified for identifying what interests the general public, packaging it for mass consumption, and making a profit; however, Hollywood is guilty of being unimaginative, borrowing characters and events from our history books, and taking creative liberties with these stories.

In their attempts to borrow people, places, and events from our past, Hollywood filmmakers highlight popular stories told from biased perspectives documented by the privileged and literate. The stories and names of immigrants, slaves, women, children, and the poor were seldom written down, and their names may have only survived on the page of a family Bible or a probate record as human property. Most of the voiceless remain unheard in both contemporary literature and in Hollywood productions. The significance of archaeology, therefore, is its ability to pull information from an unbiased context and use discarded and lost objects to reconstruct past lives and give the silent minority a stage. The current critique of both classic and modern film and television productions is that most human struggles, successes, and lessons are shown from the lives of the advantaged. This formula may be truer for Westerns than other historical-based movies; nevertheless, stories from the Other are left out of Hollywood's American history primarily because the writers' and producers' research of the people and places stops at popular histories and primary documents. In addition, stories based on famous historical figures will usually outsell films of lesser-known people and events.

To demonstrate the effectiveness of archaeology in illuminating the private space and public spheres of all people, I use three Hollywood productions, *Bonanza*, *Tombstone*, and *Deadwood*, as a stage for this discussion. The 19th-century histories of Virginia City (Nevada), Tombstone (Arizona), and Deadwood (South Dakota) are very similar despite their different geographical locations. All three settlements were founded on gold or silver strikes; large immigrant communities were drawn to these areas; and all three devolved into shadows of their former selves when the mines played out during the early 20th century. These boomtowns also have fallen victim to an oversimplified telling of their stories by Hollywood: the mining culture is glossed over, the global personality is lost, and the people remain ethnically homogeneous. Archaeology can tell the rest of the story.

Bonanza

Place: Virginia City, Nevada
Founded: 1859
Population in 1880: 10,000
Current population: 1,000

The *Bonanza* television series first aired on September 12, 1959, and ran through January 1973. It was the first Western televised in color and ranked number one with viewing audiences between 1964 and 1967 (West 1987:22). *Bonanza* cast endearing fictitious characters that included Ben Cartwright and his three grown sons, Adam, Hoss, and Little Joe. The sons had three different mothers who died before Ben acquired the Ponderosa Ranch, a handsome spread set in the Carson Valley outside of Virginia City, Nevada. Although the episodes were often filmed in the pine- and sage-covered landscape, the Cartwrights frequently made trips into town for drinking, gambling, and supplies. The *Bonanza* writers interpreted and filmed Virginia City as a dusty, false front–lined street that supported cowboys, and an occasional gentleman, strolling and loitering outside businesses, particularly saloons. Galloping horse-drawn stagecoaches provided movement in the town, and a token Native American and Chinese could be seen interacting with other background characters. The television producers introduced the Cartwrights to a variety of personalities and situations. The first season of *Bonanza* consisted of sixteen episodes, four of which were based on historical people. To their credit, the writers conducted research on the Comstock using the histories by William Wright (1967) and Eliot Lord (1883). Mark Twain (the author), Philip Diederheimer (the German inventor of square-set timbering that made mining the Comstock possible), Julia Bulette (the infamous prostitute who was murdered), and Henry T. P. Comstock (the miner who the area was named after) were incorporated into early *Bonanza* episodes. Secondary characters included women, children, Paiute Indians, Chinese, and African Americans; however, their personal stories seldom played center stage.

Tombstone

> Place: Tombstone, Arizona
> Founded: 1878
> Population in 1880s: ca. 4,000
> Current population: 1,500

Tombstone, Arizona, was settled in 1878 after the discovery of silver in the surrounding hills. The population was over 2,000 in 1880, and within two years the number of people had more than doubled (Carmony 1997:29). The film *Tombstone* (1993) starred Kurt Russell as Wyatt Earp and Val Kilmer as Doc Holliday. The movie focuses on the build up to the infamous shoot out at the O.K. Corral in Tombstone between the Earp and Clanton families. In an attempt to create an authentic Western, the production team spent considerable time researching the town, clothing, and interior furnishings of 19th-century Arizona. Replicas of buildings in Tombstone were constructed from the ground up. The set of the Oriental, an actual saloon and gambling hall, was covered in historic era–inspired wallpaper and lit with reproduction lighting patterned after historic photographs. Wardrobe designers also researched each costume to dress the characters in the correct styles, colors, and details right down to the pocket watches and diamond tie pins. Acknowledging that contemporary audiences are better educated on material culture, the producer went to extreme lengths to have his movie look the part. In fact, buckaroos were even used as movie extras (*Tombstone*

DVD). The incorporation of Western reenactors in historical films is a genuine benefit to Hollywood as the living history characters arrive on site with their own authentic costumes. The film effectively communicates the permanency and wealth of the community through large-framed buildings and a well-dressed community. Unfortunately, they used the modern Tombstone to reflect late 1870s street scenes; the original Southwest town contained a proportionate number of adobe buildings and tents.

Deadwood

> Place: Deadwood, South Dakota
> Founded: 1876
> Population in 1880s: 6,000
> Current population: 1,300

Some historians conclude that the American public has outgrown shoot-outs between cowboys and Indians, rides into the sunset, and lively music banged out on pianos; in other words, they conclude the classic Western genre is dead (Simmon 2003:xv). Recently, the Home Box Office network has successfully demonstrated with their series, *Deadwood*, that barroom brawls, prostitutes, and double crossers still have a place in Hollywood. The 21st-century Western has reinvented itself. Hollywood has sent the sensitive and romantic cowboy out to pasture and replaced the unsung hero with physically and emotionally scarred characters who conduct business like the Mafia and converse like Shakespearean pirates. Creator, writer, and executive producer David Milch researched the history of the Dakota Territory for his *Deadwood* series and concluded the place was "an outlaw community, full of misfits, and people who could not adapt to civilized society" (Milch 2004). His team, including Davis Guggenheim, director and producer, explained that the characters were based on actual people and the types of people that would have lived there. In attempts to quash the laconic cowboy image and hold true to *his* idea of the stereotypical miner and criminal element of Deadwood, Milch's characters communicate in a steady stream of obscenities. Often criticized for the relentless profanity, Milch justifies the language of the *Deadwood* characters by explaining that criminals adopt obscene language to exclude the dominant group (law-abiding citizens) in society. Through the use of vile language, Milch believes he will "get the character right" and be true to their essence.

Although *Deadwood* effectively represents members of the criminal underworld, the production excludes most immigrant characters and the ordinary human element that was prolific in a mining community. The first U.S. census of Deadwood enumerated countless numbers of foreign immigrants including a Norwegian baker, a Mexican cook, and a Scottish gunsmith (U.S. Bureau of the Census 1880). Although this census was taken four years after the setting of the *Deadwood* series, research on boomtowns suggests immigrants were prolific in these early settlements (Schablitsky 2002:92–102; Fosha 2004). Although a Chinatown filled with sojourners and caged prostitutes pays homage to part of the Western boomtown experience, the absence of an ethnically heterogeneous population limits the show's effectiveness in translating the true flavor, complexity, and multifaceted issues faced by a 19th-century global community.

Boomtowns

For the last fifty years, the movie and television productions that have focused on boomtown communities have dramatically improved their sets, props, and wardrobes. The cowboy outfits and backgrounds of *Bonanza* appear unrealistic and poorly executed by today's standards. Modern Hollywood sets, coupled with technology, leave nothing to the imagination as audiences are effortlessly transported to another place and time. Hollywood now employs well-educated prop masters to design their sets and writers dive into the archives for character names and story line inspiration. *Tombstone* and *Deadwood* are testaments to the

Western's successful evolution from generic-clothed cowboys set against a water-colored canvas to three-dimensional characters who mirror historic-period photographs.

The keen-eyed critic is no longer concerned with wrong costumes and ridiculous sets; instead, archaeologists now recognize an overemphasis and biased focus on the stories of the privileged social majority. Nineteenth-century boomtowns supported a global community of working-class Americans and immigrants who toiled in the mines and in the service industry. People representing almost every country in the world set foot in these towns to improve their lives and secure the future of their children. The struggles and triumphs of the Chinese launderer, the Irish seamstress, and the African American barber are never written into a script and shown on screen. It is true that *Deadwood*'s Godfather, Swearenger, and the Chinese merchant, Mr. Wu are blood brothers and that the Cartwrights regularly interfaced with their Paiute neighbors; however, we are not privy to the struggles of the Other or witness the growing pains of social issues and the formation of community. The ways in which immigrants and minority populations interacted and reacted to their environment are gone and not replayed for us to watch. Without their stories, we are witness to only part of our legacy, understand only a fraction of our past, and forget the lessons taught and learned by our ancestors. The value of archaeology, therefore, is not to only reveal the stories of the silent minorities ignored by Hollywood productions but, to confirm, contradict, and contribute to what is held in the written record.

The People

Despite their physical location in the United States, immigrants consciously preserved their heritage by establishing ethnic saloons, restaurants, and social organizations (Elliott 1973; Fosha 2004:49). On the Comstock in Nevada, Germans organized an athletic club by 1863, and those of Scottish heritage competed in traditional hammer-throwing events at annual picnics in Carson City (James 1998:158–159). The growth and perseverance of these ethnic clubs and gatherings was a direct result of community building. Once a mining camp was established, class distinctions based on race and social identity emerged; Chinese, people of African descent, and Native Americans immediately found themselves cast into inferior roles within the settlement. Competition between these minorities for jobs and social status could be heard and felt within the community. African Americans, and other people of African descent such as Jamaicans, also lived in western mining towns. They were never ghettoized like their later descendents and lived throughout the town in single-family homes and boarding houses. Few historical accounts have documented their lives, making it difficult to reconstruct their roles in the mining West. Their infrequent mention in the historical records is likely a result of small Black populations that did not significantly interfere with White dominance and economic attainment (James 1998:97–98). Despite their small numbers, people of African ancestry successfully integrated themselves into the community. In some instances, they owned property and ran their own businesses.

Although they were allowed to work mining dumps and tailing sites, the Chinese found steady employment in unskilled or semiskilled positions cooking food, cleaning, or washing clothes (Magnaghi 1981:136; Parker 1981:143–144). Chinese cooks were plentiful in boomtowns, and in 1880 their numbers were well over a hundred in many mining communities (U.S. Bureau of the Census 1880). They were trained to cook traditional American cuisine in boarding houses, private homes, and restaurants (Fosha 2004:48). To supplement their income, the Chinese peddled fresh vegetables from their gardens, local fish, and watercress to the citizens in Virginia City (Magnaghi 1981:137). There was stiff competition for employment between Chinese and other minority groups such as the Irish, people of African descent, and Native Americans. Many Virginians, however, preferred Chinese help, stating: "They will do things for us I would not like to ask a white person to do; besides, they never tell any family affairs like white girls do" (Matthews 1985:252). Employers in Deadwood held opposing viewpoints and sought to organize a recruiting expedition to the eastern United States for fifty servant girls to replace the Chinese work force (*Black Hills Daily Times* 1880).

In the early years of these boomtowns, Chinese were not initially marginalized into separate neighborhoods; however, eventual discrimination and zoning ordinances forced them into undesirable real estate. Chinatowns were exotic collections of homes and businesses. Since very little documentation exists on social interactions, economic exchanges, and political organization of these ethnic enclaves, archaeologists are working to identify patterns within artifact assemblages that illuminate relationships with non-Chinese and details about the process of assimilation. The archaeological excavations and historical research of Virginia City's Chinatown suggest the Chinese lived in a fairly homogeneous neighborhood away from the center of town (Thompson 1992). Despite palpable racism and their eventual residential displacement downhill, away from the central business district, the Chinese regularly interacted with non-Asian community members. The common discovery of English imported dishware in Chinese site contexts and the recovery of Chinese brown stoneware jars within the archaeological remains of a British household suggest their active participation in commerce with the non-Asian community on both commercial and neighboring levels (Schablitsky 2002:237).

Public Space

The mining towns of Virginia City, Deadwood, and Tombstone were urban, global, and wealthy for many years (Carmony 1997; James 1998; Fosha 2006:44). Families, religion, education, modern infrastructure, transportation, wealth from the mines, and European commodities transformed these early tent towns into urban settlements almost overnight.

Many visitors were surprised to see the range of amenities offered and the wealth of Virginia City. One tourist reported, "Here are the restaurants as fine as any in the world; here are drinking saloons more gorgeous in appointment than any in San Francisco, Philadelphia, or New York; and here are shops and stores which are dazzling in splendor. I have never been in a place where money is so plentiful nor where it is spent with so much extravagance and recklessness" (*New York Tribune* 1875). Those who came to Tombstone had similar experiences, "Social life in Tombstone was on par with that prevailing in communities of similar size elsewhere, even in the effete east" (Carmony 1997:39). The people living in boomtowns also *looked* rich. Those who observed Virginia City in its glory noticed all men, rich or poor, dressed in similar fashions. Even the working class cloaked their economic situation with expensive clothes and jewels created by local milliners, dressmakers, and seamstresses (*Territorial Enterprise* 1873). The *Territorial Enterprise* published a smug editorial smirking at the eastern visitors' surprise regarding style on the Comstock: "They expect to find our men dressed in buckskin breeches and gray woolen shirts, and our ladies in calico gowns, innocent of the remotest symptom of hoops" (1864). Some less-affluent residents found the vanity of Virginia City's ladies frivolous. Mary McNair Matthews stated the citizens of Virginia City were the best dressed she had ever witnessed and was sure they only went to church to show their fine clothes (1985:195).

During the 1870s and 1880s, these mining communities supported schools, churches, and documented the life of their community with daily newspapers such as Tombstone's *Epitaph*, Virginia City's *Territorial Enterprise*, and Deadwood's *Pioneer*. Their central business districts pulsed with activity; street vendors sang out advertisements, oxen-drawn prairie schooners chimed their arrival, and no less than a dozen different languages broke the dusty air. The main streets in early western towns held banks, telegraph offices, the Masonic and Odd Fellows halls, book stores, dry goods stores, and grocery stores (Matthews 1985:165). Spire churches, schools, a government seat, mansions, and Shakespeare performances gave these mining towns the mirage of a stable and immortal city. The red light district, opera houses, and Chinatowns often concentrated together on the edges of town in entertainment districts; however, saloons appeared to be ubiquitous (Schablitsky 2002).

The Hollywood saloon varies in form from a wood-plank

hovel as seen in *Deadwood*, to an elaborate gilded saloon such as the Oriental in *Tombstone*, to the stereotypical and unimaginative *Bonanza* barroom with round poker tables, clingy prostitutes, and bottomless whiskey bottles, all catering to White, U.S.-born men. In reality, the variety of ways in which Victorians dined and drank far surpassed any cinematic saloon scene. Archaeological findings and historical research in Virginia City suggest the function of the saloon was complex and that these places of leisure differed between classes and ethnic groups, and even included women.

German culture integrated the family into the saloon business through brewing their own beer and serving it over the counter and within beer gardens. The Union Brewery, which still stands along C Street, was founded by German immigrants, Charles Baker and George Duttenhoefer. Virtuous women were absent from most saloon environs, but Charles's wife, Anna, helped her husband manage his business and her presence was dutifully noted (Schablitsky 2002:127). Although Mrs. Baker was married with children and lived at home with her family, her untraditional role in the Union Brewery caused the census enumerator to record her in his ledger as a "harlot" (U.S. Bureau of the Census 1870).

The Irish also established their own saloons on the Comstock. The Hibernia Brewery was a business where draft beer was served to Irish clientele. The building had one room with plastered and painted walls and linoleum-covered floors (Hardesty 1996:14). Archaeological remains recovered from the saloon context include alcoholic and nonalcoholic bottles, shot glasses, and bar tumblers. Gambling pieces, including dice, poker chips, and cribbage pegs were also collected from the saloon remains. The presence of these bar-related objects are not surprising; however, the discovery of corset stays, glass beads, perfume bottles, porcelain doll fragments, and marbles suggest nearby occupation by women and children. On the opposite end of the spectrum of saloons in Virginia City was the Piper's Old Corner Bar located within Piper's Opera House.

Unlike the Irish watering holes, the Old Corner Bar emanated high class and elegance; fancy bar glass reflected prismatic light, decorative wallpaper adorned the walls, and an aquarium or curio displaying oddities from the sea sat among the patrons. This drinking establishment may have primarily catered to men as suggested by historic writings and confirmed by a lack of female-related artifacts (Dixon 2005:64–66, 126–129, 160–161). Despite the underrepresentation of women, the attention to detail and extra expense on décor clearly set the Old Corner Bar at the respectable end of saloons in the mining West.

One of the more unusual saloons studied was the Boston Saloon, an African American–owned and operated barroom and restaurant in Virginia City. The archaeological record revealed this establishment was similar in status to the Old Corner Bar. People of African descent drank from fancy stemware and dined on high-quality meats served on undecorated white ironstone dishes. Modern gas lighting and the presence of a trombone mouthpiece point to a comfortable atmosphere reverberating with brass band music. Discovery of feminine style buttons, beads, and female DNA on a pipe stem suggest the saloon served women as well as men (Dixon 2005:67–70). Saloon archaeology in Virginia City, along with the written record, has successfully illuminated the different functions of the saloon and the variability that can range between these places of leisure in regard to class, ethnicity, and services provided to saloon patrons.

Private Space

Mining towns were infamous for supporting hazardous and unhealthy lifestyles. Inhabitants of these settlements often battled relentless diseases and unidentifiable illnesses that required unregulated doses of pain killers. In an attempt to communicate the pain and suffering brought on by 19th-century diseases and inadequate medical care, *Tombstone* writers feature sickly characters such as the diaphoretic Doc Holiday who sputtered with tuberculosis and clutched a blood-spattered handkerchief. Mattie, Wyatt Earp's wife, is shown as a tortured soul drowning her depression in endless bottles of laudanum. The *Deadwood* series also depicts disturbing images of suffering men and women who seize with brain tumors, nurse abscesses from hypodermic drug abuse, and endure regular check-ups for venereal diseases. What is not shown are the crude tools to treat the pain and create the addiction, along with the superstitious precautions Victorians performed to protect themselves against invisible evil forces that would bring harm to them and their families. A place of protection and comfort from pain and death was the home, and this is where archaeologists look to uncover personal habits and private behavior.

On the other side of the tracks, down the hill, were the working-class homes in Virginia City, where an international community of men, women, and children lived in both single-family cottages and boarding houses. Densely occupied, ethnically heterogeneous, blue-collar neighborhoods are a natural response to urban growth. The archaeological excavation of a small dwelling house in this community revealed the burned and broken belongings of a family home, the desperate and unsanitary conditions of early medicine, and Celtic-based superstitious beliefs. The home was built during the 1860s and served as a dressmaker shop in 1873 and a residential home in 1874 before it was burned by a town fire in 1875 (Schablitsky 2002). Common household items, including Lubin perfume, a German-made porcelain doll head (Figure 11.1), and knobby tobacco pipe bowl, were discovered and associated with the British Cooper family who lived there in 1874. Deeper excavations between and below the charred floorboards revealed a variety of beads, buttons, and many straight pins, a sharp testament to the 1873 dressmaker activities. As the archaeologists excavated deeper, they discovered an inoperable glass syringe, rolled copper-alloy syringe needles, and a *Goodyear* brand, hard rubber irrigator used to flush the urethra of infectious impurities often brought on by venereal diseases such as syphilis.

Forensic tests on the hypodermic glass syringe revealed nuclear DNA signatures from at least four men and women, one of whom may have been of African descent. A gas chromatograph-mass spectrometer test recovered low levels of and/or degraded morphine within the glass syringe barrel (Schablitsky 2006:10). The discovery of an opiate within the syringe was not unexpected

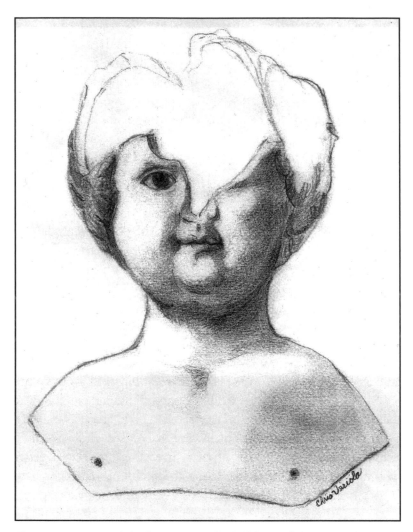

Figure 11.1. Porcelain German-made doll "Josie" discovered in the 1875 burned remains of the Cooper family home in Virginia City, Nevada. Doll head reconstructed by Susan Hopple and Drawn by Chris Uriola.

as morphine was the most common medicine injected during the last half of the 19th century. The DNA signature of at least four people, including at least one man and one woman, suggest the small home was not only used as a residence and dressmaker shop but perhaps as an earlier doctor's clinic or place of vice such as a drug den or prostitute crib. This discovery underscores the painful and unsanitary conditions endured by Victorians. These early syringes were constructed of glass, contained crudely made needles, and the injection process included lancing the skin prior to inserting the rolled copper-alloy needle into the muscle. The agony, complications, and severity of infections caused by this type of medicinal administration could never be accurately captured on film. In *Deadwood*, morphine injections are made into the vein by sharp, stainless steel syringes. Although abscesses are shown on *Deadwood* to be a side effect of injecting an opiate, the redness around an inner arm vein hardly communicates the grotesque malformation and suffering morphine addicts endured while their flesh and bone rotted away from infection (Clarke 1973:1018–1019).

In addition to the discovery of medical instruments, archaeologists also uncovered a ritual cache buried under the floorboards of this same home (Schablitsky 2002:223–231). Ritual is a common human behavior performed in myriad ways to bring about order in a world of chaos. Navigating life in a western boomtown was difficult, risky, and unpredictable. To exercise some control over unseen forces such as death and disease, people performed rituals to protect themselves (Merrifield 1987; Swann 1996). The collection of artifacts discovered under the burned northern floor boards dates to the 1860s and included: a Civil War–era boot, a ferrous padlock with a brass heart-shaped escutcheon (Figure 11.2), an empty wine bottle, a wool hat, and a piece of leather (possibly from a woman's shoe) with knife scores on one side. The context in which these particular items were discovered suggests that whoever interred the cache was attempting to bless or protect the people inside of the home.

The need for protection and the interment of ritual caches transcended borders and ethnic enclaves during the 19th century. In Deadwood's Chinatown, archaeologists discovered a two-foot-deep and over three-foot-wide bark-lined pit. It was interpreted as a ritual cache created from a deceased man's belongings and food offerings. The first items interred into the feature included deliberately broken opium-smoking paraphernalia along with fruit seeds and pits. The mourning Chinese also added personal items to the cache, which included a small leather coin purse and toothbrush. The final donations included a *sam* (upper tunic) draped atop the food; the pit was ultimately sealed with privy dirt (Fosha 2004:60).

Conclusion

The common theme among all Western shows over the past hundred years has been an emphasis on White history and an underrepresentation of minority and immigrant experiences. Boomtown screenwriters only acknowledge the settlement's

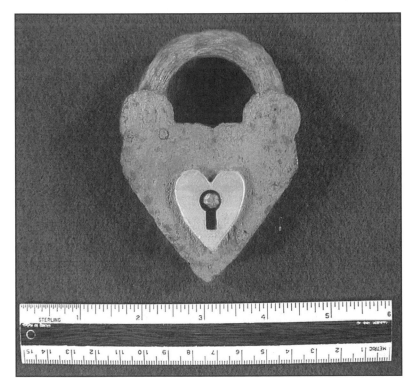

Figure 11.2. Ferrous padlock with brass-alloy heart-shaped escutcheon associated with ritual cache concealed beneath the Cooper home during the 1860s. Padlock conserved by Ken Hopple and photo by Julie M. Schablitsky.

194

global flavor through the introduction of physically unique characters in the background or through guest appearances. The most popular and visually exciting immigrant group to Hollywood has been the Chinese. The Cartwright family employed a Chinese servant, Hop Sing; *Tombstone* placed Chinese extras dressed in traditional clothing wearing a queue in street scenes and had secondary characters discuss the Anti-Chinese League; and the ambitious *Deadwood* series introduced the audience to the underworld of Chinatown and the mysterious character of Mr. Wu. Despite the inclusion of this ethnic group, the role of the larger immigrant community, extent of their culture, and personal stories remain unexplored and ambiguous.

In addition to the problem with homogeneous characters, Hollywood commonly downplays complexities and multidimensional aspects of life in boomtowns and producers of Westerns keep storylines simple and details obscured. An exception to this rule may be David Milch's *Deadwood* series. Although his episodes focus on the ambitions of White males, Milch's research into the *Pioneer* and inclusion of actual people and places has facilitated his ability to authenticate a realistic Western. As the characters and community of *Deadwood* grow, perhaps the depth and variety of characters will evolve along with the story. Already, Milch is beginning to introduce elements that suggest the presence and growth of community. Gathering for a child's funeral, swinging arm in arm at a town dance, and ritually serving canned peaches at each town meeting are all signatures of stability and kinship. The formation of organized societies, a strong symbol of town permanence, is hinted at in *Deadwood*. After leaving a restaurant, A. W. Merrick, newspaper editor of the *Pioneer*, suggests to his comrades as they clomp along the boardwalk that they should form a private club. Grasping for an idea, he suggests they meet to stroll about town. They pay little attention to his suggestion and walk away in different directions; still in thought, he wonders aloud … perhaps, the "Amblers."

Although Hollywood and archaeologists often study and disseminate stories from our past, our missions are not congruent. Admittedly, the archaeologist's responsibility is to dig in the archives and the ground, analyze those data, and reveal the stories about everyday life, the unrepresented minorities, and the environment in which these people and events played out. Publications on the rich diversity among saloons, research on the personal behavior of working-class Victorians, and the recognition of the complexities of Chinatowns are collectively adding to our knowledge of 19th-century boomtowns. These investigations have advanced our perception of the frontier from a prostitute-strewn saloon environ to a human experience that longed for comfort, protection, and community. Although producers and writers are not expected to deliver intricate details and mundane history, it is hoped they will take a closer look at the underrepresented lives of the people who helped build our American culture and incorporate them into their storytelling.

References

Black Hills Daily Times
    1880   *Black Hills Daily Times* (Deadwood, SD), May 19.
Carmony, Neil B., editor
    1997   *Apache Days and Tombstone Nights, John Clum's Autobiography, 1877–1887.* High-Lonesome Books, Silver City, NM.
Carnes, Mark C., editor
    1995   *Past Imperfect, History According to the Movies.* Henry Holt and Company, New York.
Cawelti, John G.
    1968   The Gunfighter and Society. *American West* 5(2):30–35, 76–78.
Clark, Walter Van Tilburg, editor
    1973   *The Journals of Alfred Doten, 1849–1903.* University of Nevada Press, Reno.

Dixon, Kelly J.

   2005   *Boomtown Saloons, Archaeology and History in Virginia City*. University of Nevada Press, Reno.

Elliott, Russell R.

   1973   *History of Nevada*. University of Nebraska Press, Lincoln.

Fosha, Rose Estep

   2004   The Archaeology of Deadwood's Chinatown: A Prologue. In *Ethnic Oasis, The Chinese in the Black Hills*, Liping Zhu and Rose Estep Fosha, editors, pp. 44–68. South Dakota State Historical Society Press, Pierre.

   2006   The Chinese Experience in Deadwood, South Dakota: Life on the Edge of the Interior Western Frontier. Paper presented at the 39th Annual Society for Historical Archaeology Conference, Sacramento, CA.

Hardesty, Donald L., with Jane E. Baxter, Ronald M. James, Ralph B. Giles Jr., and Elizabeth M. Scott

   1996   Public Archaeology on the Comstock. University of Nevada, Reno, report prepared for the State of Nevada Historic Preservation Office, Carson City.

James, Ronald M.

   1998   *The Roar and the Silence, A History of Virginia City and the Comstock Lode*. University of Nevada Press, Reno.

Lord, Eliot

   1883   *Comstock Mining and Miners*. Reprint, Washington DC: U.S. Geological Survey, Government Printing Office (1959).

Magnaghi, Russell M.

   1981   Virginia City's Chinese Community, 1860–1880. *Nevada Historical Society Quarterly* 24(2):130–157.

Mathews, Mary McNair.

   1985   *Ten Years in Nevada or Life on the Pacific Coast*. Reprint, University of Nebraska Press, Lincoln.

Merrifield, Ralph

   1987   *The Archaeology of Ritual and Magic*. New Amsterdam Books, New York.

Milch, David

   2004   Interview on *Deadwood*. DVD.

New York Tribune

   1875   *New York Tribune*, August 27.

Parker, Wattson

   1981   *Deadwood, The Golden Years.* University of Nebraska
   Press, Lincoln.

Peterson, Richard H.

   1996   The Western Rides Again. *Journal of the West*
   35(1):54–58.

Sarf, Wayne Michael

   1983   *God Bless You, Buffalo Bill: A Layman's Guide to History
   and the Western Film.* Fairleigh Dickinson University Press,
   Madison, NJ.

Schablitsky, Julie M.

   2002   The Other Side of the Tracks, The Archaeology and
   History of a Virginia City, Nevada Neighborhood. Ph.D. disser-
   tation, Department of Urban Studies, Portland State University,
   Portland.

   2006   Genetic Archaeology: The Recovery and Interpretation of
   Nuclear DNA from a Nineteenth-Century Hypodermic Syringe.
   Historical Archaeology 40(3):8–19.

Simmon, Scott

   2003   *The Invention of the Western Film, A Cultural History
   of the Genre's First Half-Century,* Cambridge University Press,
   London.

Swann, June

   1996   "Shoes Concealed in Buildings." *Costume Society Journal*
   30:56–59.

Territorial Enterprise

   1864   *Territorial Enterprise* (Virginia City, NV), June 14.

   1873   *Territorial Enterprise* (Virginia City, NV), March 14.

Thompson, Judy Ann

   1992   Historical Archaeology in Virginia City, Nevada: A Case
   Study of the 90-H Block. Unpublished Masters thesis, Department
   of Anthropology, University of Nevada, Reno.

Toplin, Robert Brent

   2002   *Reel History, In Defense of Hollywood.* University Press of
   Kansas, Lawrence.

Tuska, Jon

   1985   *The American West in Film: Critical Approaches to the
   Western.* Greenwood Press, Westport, CT.

U.S. Bureau of the Census

1870   *Population Schedules of the Ninth Census of the United States, 1870.* Nevada State Archives, Carson City.

1880   *Population Schedules of the Tenth Census of the United States, 1880.* Nevada State Archives, Carson City.

Walker, Janet, editor

2001   *Westerns: Films through History.* Routledge, New York.

West, Richard

1987   *Television Westerns: Major and Minor Series, 1946–1978.* McFarland and Company, Jefferson, NC.

Wright, William (Dan De Quille)

1967   *The Big Bonanza.* Reprint of 1876 edition. Alfred A. Knopf, Inc., New York.

CONTESTING HOLLYWOOD'S CHINATOWNS

Bryn Williams and Stacey Camp

● ●

Chinatowns have long been used in American media as a geographic signifier for dark, mysterious, and dangerous people. Common media images of life in Chinatowns include the lascivious depictions of opium dens, prostitution, and gambling. Archaeological research on historic Chinese communities promises to nuance these oversimplified and racial stereotypes. Not only can archaeologists challenge inaccurate conceptions of history and the past, they can also interpret material culture in a way that illuminates why these representations had traction in past films and are perpetuated in the present. In addition to confronting Hollywood's mythic Chinatowns, the history behind how these myths were created and their persistence into present-day debates is explored using primary documents. Historical archeology, in particular, with its unique emphasis on both the daily lives of individuals and cultural processes, provides a powerful forum for these discourses to be discussed, challenged, and mediated.

Nations are imagined communities that tie individual subjects to specific regimes of sovereignty (Anderson 1983). Like other social groups, nations are constituted through social processes of inclusion and exclusion that often fracture along lines of gender, race, and sexuality (Stoler 2002). In the western United States, Chinese were often used as exemplary Others against which a racialized Anglo American national identity was formed (Shah 2001). Non-Chinese fears of Chinese immigration into the United States and resulting anxiety about the demographic constitution of the nation can be witnessed in media representations of Chinatowns. Themes depicting the Chinese as antagonistic to the health and security of the nation were associated with a post–Civil War depression that began in the 1870s, which forced Anglo Americans out of work.

Claiming that cheap Chinese labor was contributing to Anglo American unemployment, federal politicians passed laws that excluded Chinese from immigrating to and becoming citizens of the United States (Daniel 1991). These acts included the Naturalization Act of 1870, which banned Chinese from becoming naturalized citizens of the United States (Daniel 1991:245; Ngai 2004:38), and the 1882 Chinese Exclusion Act, which "made the Chinese, for a time, the only ethnic group in the world that could not freely immigrate to the United States" (Daniel 1991:246). State laws also targeted noncitizens; for example, the 1913 California Alien Land Law prohibited nonnaturalized immigrants from owning their own land (Guerin-Gonzales 1994:16). This law built into the legal structure of California exclusionary practices targeted at Mexican and Chinese immigrants that had been in place since the late 1800s (Haas 1995; Garcia 2001). The media's interpretations of and role in creating these historical events were and continue to be materially articulated in political cartoons, films, and television shows. The archaeological endeavor can build on, challenge, and/or contextualize these themes by juxtaposing archaeological evidence against the rhetoric reiterated in this media.

Although this discussion specifically focuses on the archaeology of Chinatowns in California, many of these observations can be extended to other Chinatowns. Locally situated media that defined the Chinese in threatening and dangerous ways had national and even international reverberations (Eng 2001; Shah 2001). Despite this international salience, all generalizations must be evaluated against the historical circumstances of local situations. The Chinese experience in other areas of the country and the world followed different historical trajectories because of different economic, social, and political conditions (Takaki 1989; Wegars 1993; Lydon 1999; Fosha 2004; Gardner et al. In press).

California Chinatowns

The Chinese presence in California extends back to the Spanish period of the late 18th century when several Chinese individuals accompanied the Spanish in their colonization of "Alta California" (Lydon 1985). Additionally, both Chinese and non-Chinese Californios made extensive use of Chinese goods, primarily porcelains, imported to Mexico from the Manila galleon trade (Mudge 1986; Voss 2002). Although there was a definite Asian presence, the number of Chinese in California remained small until the mid-19th century, when the Chinese population in the state rapidly expanded. This expansion was due to a number of historical factors in both China and the United States, including the Taiping rebellion in China and the California Gold Rush. This migration was part of the broader formation of a transnational diaspora as Chinese moved to countries around the Pacific Rim and beyond (Ong 1999).

In California, the Chinese quickly grew to become one of the largest non-White immigrant populations. For as many as 20% of the miners working in California during the mid-1850s (Rohe 2002), the journey to California was not a westward journey over land or a trip around the Cape of Good Hope, but a journey east across the Pacific to "Old Gold Mountain," the name still used in China for San Francisco.

California was a place with a large variety of ethnic groups, many of whom lived in segregated neighborhoods (Lotchin 1997). Nonetheless, the popular media have given a particular prominence to Chinatowns, presenting them as completely ethni-cally homogeneous and exotic places with rigid boundaries. Many of the Chinese who came to California settled in Chinatowns, and every major western city had one. The larger cities—San Francisco, San Jose, and Sacramento—tended to have correspondingly large Chinatowns, with San Francisco being home to an upwards of 20,000 overseas Chinese (Shah 2001:25).

In the late 1800s, a variety of factors led to the destruction and disbandment of many Chinatowns. Changing social and econom ic conditions in both the United States and China and increas-ing racial conflict and violence also threatened these communi-ties (Allen et al. 2002). Historian Connie Yu (1991:27) explains how "racist attitudes and ridicule of the Chinese" become "part of popular vocabulary," manifested in anti-Chinese newspapers, violent acts against the Chinese, and increasingly stringent anti-Chinese laws. Racist anti-Chinese laws were extended to the national stage with the passage of the Chinese Exclusion Act of 1882 (Daniel 1991). After the passage of this law, the return home of many Chinese, and the passing away of elderly bachelors, the Chinese population dwindled by the late 19th century. Despite these historical difficulties and pressures, some Chinatowns (such as those in San Francisco and New York) continue to exist as cen-ters of contemporary Chinese and Chinese American culture in the United States.

San Jose's Market Street Chinatown

Located in downtown San Jose, the Market Street Chinatown was a gathering site for the nearly 3,000 Chinese immigrants living in and around Santa Clara County during the late 19th century (Yu 1991:29). During its time, the Market Street Chinatown was the largest Chinese community south of San Francisco. The Market Street Chinatown was not the first Chinese community in San Jose. At the same location, a previous Chinatown was formed in the 1860s and was occupied until 1869 when the wooden buildings of this community burned to the ground (Yu 1991:21). Members of the Chinese community built another, temporary

Chinatown in San Jose and lived there until the Market Street Chinatown was rebuilt in 1872 (Yu 1991:21). On May 4, 1887, an arson-sparked fire inspired by anti-Chinese sentiment burned the Chinese buildings to the ground. Rather than be driven away, the Chinese in San Jose regrouped and founded new Chinatowns in two separate locations. One community was attached to a factory and became known as the "Woolen Mills Chinatown." The other community, the "Heinlenville Chinatown," was located on the outskirts of town (Allen et al. 2002).

Although artifacts from Market Street Chinatown were excavated in 1985, 1986, and 1988, the cultural material from the site was never fully analyzed. History San José, a nonprofit organization, gained control of the collection in 2002 and entered into a joint project with Stanford University to process the artifact assemblage. Preliminary research has led to the publication of a number of reports based on materials from the site. These reports range from in-depth studies of single features (Clevenger 2004) to examinations of classes of artifacts across the site that include ceramics with "peck marks" (Michaels 2005), gaming pieces found at the site (Camp 2004; Chang 2004), tiny cups (Simmons 2004), and opium paraphernalia (Williams 2003). Additionally, archaeological materials from the site have been used as a case study to discuss overseas Chinese archaeology (Voss 2005) and the archaeology of masculinity (Williams 2006).

Hollywood's Chinatown

Hollywood has long used Chinatowns and Chinese Americans to both create and convey cultural anxieties about the constitution of U.S. national identity. These tropes permeate historical and contemporary media and infiltrate archaeological interpretations of overseas Chinese communities. Although other forms of media are briefly considered (political cartoons), this analysis primarily focuses on three films: *Broken Blossoms*, from the age of silent cinema, *Mr. Wong in Chinatown*, from the late 1930s, and *The Corruptor*, a contemporary film released in 1999. Two powerful and intertwined discourses that echo throughout these films and represent imagined Chinese threats to America are the portrayal of Chinatowns as dangerous places outside of law and the imagination of Chinatowns as "beachheads" for the cultural invasion of America. The depictions of the Chinese and Chinatowns that emanate from Hollywood do not emerge sui generis from the minds of producers and directors. They are both generated by and generative of long-standing discourses regarding Chinatowns.

In many films, Chinatown has been depicted as a mysterious and dangerous space, existing outside of the rules and regulations of "normal America." In contrast, Chinese immigrants who leave Chinatowns or live outside them are often depicted as ideal, moral, and assimilated U.S. citizens. The Chinese Americans who remain in Chinatowns are shown as envious or as harboring hatred toward the assimilated.

Mr. Wong in Chinatown (1939) is an installment of the serialized film series "Mr. Wong" starring Boris Karloff, as Mr. Wong. Set in San Francisco, Mr. Wong is a Chinese American private detective who solves various crimes involving the San Francisco Chinatown and the Chinese community. In this particular episode, Mr. Wong helps the San Francisco police investigate the murder of a Chinese "princess" who was in California attempting to buy military airplanes for the wars in China. Mr. Wong uses his connections with the Tongs—Chinese gangs commonly associated with crime, drugs, and prostitution by the media—in Chinatown to help solve the case. Throughout the series, Mr. Wong is the "Americanized" Chinaman who serves as a liaison between the separate worlds of Euro American San Francisco and the foreign Chinatown.

In *Mr. Wong in Chinatown*, the Chinatown is primarily visited when a crime or other misdeed has been committed. The Chinese who live there are depicted as backward and foreign, whereas those living outside of Chinatown are more civilized, less prone to violence, and culturally "Whiter" (and, in Mr. Wong's case, physically Whiter). The portrayal of the Chinese community in the film insinuates that it is the Chinatowns themselves that keep the Chinese from assimilating into American culture. To further accentuate the danger of these places, the only economic activities that seem to take place (aside from the ubiquitous Chinese restaurants) are smuggling, prostitution, and drug use.

James Foley's *The Corruptor* (1999) is a story about Danny, a New York City police officer (Mark Wahlberg), assigned to "work the beat" in Chinatown. He is the only non-Chinese officer working in the precinct. Another experienced officer, Nick (Chow-Yun Fat), serves as the link between the seedy and unregulated world of Chinatown and the New York police force. Toward the end of the movie, we find that Nick is corrupt and has many connections with the Tongs. In the end, Nick is forced to choose between his loyalty to the police force and his allegiance to the Tongs. Though Tongs were important parts of life in many Chinatowns, they are better characterized as community organizations. The Tongs' criminal connections lasciviously used in the media, are overstated and rest on "very little reliable evidence" (Daniel 1991:245).

The Corruptor paints a similar picture of the New York Chinatown. The streets of the community are liminal legal spaces where crimes easily go unpunished by official authorities who must rely on sympathetic insiders to maintain order. This film also explicitly deals with Chinatown issues that were only hinted at in the older films: filth, moral depravity, and drug use. Whereas early silent films, such as *Broken Blossoms* (1919), often showed Chinese characters smoking opium, and the serialized movies made reference to opium dens and women of ill repute, the Foley movie is quite explicit in its depiction of drug use, gambling, and prostitution. In this film, several scenes take place in brothels, violently depicted murders occur at an alarming pace, and the officers regularly visit gambling halls as part of their "beat."

Symbolism and imagery have also sent a strong message about the danger, vice, and corruption of Chinese enclaves. Choy et al. (1994:102) explain how in political cartoons, the Chinese were "ridiculed ... as cultural inferiors, physically grotesque, morally depraved, and carriers of the deadliest diseases." In fact, in 1903 "the presence of the bubonic plague was a deliberate scare fabricated by the Board of Health in a campaign to convince San Franciscans of the necessity to get rid of the Chinese and to burn

Chinatown" (Choy et al. 1994:102). Cartoons helped further San Francisco's Board of Health's political campaign, with captions reading, "The Bubonic Plague in San Francisco, Chinamen, Confined within the Chinese Quarter." By the time the epidemic had been dismissed by federal courts as nothing more than a "political and labor maelstrom" (Molina 2006:28) related to the mayor of San Francisco's political platform, Anglo Americans' fear of the Chinese, which had its origins from the time the Chinese begin to enter the United States, increased by manifolds (Saxton 1970; Shah 2001). Cartoons frequently sensationalized Chinatowns, often showing Chinese Americans engaging in prostitution, smoking, gambling, smoking, and the "debauchery of White women" (Choy et al. 1994:102).

The portrayal of Chinatowns as dens of vice and crime in both film and other media venues creates a mythic place that bears little resemblance to actual Chinatowns. Archaeological research provides the tools to address this discrepancy. The most direct way to illuminate a more nuanced understanding of Chinatowns is by challenging these depictions on a factual level. For example, Chinatowns were not the "seedy dens of opium consumption" presented in these movies and cartoons. Material culture relating to opium production and prostitution, although present, reflects only a small percentage of the Market Street Chinatown's archaeological assemblage and was undoubtedly not the primary commercial activity within the Chinatown. This pattern seems to be consistent with archaeological evidence from other overseas Chinese communities (Wylie and Fike 1993). During the 19th century, opiate consumption in the form of opium, laudanum, and morphine was common in the United States (Courtwright 1982) and Canada (Anderson 1987:592). Although opiate use is commonly linked with Chinese use, "only 20% of the opium imported into the United States during the late 19th century was smoked by Chinese" (Wylie and Fike 1993:258).

Furthermore, opium pipe tops (also called pipe "bowls") at the Market Street Chinatown were found in features that were associated with a wide variety of depositional contexts, including residential, commercial, and mixed-use sites (Williams 2003) (Figure

12.1). Although it is true that patterns of disposal do not necessarily directly correlate with patterns of use, the variable contexts in which the pipe tops were found suggest a pattern of use most congruous with the idea that opium was consumed in different contexts, including commercial opium dens, general stores, and domestic residences. This implies that opium products at the Market Street Chinatown were not consumed exclusively or even primarily in concentrated locales and "dens," but were instead consumed over wider spatial and social contexts and perhaps, as historical documents confirm, by non-Chinese. In their research,

Figure 12.1. Opium pipe tops (bowls).   Photo by Bryn Williams.

Wylie and Higgins also come to a similar conclusion. They argue that opium was consumed in different locations corresponding to different social contexts, including recreational smoking, work-related smoking, and social smoking in residences (Wylie and Higgins 1987:365).

Smoking opium was a common feature in American societies after 1875 and was "considered particularly fashionable by White females" (Wylie and Fike 1993:258). Additionally, Schablitsky (2002:279) notes, "when compared with public intoxication and alcoholism, morphine was viewed by Victorian society as the lesser of the two evils." She similarly observes that "morphine addicts were often found in the middle and upper class circles" and that "opiate addiction was considered a malady of middle life" (Schablitsky 2002:284). An 1880 issue of *Harper's Weekly* notes this trend, writing, "The consumption of opium in this country is by no means confined to the Chinese. It is spreading to an alarming extent among people of American birth" (Wylie and Fike 1993:258). This is not to say that Chinatowns were drug free. As Lydon (1985) and Raven (1987) both point out, many Euro Americans frequented Chinatowns in search of opium. This challenges the idea that the drug use in Chinatowns was worthy of the exoticization and excessive focus in Hollywood depictions of Chinatowns.

If, as archaeologists have demonstrated, Chinatowns were not the dangerous smoke-filled opium havens that Hollywood has implied and San Francisco's contemporary Chinatown is one of the safer areas of the city (Resource Development Associates 2002:37), why did these images hold such power in the past and, more importantly, why do they remain so powerful today? Perhaps imagining Chinatowns as dangerous places where moral depravity is the norm lends rhetorical weight and a sense of urgency to the trope that Chinatowns as predatory spaces threaten the sanctity of the United States.

Predatory Chinatowns

Through the lens of Hollywood, Chinatowns are not only places of grave danger, but are also often imagined as "outposts" of a foreign and predatory culture that pose an imminent threat to the imagined purity of the country. Like many other nationalist discourses, this trope is deeply embedded in complex class and gender relations and often revolves around anxieties about masculinity and the working class (McClintock 1995; Enloe 2000). In the context of media depictions of Chinatowns, this fear often focuses on the perceived threat to White working-class men by Chinese competitors.

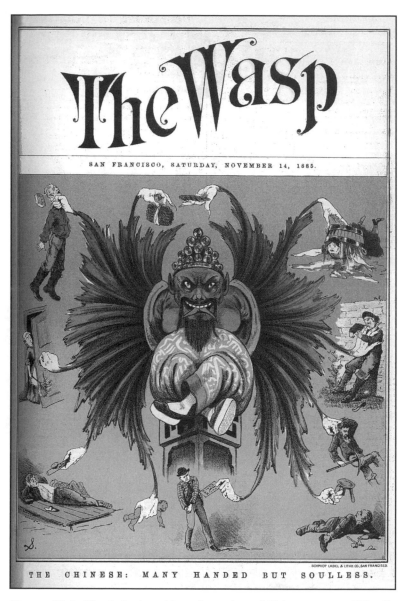

Figure 12.2. The "all-absorbing character of Chinese competition" wreaking havoc on American soil (Choy et al. 1994: 1990).

Media representations of this fear reach back to at least the late 19th century. For example, in an 1885 issue of the magazine *The Wasp*, a political cartoon depicts a grotesque Chinese figure

210

with multiple arms and hands engaged in various forms of labor with the caption "all-absorbing character of Chinese competition" (Figure 12.2). Beside the cartoon, *The Wasp* writes:

> On all sides it is reaching out for trades that it can master and a crushing our opposition is the inevitable result. ... Our workingmen and women dependent upon their own hands and arms for support look with sad hearts upon this iconoclastic breaking down of all their employments, and in bitterness of soul cry aloud, "How long, O Lord, how long." [Choy et al. 1994:90)]

Beginning clockwise, one sees the multiple hands of the Chinese man overtaking the United States by selling opium, increasing taxes, and taking Anglo American miners', launderers', and housekeepers' jobs away.

Anxieties about competition between Anglo Americans and Chinese Americans for employment are also demonstrated in a cartoon entitled, "The Consequences of Coolieism" (Choy et al. 1994:125). In this cartoon, the purposed dominance of the Chinese in the labor market results in the "ruination of the American family: the father commits suicide, the son is caught stealing bread, the mother is in despair, and the daughter is hooked on opium" (Choy et al. 1994:124). The nationalist implications of this trope are obvious; a Chinese man replaces the Statue of Liberty, the sky appears dark and ominous, and the harbor's waters look polluted, implying that the future of the country is questionable. Rather than being a beacon of light and liberty, this statue's luminance projects ideologies of "filth, immortality, diseases," and ruin to White labor (Choy et al. 1994:136).

Filmmakers quickly adopted the idea that Chinatowns are predatory "extra-territorial" spaces existing outside of the rules and regulations of "America." D. W. Griffiths's 1919 film *Broken Blossoms* is a particularly strong example of this theme. This film, which presents one of the earliest images of a Chinatown in the media, can be viewed as a cautionary tale against White moral failure. In *Broken Blossoms*, a character known only as "Yellow

Man," moves to the West on a missionary expedition to "take the glorious message of peace to the barbarous Anglo-Saxons, sons of turmoil and strife." After moving to London, he opens a general store in the heart of Chinatown. One of his regular customers is Lucy, a young White girl who is regularly abused by her father, Battling Burrows. After one particularly bad beating, she stumbles into Yellow Man's store and passes out. Yellow Man nurses her back to health, dressing her in his old "magical" Chinese robe. The robe symbolizes Chinese culture and by enveloping Lucy in his robe, the Yellow Man ritually turns her Chinese. A friend of Burrows discovers that Lucy is staying with Yellow Man. Burrows, as we learn in the movie, "suddenly discovers parental rights:—a Chink after his kid! He'll learn him!" He rushes into Yellow Man's store, finds his daughter, and drags her back to his house before beating her to death. Yellow Man follows Battling to his house and, finding Lucy dead, shoots him. He then returns to his store with Lucy's body, prays to Buddha, and commits suicide.

When the White father is not fulfilling his duties, and becomes abusive, his daughter, Lucy, runs to a Chinatown. There, the caring arms of an Asian man, "Yellow Man," await her. This same sentiment resonates today in dire warnings of Asian Americans outperforming White Americans in universities and the current fear of outsourcing manufacturing and technology jobs to China. The message is that if White people falter or stumble, their jobs, their children, and the soul of their nation will be taken over by hard-working Asians.

Underneath Mr. Wong's Chinatown, there are numerous tunnels that the Chinese use to smuggle goods and people, both within the Chinatown and to the docks of San Francisco. These tunnels symbolize the secretive underworld of the Chinese. They are particularly significant because the passages suggest a direct physical link from the San Francisco Chinatown to China via the ships waiting at the end of the tunnel. Goods and people can enter the Chinatown without even setting foot on U.S. soil, further emphasizing the "foreignness" of the Chinese.

There is no evidence of an extensive network of tunnels underneath the Market Street Chinatown in San Jose (and because of its complete excavation, it is almost certain that tunnels would have been found had they existed). Several towns, such as Pendleton, Oregon, advertise tunnels underneath old Chinatowns as tourist attractions. According to Priscilla Wegars (2006 pers. comm.), director of the Asian American Comparative Collection, these tunnels are primarily sidewalk vaults that were used for general delivery, to admit light into basements, and were common features of urban commercial buildings during the time. Claims for tunnels underneath Chinatowns are based mainly on innuendo, rumor, and clearly biased contemporary newspaper accounts. For example, the evidence mustered for tunnels underneath the El Paso Chinatown are derived from early 20th-century English newspaper accounts (Farrar 1972:20–21). The difficulty in finding verifiable archaeological evidence for these tunnels highlights their scarcity and the fact that they were clearly not central features of life in Chinatowns. Archaeologists have investigated enough Chinatowns to determine that if there were tunnels underneath some Chinatowns, they were the exception rather than the rule.

The Chinese did live in separate and sometimes isolated communities where they found safety in surrounding themselves with people from their own country who spoke their language, ate the same foods, and dressed in similar clothes. Their marginalization from the non-Chinese community was reinforced by numerous state and federally imposed acts and laws banning them from reaping the benefits of being naturalized U.S. citizens. This legislation created a social and psychological barrier between Chinatowns and the rest of these western cities.

The archaeological record, however, illuminates a more complex series of interactions between the Chinese and their neighbors. Alongside the Chinese medicine bottles and cookware, a number of U.S. patent medicine bottles were found, as well as a large number of European-produced cookware. Store ledger records from general stores surrounding the Market Street community document extensive and persistent relationships between residents of the Market Street community and the surrounding neighbors. Rather than being two isolated worlds, the Market Street Chinatown and the rest of downtown San Jose formed a synergistic relationship. This is not to imply that conflict did not take place between the Chinese and non-Chinese residents of the city. Rather, it shows that there were many nuanced, varied, and complex connections between the Market Street Chinatown and the surrounding community.

This pattern is seen in other Chinatowns across the world. Clearly, economic and social interactions beyond those pictured on film took place between the "exterior" Euro American communities and "inner" Chinatowns. Historian Sandy Lydon (1985) stated the Chinese in California had extensive formal relationships with local White officials and businessmen and that White Californians would often testify in court during immigration cases on behalf of Chinese neighbors. Julie Schablitsky (2002) has demonstrated that commodities were exchanged between Chinese and non-Chinese residents of Virginia City, Nevada. Praetzellis and Praetzellis's (2001) examination of notions of "gentility" in Sacramento, California, illustrates that a Chinese merchant family purchased and displayed ceramic wares produced in Staffordshire to convey the image of middle-class respectability to their non-Chinese neighbors and to foster commercial relationships with the non-Chinese community.

This adoption of non-Chinese ceramics does not appear the result of simple assimilation (the act of becoming non-Chinese that Hollywood has painted as the antidote to the dangers of Chinatown). On the contrary, these adaptations were part of an uneven refiguring of identity that transformed both the Chinese and their non-Chinese neighbors in unique ways (Praetzellis and Praetzellis 2001). Australian archaeologist Jane Lydon (1999) has similarly looked at the strategies that the overseas Chinese in Australia used in their negotiation of a foreign culture. For example, many Chinese merchants would throw charity banquets for "patriotic" causes, acts that showcased their role as "good citizens" (Lydon 1999:146). This interaction moved beyond formal events and strictly commercial exchanges. In Sydney, there were even several European women who lived with Chinese men (Lydon 1999:138–140).

Figure 12.3. Chinese gaming pieces.

Photo by Bryn Williams.

Camp's study (2004) of gaming pieces found in the Market Street Chinatown challenges the notion that gambling took place in isolated opium dens. Artifacts such as dominoes, die, chess, and other Chinese gaming pieces were found in several different contexts (Figure 12.3). Based on her spatial analysis and historical research, she suggests that gaming activities often took place in outdoor, communal areas where families gathered and shared food. Researchers have also pointed out that Euro American "outsiders" often ventured to Chinatowns; an observer of these activities recalled, "dollars in gold passed hands—often from the white hand to the yellow—and often, too, from yellow to white" (Lydon 1985:206).

Although it is true that Chinatowns are distinct locations, with identifiable material differentiating them from surrounding areas, this difference is never a totality. Archaeologists can challenge these formulations by studying topics that are likely to comment on, contest, or add nuance to these tropes.

Conclusion

Nationalism is a social process that plays a key role in the constitution of identities and social difference (McClintock 1995). With this in mind, these Hollywood depictions of Chinatowns as dangerous and predatory spaces make sense when they are understood to discursively delineate the edges and boundaries of the nation. The idea of the Chinatown as a dangerous place legitimates and accentuates the threat to the nation that the predatory Chinatown poses.

The historical persistence of these tropes and their presence across a wide range of media implies that they were not simply *created* by Hollywood but were formed through recursive relationships between the media, the legal structure, and daily interactions between Chinese and their neighbors. As Anderson (1987) reminds us, the concept of a "Chinatown" is reliant on the historically situated and culturally loaded idea that identities can be given a spatial and temporal location. In reality, Chinatowns, like most places, were spaces of multiethnic interaction, where people with different dialects, genders, ethnic affiliations, and ages congregated. Archaeology is equipped to untangle some of the ways these identities were constituted at a material level by contextualizing and historicizing the Chinese American experience in the United States.

Although the borders of nations and the delineations of who is and who is not a national subject may appear rigid in cinema, the contrary seems to be true in archaeological descriptions of history. Archaeological materials recovered from Chinese American neighborhoods must therefore be understood in relationship to the historical events surrounding them, and not simply used to measure acculturation or isolationist tendencies. This is not to say that the very real violence and discrimination that the Chinese faced on a daily basis should be ignored. The complex interactions between the Chinese and their non-Chinese neighbors must also be understood in the context of the potent power relationships of the time.

As research at the Market Street Chinatown and similar investigations in turn-of-the-century America illustrates, Chinatowns were not simply, as Hollywood has asserted, lawless and foreign nations within a nation. There is no conclusive evidence for opium dens, tunnels, or brothels at the Market Street Chinatown; however, we know from historical documents, photographs, and similar archaeological work that these places existed. If, as some of these forms of media imply, these types of activities primarily supported the economies of the Chinatowns, a preponderance of archaeological evidence should have attested to these activities. Instead, what archaeological evidence does reveal are multiple, complex relationships between the residents of Chinatowns and their non-Chinese neighbors. This is only the beginning of an establishment of an archaeological model of the relationship of Chinatowns to the surrounding community that is based on interaction, mediation, conflict, and negotiation and not simply of exclusion and separation.

References

Allen, Rebecca, Scott Baxter, Anmarie Medin, Julia Costello, and Connie Young Yu

2002 *Excavation of the Woolen Mills Chinatown (CA-SCL-807h), San José*. Report to the California Department of Transportation, Oakland, from Past Forward Inc., Richmond, CA.

Anderson, Benedict

1983 *Imagined Communities: Reflections on the Origin and Spread of Nationalism*. Verso, London.

Anderson, Kay J.

1987 The Idea of Chinatown: The Power of Place and Institutional Practice in the Making of a Racial Category. *Annals of the Association of American Geographers* 77(4):580–598.

Camp, Stacey

> 2004 An Examination of Gaming Pieces in the Market Street Chinatown Archaeological Assemblage. In *Market Street Chinatown Archaeological Project 2003–2004 Progress Report*, Barbara Voss, Stacey Camp, Liz Clevenger, and Bryn Williams, editors, Appendix D. Stanford Archaeology Center and the Department of Cultural and Social Anthropology, Stanford, CA.

Chang, Beverly

> 2004 Gambling and Gaming Pieces in the Market Street Chinatown Community. In *Market Street Chinatown Archaeological Project 2003–2004 Progress Report*, Barbara Voss, Stacey Camp, Liz Clevenger, and Bryn Williams, editors, Appendix D. Stanford Archaeology Center and the Department of Cultural and Social Anthropology, Stanford, CA.

Choy, Philip P., Lorraine Dong, and Marlon K. Hom

> 1994 *Coming Man: 19th Century American Perceptions of the Chinese.* University of Washington Press, Seattle.

Clevenger, Elizabeth

> 2004 Reconstructing Context and Assessing Research Potential: Feature 20 from the San José Market Street Chinatown. Master's thesis, Department of Cultural and Social Anthropology, Stanford University, Stanford, CA.

Courtwright, David T.

> 1982 *Dark Paradise: Opiate Addiction in America before 1940.* Harvard University Press, Cambridge, MA.

Daniel, Roger

> 1991 *Coming to America: A History of Immigration and Ethnicity in American Life.* HarperPerennial, New York.

Eng, David

> 2001 *Racial Castration: Managing Masculinity in Asian America.* Duke University Press, Durham, NC.

Enloe, Cynthia

> 2000 *Bananas, Beaches, and Bases: Making Feminist Sense of International Politics.* University of California Press, Berkeley.

Farrar, Nancy

> 1972 *The Chinese in El Paso.* Texas Western Press, El Paso.

Fosha, Rose

> 2004   The Archaeology of Deadwood's Chinatown: A Prologue. In *Ethnic Oasis: The Chinese in the Black Hills*, Liping Zhu and Rose Fosha, editors, pp. 44–68. South Dakota State Historical Society Press. Pierre.

Garcia, Matt

> 2001   *A World of Its Own: Race, Labor, and Citrus in the Making of Greater Los Angeles, 1900–1970.* The University of North Carolina Press, Chapel Hill.

Gardner, Dudley, Martin Lammers, Laura Pasacreta, and Seth Panter

> In press Women and Children in the Evanston Chinatown. *The Wyoming Archaeologist* 48(2).

Guerin-Gonzales, Camille

> 1994   *Mexican Workers and American Dreams: Immigration, Repatriation, and California Farm Labor, 1900–1939.* Rutgers University Press, New Brunswick, NJ.

Haas, Lisbeth

> 1995   *Conquests and Historical Identities in California: 1769–1936.* University of California Press, Berkeley.

Lotchin, Roger

> 1997   *San Francisco, 1846–1856: From Hamlet to City.* University of Illinois Press, Urbana.

Lydon, Jane

> 1999   Pidgin English: Historical Archaeology, Cultural Exchange and the Chinese in the Rocks, 1890–1930. In *Historical Archaeology: Back from the Edge*, Pedro Paulo A. Funari, Martin Hall, and Siân Jones, editors, pp. 255–283. Routledge, New York.

Lydon, Sandy

> 1985   *Chinese Gold: The Chinese in the Monterey Bay Region.* Capitola Book Company, Capitola, CA.

McClintock, Anne

> 1995   *Imperial Leather: Race, Gender, and Sexuality in the Colonial Contest.* Routledge, New York.

Michaels, Gina

> 2005   Peck-Marked Vessels from the San José Market Street Chinatown: A Study of Distribution and Significance. *International Journal of Historical Archaeology* 9(2):123–134.

Molina, Natalia

2006   *Fit to Be Citizens? Public Health and Race in Los Angeles, 1879–1939.* University of California Press, Berkeley.

Mudge, Jean McClure

1986   *Chinese Export Porcelain in North America.* Riverside Book Company, New York.

Ngai, Mae M.

2004   *Impossible Subjects: Illegal Aliens and the Making of Modern America.* Princeton University Press, Princeton, NJ.

Ong, Aihwa

1999   *Flexible Citizenship: The Cultural Logics of Transnationality.* Duke University Press, Durham, NC.

Praetzellis, Adrian and Mary Praetzellis

2001   Mangling Symbols of Gentility in the Wild West: Case Studies in Interpretive Archaeology. *American Anthropologist* 103(3):645–654.

Raven, Shelly

1987   Red Paper and Varnished Ducks: Subjective Images of Riverside's Chinatown. In *Wong Ho Leun: An American Chinatown Vol. I*, pp. 215–265. The Great Basin Foundation, San Diego, CA.

Resource Development Associates

2002   San Francisco Gang-Free Communities Initiative Assessment Report. Report to the San Francisco Department of Children, Youth, and their Families, San Francisco Juvenile Probation Department, and the Mayor's Office of Criminal Justice, Lafayette, CA.

Rohe, Randall.

2002   Chinese Camps and Chinatowns: Chinese Mining Settlements in the North American West. In *Re/Collecting Early Asian America: Essays in Cultural History*, Josephine Lee, Imogene L. Lim, and Yuko Matsukawa, editors, pp. 31–54. Temple University Press, Philadelphia.

Saxton, Alexander

1970   *The Indispensable Enemy: Labor and the Anti-Chinese Movement in California.* University of California Press, Berkeley.

Schablitsky, Julie M.

2002   The Other Side of the Tracks: The Archaeology and History of a Virginia City, Nevada Neighborhood. PhD. dissertation, Department of Urban Studies, Portland State University, Portland.

Shah, Nayan

2001   *Contagious Divides: Epidemics and Race in San Francisco's Chinatown.* University of California Press, Berkeley.

Simmons, Erica

2004   Drinking Practices in San Jose's Market Street Chinatown: A Study of Cups. In *Market Street Chinatown Archaeological Project 2003–2004 Progress Report*, Barbara Voss, Stacey Camp, Liz Clevenger, and Bryn Williams, editors, Appendix D. Stanford Archaeology Center and the Department of Cultural and Social Anthropology, Stanford, CA.

Stoler, Ann

2002   *Carnal Knowledge and Imperial Power: Race and the Intimate in Colonial Rule.* University of California Press, Berkeley.

Takaki, Ronald

1989   *Strangers from a Different Shore.* Little Brown and Company, New York.

Voss, Barbara

2002   The Archaeology of El Presidio de San Francisco: Culture Contact, Gender, and Ethnicity in a Spanish-Colonial Military Community. PhD. dissertation, Department of Anthropology, University of California, Berkeley. University Microfilms International, Ann Arbor, MI.

2005   The Archaeology of Overseas Chinese Communities. *World Archaeology* 37(3):424–439.

Wegars, Priscilla, editor

1993   *Hidden Heritage: Historical Archaeology of the Overseas Chinese.* Baywood, Amityville, NY.

Williams, Bryn

2003   Opium Pipe Tops at the Market Street Chinese Community in San José. In *Market Street Chinatown Archaeological 2002–2003 Progress Report*, Barbara Voss, Stacey Camp, Liz Clevenger, and Bryn Williams, editors, Appendix C. Stanford Archaeology Center and the Department of Cultural and Social Anthropology, Stanford, CA.

2006   Chinese Masculinities and Material Culture. Society for Historical Archaeology 39th annual conference, Sacramento, CA.

Wylie, Jerry and Richard Fike

1993   Chinese Opium Smoking Techniques and Paraphernalia. In *Hidden Heritage: Historical Archaeology of the Overseas Chinese*, Priscilla Wegars, editor, pp. 255–303. Baywood Publishing Company, Amityville, NY.

Wylie, Jerry and Pamela Higgins

1987   Opium Paraphernalia and the Role of Opium Riverside's Chinatown. In *Wong Ho Leun: An American Chinatown, Vol. II, Archaeology*, pp. 317–385. The Great Basin Foundation, San Diego, CA.

Yu, Connie Young

1991   *Chinatown, San José, USA*. History San José, San Jose, CA.

WHEN THE LEGEND BECOMES FACT

RECONCILING HOLLYWOOD REALISM AND ARCHAEOLOGICAL REALITIES

Vergil E. Noble

• •

[M]ythology is an art form that points beyond history to what is timeless in human existence, helping us get beyond the chaotic flux of random events, and glimpse the core of history.

—*Karen Armstrong (2005)*

This is the West, sir. When the legend becomes fact, print the legend.

> —*Shinbone Star reporter Maxwell Scott's (Carleton Young) reply to Senator Ransom Stoddard (James Stewart), when asked if he would publish Stoddard's true account of his own rise to public prominence, in John Ford's The Man Who Shot Liberty Valance (1962)*

Introduction

When Julie Schablitsky first told me of her plans to organize a symposium called "Screening the Past" for the 2004 Conference on Historical and Underwater Archaeology, I was immediately interested because the general theme seemed to present a close parallel to the equally controversial topic of site reconstruction. Many archaeologists once complained that the past is simplified, sanitized, and otherwise misrepresented at reconstructed archaeological sites, in spite of the fact that we experts are often directly involved with realizing the mission of heritage tourism. I have observed, however, that this uneasy relationship between archaeologists and those who create such illusory recreations has eased in recent years, owing partly to a growing acceptance that absolute historical authenticity is not possible to achieve at reconstructed sites. Nor is it essential when typical site visitors tour them more for recreation than education (Noble 2004).

A more personal reason for my interest in Hollywood's handling of the past, though, is that I have been a movie fanatic for as long as I can remember. Indeed, if I had any real creative talent, I might have enrolled in film school years ago with the ambition to become a director. Ironically, it was through film that I formed my earliest impressions of archaeology from the most unlikely of inspirations. That first memorable glimpse of our profession, at age nine or ten, was obtained while watching the Three Stooges short *We Want Our Mummy* (1939), a popular (at least in some circles) Egyptian-themed Hollywood production not among the titles considered in Stuart Tyson Smith's thoughtful chapter on the subject. While I laughed in delight as Larry, Moe, and Curly ran amok through King Rutentuten's tomb, terrorized by villains bent on plundering the mummy's treasure, I also gaped in wonderment at the exotic settings and imagined what it might be like to pursue the past through archaeology. Soon thereafter, I would become an avid reader of such classics as C. W. Ceram's (1951) *Gods, Graves, and Scholars* and similar books that illustrated the scholarly adventure of archaeology in romantic style.

I learned long ago, of course, that there is much more to doing archaeology than what I saw on screen as a child—much more than what I read in popular books on the subject, for that matter. But nearly fifty years hence, I readily acknowledge the significant role that just one film—albeit a knock-about comedy—played in shaping the course, if not the outcome, of my own professional life. Accordingly, I must also acknowledge that the movies can and do play a significant role in shaping the untutored public's impressions of our shared past. But is that something that should worry us in the archaeological profession, or should we perhaps be grateful to the filmmakers for popularizing historical themes in their work even if they might get it so dreadfully wrong at times?

The Past on Film

Movies set in the past have been popular since motion pictures were in their infancy, and many of those movies are among the greatest artistic achievements ever captured on film. Edwin Porter's pioneering production of *The Great Train Robbery* (1903), made only a decade after Thomas Alva Edison established the first commercial motion picture studio, foreshadowed what would eventually become the classic Western movie genre and promised great things for the fledgling movie industry (Brownlow 1968; Everson 1998). More to the point, the story told in *The Great Train Robbery* was based loosely on real historical events, while drawing liberally from published fiction and the filmmaker's own creative imagination.

A dozen years later, D. W. Griffith fulfilled that promise with *The Birth of a Nation* (1915). Controversial then and now for its depiction of African Americans during the U.S. Civil War and Reconstruction, the picture also received high praise for its sweeping historical spectacle at its release. It also made a lot of money for its producers, partly because of the intense national controversy it stirred. Today, in spite of its offenses to sensibility, *The Birth of a Nation* is recognized as a major landmark in the development of film as art and industry. Noted film historian William K. Everson

(1998), in arguing for its artistry, also points out that the film's objectionable content must be understood in light of its vitriolic published source material, which Griffith toned down considerably in his adaptation. He further notes that the director's intent was to show the Civil War and its immediate aftermath not objectively, but from a distinctly Southern point of view.

A century later, average moviegoers and even the most discriminating film critics still adore historical films, whether they focus on actual events and personages or are simply fictional tales set against the exotic backdrop of our shared past. By my own count, during the twenty-five-year period from 1981 through 2005, more than half of the 125 films nominated for Best Picture by the Academy of Motion Picture Arts and Sciences were set in a time before the present. Moreover, in seventeen of those twenty-five years, two-thirds of the time, the Academy honored such films with the Oscar©. Those justly celebrated productions span some 2,000 years in subject matter, from the Roman Empire to the Vietnam War, and represent practically all the major film genres. In fact, if we were to expand our scope to include fantasy, we could factor in the *Lord of the Rings* trilogy, which evokes the distant fictive past of Middle Earth's Third Age. Such a liberal interpretation would add three more Best Picture nominees and one winner, *Lord of the Rings: The Return of the King* (2003), to our elite list of recent historical films.

Most historical films made in the past century, of course, are not revered as great or memorable works of art, yet many endure to this day. Unlike early dime novels, pulp fiction, and other pop culture products of the print media—ephemera for the most part lost to most modern readers—many of the formulaic B pictures and serials cranked out under the old studio system are still enjoyed. Although I have seen alarming statistics that suggest the loss of fully half the films produced before use of safety film became common in the 1950s, those that do survive are now more accessible than ever. Indeed, with the advent of home videotape and DVD players, as well as dozens of cable and satellite TV channels devoted exclusively to showing movies, formerly obscure and rarely appreciated films of earlier eras are now readily available to those who seek them out.

It should be obvious that imperfect scholarly comprehension of the past and much cruder available technology would hamper even the best attempts at historical accuracy in earlier major releases, but the lesser films that survive from that period suffered even more from low budgets and almost indifferent assembly-line production. As measured against any standard, far too many bad movies fraught with broad stereotypes and standard plot devices have been made over the years. Accordingly, the authors of this book's chapters for the most part wisely restricted their comments to better productions of more recent vintage, but all of them could have carped about some real stinkers. *The Norseman* (1978), for example, combines in one otherwise unremarkable film the most hackneyed images of both Vikings and Native Americans that one could possibly imagine. Certainly, there would be no point in criticizing such forgettable films for their lack of authenticity, but a few insomniacs can still catch them on late-night TV.

Of course, Hollywood has always been keen to capitalize on the popularity of certain movies with sequels or remakes that tend to perpetuate historical errors of the earlier films that inspired them, though they generally include distinctive variations on the original theme. Several of the contributors to this book discuss films that fall into this category, including *The Mummy* (1932 and 1999) and *Stagecoach* (1939, 1966, and 1986). It is worth noting that, although the essential story of the original is retained, *The Mummy* remake differs in many details, including the introduction of an American protagonist. Further, the all-star 1966 version of *Stagecoach* has a Sioux raiding party under Crazy Horse attack the hapless passengers on the road from Deadwood to Cheyenne, instead of Geronimo's Apaches pursuing the stage through southeastern Arizona to Lordsburg, New Mexico, as depicted in the original 1939 and later 1986 productions.

Notable foreign films dealing with historical themes also have been redone with settings more familiar to American audiences substituted for the more obscure originals. Thus, the same basic story presented in Akira Kurosawa's *Seven Samurai* (*Scichinin no Samurai*, 1954), set in Japan's exotic warrior past, translated into

John Sturges's Western, *The Magnificent Seven* (1960). Similarly, *The Return of Martin Guerre* (*Retour de Martin Guerre*, 1982), a true story of 16th-century rural France well known to many throughout Europe, became the Civil War romance *Sommersby* (1983) for American audiences. By the same token, Shakespeare's *Romeo and Juliet*, a tragedy of star-crossed lovers written more than 400 years ago, has been remade faithfully for the screen, as Franco Zeffirelli did in 1968, retold as a contemporary tale of competing New York street gangs in the musical *West Side Story* (1961), or updated still further to a modern urban setting for today's teenaged demographic in *Romeo and Juliet* (1996).

Whether such adaptations that change time period and location should succeed or fail in the eyes of critics, their very existence is telling. Their popularity underscores the fact that, for the filmmaker and for most audiences, specific historical details are only incidental to a more general exploration of humanity in triumph and adversity. As several contributors to this book acknowledge, films set in the past are not about the past at all. Instead, they are intended to address much broader questions of what it means to be human through stories that deal with such universals as courage and cowardice, betrayal and redemption, altruism and greed.

Stagecoach, after all, is not about an Indian attack, and its purpose is achieved no matter what tribe is depicted or how they behave. The film is about such familiar themes as revenge and redemption, social prejudice, the duality of public image and private behavior (nobody on the stage is what he or she seems), and the revelation of true character through danger. The Indian attack is important to the story only as an obvious and sustained threat. In fact, director John Ford once famously conceded that a real attack would have dispatched the stagecoach quickly, but then that would have ended the picture (Bogdanovich 1978:72). Another director might have explored the same themes by using a shark at sea, aliens in space, or even snakes on a plane.

Moreover, films set in the past are likely to tell us more about the social issues and public tastes prevalent during the times in which they were made than about the times they depict on screen.

Earlier films that featured the Battle of the Little Bighorn, such as the greatly fictionalized *They Died with Their Boots On* (1941), produced on the eve of U.S. entry into World War II, emphasized heroic adventure and glorious death.

More recent films like *Little Big Man* (1970) and the television movie *Son of the Morning Star* (1991), on the other hand, have been more inclined to examine the injustices of late 19th-century westward expansion and view Custer's exploits from a Native American perspective. In fact, *Son of the Morning Star* achieves some measure of balance in telling Custer's story through the subtly contrasting recollections of his wife and a Native American woman. In a similar vein, *Little Big Man* is the oral history account of fictional old timer Jack Crabb, a White centenarian raised by the Cheyenne, who recalls historical events from his unique perspective and paints Custer as an incompetent buffoon.

Similarly, although all major films dealing with the loss of the steamship *Titanic* are parables on the price of hubris, *A Night to Remember* (1958) focuses largely on actions of the crew, particularly the heroic first officer, with only fleeting vignettes afforded to the passengers. The fictional story line in *Titanic* (1997), however, is the more personal tale of what might have been one of many mundane dramas among the passengers that played out against the momentous events of that night. Further, it delves into issues that perhaps have much greater resonance with modern audiences, such as the inequities of class, survival and the affirmation of life in the wake of profound loss, and, above all, the endurance of love.

All authorities would agree that *Titanic* depicts the actual vessel loss with much greater accuracy than *A Night to Remember*. The former, after all, benefited from the archaeological evidence available to James Cameron, whereas the latter was drawn from author Walter Lord's 1955 book based on various survivor accounts. But that nuance matters only to a few. It was the story of love suddenly found and just as suddenly lost—related in a fictional survivor's oral history of the sinking—that made *Titanic* the biggest box phenomenon in movie history.

A Critical Look at the Movies

Although the chapters in this book combine to represent the first major published commentary on the subject from members of our profession, historians now have been grappling in print with this thorny issue of Hollywood's view of the past for more than thirty-five years. In 1971, the Historians Film Committee, an affiliated society of the American Historical Association, began publishing *Film & History: An Interdisciplinary Journal of Film and Television Studies*, and one of the earliest scholarly books devoted to the subject was Pierre Sorlin's (1980) *The Film in History: Restaging the Past* (Toplin 2002:207). Many more volumes have since contributed to an ever-growing academic and popular literature aimed at the way our collective past is portrayed on both the big and small screens (e.g., Carnes 1995; Rosenstone 1995a, 1995b; Sanello 2003; McCrisken 2005; Vankin 2005).

Even cable television has addressed this subject with a History Channel film series, *Movies in Time*, which interspersed authoritative commentary with the airing of a featured historical film. Its hour-long documentary series, *History vs. Hollywood* (2001–2005), also examined the historical basis for major motion pictures like Martin Scorsese's *Gangs of New York* (2002), which Rebecca Yamin and Lauren Cook address in this book. The success of those hit television shows, as well as other documentaries, newspaper articles, and web sites that certain films stimulate into production, clearly demonstrates the public hunger for authoritative information about the historical periods interpreted for presentation on screen.

Many historians have been highly critical of the film industry for oversimplifying the past. Some have gone even further in condemning what they perceive to be cases of intentional misrepresentation—for example, speculation on motives in the absence of clear historical evidence or, worse, direct contradiction of what is objectively known to be factual. One recent analysis of classic Hollywood productions even argues that some of our most noted major filmmakers purposefully sought to create their own versions of history (Smyth 2006).

Other historians, particularly Robert Brent Toplin (1996, 2002), argue that film must be appreciated on its own terms, according to its unique conditions, and should not be judged by the same standards as academic history. As Toplin points out, the very nature of filmmaking and the practical limitations of what an average audience will tolerate in many cases demand that the past be modified to tell a compelling story that can be readily followed and meet audience expectations. Accordingly, time may be collapsed to advance the story; the actual actions of multiple persons may be represented by one real historical figure or a composite fictional character in heroic fashion; and locations may be substituted for their visual appeal or to overcome logistical difficulties.

Archaeologists, for their part, have a different take on the movies. One might think that a common pet peeve would concern a particular film's use of material culture that is inappropriate to the time period. Indeed, Charles Haecker's contribution does make the important point that historic Native American tribes quickly adopted a much wider variety of Euro American goods than what is usually believed. But the fact that archaeologists are rarely heard to complain about the placement of anachronistic artifacts in contemporary film attests to the more thorough research contributing to set decoration today. Instead, as Julie Schablitsky on western boomtowns, Rebecca Yamin and Lauren Cook on New York City, and Bryn Williams and Stacey Camp on Chinatowns all show, archaeologists are more prone to focus on the people and activities that are present (or absent) in the background of most historical films.

The historian's lament usually boils down to the incontrovertible fact that the past was far more complicated than is typically portrayed in movies. They emphasize the complex sequences and interconnectedness of historical events, as well as the particular roles of individuals who influenced the outcomes of those events. The discipline of archaeology, however, rarely has the opportunity to shed light on such specifics.

In certain instances, tactical maneuvers executed at battles engaged on land and water may be inferred through archeological investigations, as with Little Bighorn or the encounter between *H. L. Hunley* and *Housatonic* that Robert Neyland describes. The particular circumstances of certain catastrophes at times can also be revealed, as with the shipwrecks described by James Delgado or Charles Ewen and Russell Skowronek. In most cases, however, archaeological evidence can contribute precious little new information about major events beyond the traditional historian's interpretation derived from other sources.

Archaeology is even more limited in its ability to tell us much about a specific historical personage or that individual's role in particular events. In unusual instances where one can examine the skeletal remains and directly associated possessions of a known person, as in the case of the *Hunley*'s crew, we may be able to draw conclusions about the life history, health, and perhaps personal habits of the individual, but in most cases we must speak in generalities about communities or cultures. As Randy Amici points out, archaeology can tell us nothing about Pocahontas herself, but it can tell us a great deal more about the society of which she was a part than we could learn by researching documentary records left by European observers of the period.

When archaeologists talk about the past being more complicated than it is shown in most movies, we mean that the conditions at a particular place and time in question were much more diverse and more richly textured than most two-dimensional film versions. As all the contributors to this book would agree, the typical historical film pays too little attention to the mundane everyday aspects of life. Of course, that shortcoming is also a shortcoming of films set in our own time. *Gangs of New York*, in focusing on one element of the Five Points district, may indeed fail to show the mass of ordinary people engaged in useful occupations. Nevertheless, *Do the Right Thing* (1997), a film set in New York's Bedford-Stuyvesant neighborhood of today, is no better in that regard. Of the neighborhood men, only the protagonist, Mookie (Spike Lee), appears to be gainfully employed.

Moreover, the same criticism pertaining to focus also applies to most historical research, which is largely dependent on documents produced by literate observers representing the controlling elite and, therefore, deficient or even biased in addressing the mass of humanity. Although historians long ago extended their scope and purpose beyond the recounting of momentous events or the actions of great men, the origins and contents of documentary sources do set limits to their reach. Archaeologists have the advantage of access to a wide variety of sites containing materials left in the ground directly by people of all races, all ethnic groups, and all walks of life, granting us the ability to achieve a more comprehensive view of any particular time period.

Even so, archaeological interests in many of the subjects addressed in this book are of relatively recent genesis, so it should not be surprising that Hollywood has not yet followed our lead. As Stuart Tyson Smith notes, archaeologists have just begun looking beyond the tombs and sacred sites of ancient Egypt to the village sites that are more revealing of the laborers who built them. By the same token, underwater archaeologists dealing with maritime history acknowledge that research into shipwreck remains alone can tell only a narrow part of the story, which must be augmented with research on land like that now being done on Viking village sites. Further, American historical archaeologists, who once readily dismissed 19th-century ranches, farmsteads, urban neighborhoods, and modern industrial sites as being too recent to investigate, have now come to see their value.

Mythic Pasts and Cultural Stereotypes

It is often said that the movies have contributed to the creation of a mythic past, and to some extent that complaint is valid. Certainly, if your introduction to the late 19th-century American West were gained from watching movies, your initial impressions of what life was like in that particular time and place would be formed accordingly. The movies, however, are more often consumers of myth than creators, exploiting those that were already well developed in our psyche long before the rise of motion pictures.

Indeed, the Old West, as it is depicted in most movies and television programs, in many ways is a product of those who actually lived or directly witnessed it. Thrilling tales of fierce Indian raids and violent shootouts between heroic sheriffs and desperate outlaws were repeated and exaggerated in countless newspaper accounts and dime novels of the day. Plays were written and produced for curiosity-seeking eastern audiences, and some even featured real frontiersmen, like Wild Bill Hickock and Buffalo Bill Cody, who capitalized on their growing notoriety by playing overstated versions of themselves.

George Armstrong Custer did much to burnish his own myth by publishing a series of magazine articles eventually compiled as the autobiography, *My Life on the Plains*. Moreover, after Little Bighorn, his widow made certain that Custer's idealized version of taming the West was perpetuated well into the next century. Similarly, the famous exploits of William F. Cody, though sprinkled amply with nuggets of fact, were largely inventions of the dime novelist and playwright Ned Buntline.

Cody himself helped create the mythic West in staging Buffalo Bill's *Wild West* during the decades surrounding the turn of the 20th century. He employed such notable contemporaries as Chief Sitting Bull, Calamity Jane, and Wild Bill Hickock, and the show included spectacular reenactments of stagecoach attacks, gunfights, and even Custer's Last Stand, effectively blurring the line between historical reality and showmanship and influencing the style and content of later movie Westerns. In his later years, Cody even starred as himself in a silent picture, *The Adventures of Buffalo Bill* (1914), which placed him at the center of several history-making events of the Old West. Arguably our first entertainment superstar, Cody has probably now appeared in more film and television plays than any other Western figure—most uncharacteristically played by Paul Newman, the greatest film superstar of his era, in Robert Altman's anti-Western study of celebrity, *Buffalo Bill and the Indians, or Sitting Bull's History Lesson* (1976).

Many of the films discussed in this book are founded on

myths that have been with us for centuries. As Smith notes, *The Mummy*, and films like it, owe a great deal to faulty translations and other early misconstructions of ancient texts as well as to the sensational style of journalism that reported on the early archaeological discoveries in Egypt. The ancient Norse sagas certainly influence the depiction of Vikings on film, as Mark Tveskov and Jon Erlandson point out, and the Old English epic poem *Beowulf* served as the inspiration for Michael Crichton's novel, *Eaters of the Dead*, adapted for film as *The 13th Warrior* (1999).

It is also true that certain ethnic and racial stereotypes, which moviemakers have exploited unabashedly for a hundred years, are endemic in our society and of long standing. The way in which African slavery is presented on film has changed in step with social movements of the last fifty years (Davis 2002), with *Amistad* (1997) showing the misery of the slave trade in shocking images and endowing its victims with great dignity and intelligence. Paul Mullins observes, however, that some depictions of African Americans on film today are still not far removed from the characterizations of old minstrel shows. Others have shown that standard movie images of Native Americans can be traced back practically to 1492 (Berkhofer 1978; Kilpatrick 1999), and Asian immigrants were viewed negatively as the "yellow peril" and stereotyped as fiendish undesirables in many Western countries long before D. W. Griffith ever thought about making the silent classic *Broken Blossoms* (1919).

Indeed, if we accept the general proposition that we live in a racist society, we can hardly expect our cinema to be any different. Many would argue that, whether we are conscious of it or not, race has a pervasive influence on our daily lives, and there is no reason to think that filmmakers are free from those effects. Most major filmmakers are wealthy White males, after all, and given their backgrounds even those with the purest of intentions and greatest ability may resort to common misconceptions in depicting the lives of other groups not of their company. If there were more African American filmmakers, the Black experience perhaps might be told more consistently and with much greater truth, but only a few—most notably, Gordon Parks, Sidney Poitier, and Spike Lee—have had a major impact on Hollywood in the past fifty years (Donaldson 2003). This is not to say that a White director is incapable of telling a Black story (or any other non-White story) accurately and well, but surely such efforts that transcend one's own experience present a substantial challenge. Most might fail in the eyes of others.

Director Stanley Kramer has been praised for his groundbreaking message pictures, several of which deal with Black-White relations, and criticized by others for not depicting Blacks accurately and for not going far enough in those efforts. Kramer's film *The Defiant Ones* (1958), which Mullins discusses, perhaps presents a false view of race relations when it is viewed as a commentary on society at large. The basic premise of two men chained at the wrist grudgingly cooperating with each other to escape their pursuers, however, is believable. Certainly that aspect of the film is far more convincing than the actions of a single mother, encountered by the duo in her remote cabin, who gives herself freely that same night to handsome Tony Curtis's character and then schemes to run away with him. Though the convicts do eventually achieve a level of ease with one another, both escapees act entirely out of self-interest and are merely reluctant partners against a mutual enemy. Indeed, the one honorable act of the bigoted White to make amends for the woman's treachery is as much an act of defiance toward her as it is an act of compassion toward his Black companion.

A different director, of course, would have made a much different film of the story, and one wonders how an African American filmmaker would resolve the racial tension manifest in almost every frame. As it happens, Spike Lee tells basically the same story forty years later in his film, *Do the Right Thing*, although here the Black and White protagonists are bound up in an essential but uneasy economic alliance instead of physically shackled. The increasing strain between Mookie, a young Black pizzeria worker, and his White employer (Danny Aiello), is symptomatic of racial tensions in the neighborhood and ultimately leads to a riot that destroys the business and Mookie's livelihood. The viewer, however, is left to ponder whether his more radical choice of a violent resolution is, in fact, the right thing to do.

It is also worth noting, as an aside, that the depiction of Italian American characters in *Do the Right Thing* engendered criticism of writer-director Lee every bit as harsh as that prominent African Americans leveled against Kramer for *The Defiant Ones*. Even filmmakers who deal with contemporary stories have the ability to displease any identifiable group (whether an ethnic, racial, professional, political, or some other group) who feel that they have not been depicted fairly, just as we who hold dear our study of the past may object to how it is depicted in film. Which raises one more important point: watching movies is not a passive activity.

Every film is subject to interpretation, influenced by the viewer's own frame of reference and life experiences as much as the filmmaker's craft. Each individual may take different messages from the same film, depending on his or her own point of view, and the viewer's interpretation may be completely different from the filmmaker's intended message. One can see Griffith's *Broken Blossoms*, for example, as a cautionary tale about potential loss of Whites' presumed birthright to foreign immigrants, as observed in the Williams and Camp chapter on Chinatowns; however, the film can also be seen as a condemnation of racial intolerance, as a story about the corrupting influences of Western society, or as a poetic tragedy of forbidden love.

To enjoy a film, the viewer must also suspend disbelief to some degree and accept contrived story lines, ignore the physical impossibility of certain stunts, and believe in the performances of talented actors appearing in widely disparate roles from one film to another. While watching a good film we invest a certain amount of ourselves, immersed in the sights, sounds, and story, forming attachments to some characters and disliking others, seeing ourselves or our acquaintances in certain roles or situations. When we put ourselves in the context of a compelling film story, identifying with its characters, and vicariously experiencing familiar or exotic situations, it is part of our continuous search to achieve a better understanding of our own lives.

In comparing the function of modern novels to classical

myth, author Karen Armstrong (2005:149) underscores the fact that readers know full well that the fictional world is not real, but as one is absorbed in the story it becomes compelling. She points out that a novel, like classical myth, "teaches us to see the world differently; it shows us how to look into our hearts and to see our world from a perspective that goes beyond our own self-interest" (Armstrong 2005:149). The same can be said of motion pictures. Although they may not create myth, movies most assuredly play the same role in modern society that myth did in earlier times by making us question our behavior and allowing us to feel empathy for others. As Armstrong says of myth, movies are "true" if they are effective in stimulating self-examination, not because they present the literal truth in factual terms.

The Convergence of Art and Archaeology

Since at least the time of Aristotle's treatise on *Poetics*, it has been understood that the artistic representation of something is not the thing itself. It took the Belgian surrealist René Magritte to point out the irony in that fact with his famous painting, *The Betrayal of Images (La trahison des images)*, which depicts a smoking pipe rendered in a most realistic manner. Beneath the image appears the simple phrase, *Cici n'est pas une pipe* ("This is not a pipe"), thus declaring unambiguously that what you see is not the real thing but merely a picture of a pipe. That paradox surely applies to the movies, but instead of a disclaimer warning us that all we are about to see is not the literal truth, most movies featuring actual historical events or personages tend to emphasize their general basis in fact without indicating where poetic license is taken.

The same paradox, however, also applies to archaeology. Through scientific investigations we strive to achieve an understanding of the past, but we are limited to interpreting what remains as a reflection of it in the archaeological record—and that record is both imperfect and incomplete. Accordingly, our versions of the past are also imperfect and incomplete. Certainly we can get at aspects of the past that elude even the best historians, because the data we use are qualitatively different and provide different insights, but there is just as much that eludes us. We may be able to learn a great deal about the shipboard life of pirates by investigating a wreck site, but pirates did not spend all their lives at sea and it would be difficult to distinguish piratical activities from any other on land through archaeology. Ritualistic caches left by African American slaves and recovered archaeologically may tell us something about their means of coping with adversity through the private retention of traditional practices, but we can only imagine the cruelty of life in the plantation fields.

An essential difference between filmmaking and doing archaeology is that the former is a subjective and intensely personal undertaking, whereas those who practice archaeology seek objectivity as the ideal. A film director puts his or her own stamp on each project, deciding at every turn what to emphasize in making a point, and the great ones impart an individual style that can immediately be recognized by a discerning viewer. Thus, a John Ford Western is different from that of Sergio Leone or Clint Eastwood, and the New York City of Martin Scorsese differs radically from that of Spike Lee or Woody Allen. Some archaeologists might say that there is one true past waiting to be gleaned, but most filmmakers would likely argue that the past holds many truths, and each director has a unique vision of what that might be. This is not to say, however, that all archaeologists view the past in the same way, for each of us interprets the past through a lens of theory and personal experience.

It would be wonderful, of course, if more directors were to use a wider lens in capturing the essence of the past, but commercial interests and audience tastes do play a significant role in determining what stories reach the big screen and how they are told. A relatively obscure independent film like *Heartland* (1979) deserves high marks for its stark portrayal of the ranching life in 1910 Wyoming, but if few people see it the impact on public consciousness is slight. Episodic series television, perhaps, has more freedom to explore the lesser-known corners of our past and can reach many if the program finds an audience and becomes a perennial favorite. In spite of its perceived deficiencies, over its long run *Bonanza* (1959–1973) did manage an occasional glimpse at the lives of Others through their encounters with the Cartwrights (it should also be remembered that the series was atypical in its focus on a family of ranchers, instead of a heroic lawman, and featured many scenarios taken from everyday domestic life). We can hope, as Schablitsky does, that the makers of *Deadwood* and other programs like it will eventually broaden their scope, but we should not be surprised or disappointed if they fail to do so.

We experts on the past perhaps should be more concerned with what we do to advance our own discipline than what we can do to change or improve Hollywood productions. That is not to say that we should reject participation as consultants on film productions as wasted effort, but we should not hold false hope of remaking the film industry according to our lights. Instead of lobbying for change in Hollywood, we would be smart to take a lesson from the movies and adjust our own style.

Historian Natalie Zemon Davis, who collaborated on *The Return of Martin Guerre*, appears to have done just that in her own research. While working on this French film, Davis was inspired to research a well-received scholarly examination of the actual 1560 trial of a Pyrenean villager accused of being an impostor. Like many technical advisors, she was troubled by the film's occasional departures from historical fact, but she also admits to having taken certain liberties in her own presentation of the story (Davis 1983:5): "What I offer you here is in part my invention, but held tightly in check by the voices of the past." The importance of Davis's book, of course, does not hang on the specific details of the cuckold Martin Guerre's life or that of his clever impostor, Arnaud du Tilh. Rather, her book is a meaningful contribution to the historical literature for what the story also tells about the day-to-day lives of peasants in early modern Europe, as well as the legal system and societal norms governing that time and place.

By embroidering on the documentary record to present a more colorful account consistent with what is demonstrably knowable, Davis engages in what some historical archaeologists have come to call "storytelling." The term implies following the guidance of one's own experience, intuition, and imagination beyond the limits of basic empirical evidence toward the creation of a more compelling presentation of our rather lifeless archaeological data (Praetzellis 1998), and it seems to me that the approach is not too far removed from what filmmakers do when crafting a purely fictional story played out in the context of actual events. Although many archaeologists still balk at the notion of such liberal readings of the archaeological record, those who do advocate this alternate way of telling a site's story remind us that all archaeological conclusions are analytical interpretations drawn from circumstantial evidence (Praetzellis and Praetzellis 1998).

Those of us committed to more traditional approaches and less inclined toward the creative writing of storytelling can at least take a cue from Hollywood and make our work more accessible and more interesting to the public. It is a pity that the conclusions of our research are so often buried in dry technical reports beneath pages upon pages of background material that is of little use to anyone beyond a small circle of professional colleagues. We typically cram our reports with long-winded descriptions of field methods and previous research, then we systematically describe the findings in mind-numbing detail, arguing for their significance with arcane comparisons and incomprehensible tables—all in a rather soporific style that fails to convey the importance of our work to the public.

It is unlikely that we can ever present the products of archaeology in a fashion that is as entertaining as the visual artistry of good film, but there is no excuse for being boring. Like us, our colleagues in history convey the results of their endeavors with the written word, but many of their scholarly publications become best sellers while ours rarely reach beyond academia to capture the public's attention. Fortunately, more archaeologists are now writing expressly with a broader readership in mind, and we can hope that the prospects for publishing that type of book will continue to improve.

There are many other ways, of course, to get our interpretations of the past across to a larger audience, and the Internet provides ample opportunities in that regard. Web sites, like the one that Yamin and Cook cite for the Five Points archaeological project, not only have the ability to reach anyone with access to the computer, they can be revised and expanded almost infinitely with new information designed to satisfy the curious. Thanks to the proliferation of specialized cable television channels, there are also more opportunities than ever for archaeologists to collaborate with documentary film producers on projects of mutual interest and broad appeal.

Epilogue

Scholars can fault Hollywood for showing us only selected aspects of the past, however, it also deserves our praise for exhibiting certain universal qualities of humanity that neither history nor archaeology can effectively address. Negative cultural stereotypes can be hurtful, to be sure, but there is nothing inherently wrong with a little mythic imagery and fanciful history. We need heroes to help us make sense of our lives just as much as we need to know the truth about our collective past. We need not choose between legend and fact, but should embrace the complementary qualities of both.

References

Armstrong, Karen
    2005   *A Short History of Myth*. Canongate, New York.
Berkhofer, Robert, Jr.
    1978   *The White Man's Indian: Images of the American Indian from Columbus to the Present*. Alfred Knopf, New York.

Bogdanovich, Peter

1978   *John Ford* (revised and enlarged edition). University of California Press, Berkeley.

Brownlow, Kevin

1968   *The Parade's Gone By.* University of California Press, Berkeley.

Carnes, Mark C., editor

1995   *Past Imperfect: History According to the Movies.* Henry Holt, New York.

Ceram, C. W.

1951 *Gods, Graves, and Scholars: The Story of Archaeology.* Alfred J. Knopf, New York.

Davis, Natalie Zemon

1983   *The Return of Martin Guerre.* Harvard University Press, Cambridge, MA.

2002   *Slaves on Screen: Film and Historical Vision.* Harvard University Press, Cambridge, MA.

Donaldson, Melvin

2003   *Black Directors in Hollywood.* University of Texas Press, Austin.

Everson, William K.

1998   *American Silent Film.* Da Capo Press, New York. Reprint of 1978 volume originally published by Oxford University Press.

Kilpatrick, Jacquelyn

1999   *Celluloid Indians: Native Americans and Film.* University of Nebraska Press, Lincoln.

McCrisken, Trevor B.

2005   *American History and Contemporary Hollywood Film.* Rutgers University Press, New Brunswick, NJ.

Noble, Vergil E.

2004   The Value of Reconstructions: An Archaeologist's Perspective. In *The Reconstructed Past: The Role of Reconstructions in the Public Interpretation of Archaeology and History,* John H. Jameson, Jr., editor, pp. 273–286. AltaMira, Walnut Creek, CA.

Praetzellis, Adrian

1998   Introduction: Why Every Archaeologist Should Tell Stories Once in a While. *Historical Archaeology* 32(1):1–3.

Praetzellis, Adrian and Mary Praetzellis, editors

    1998   Archaeologists as Storytellers. *Historical Archaeology* 32(1):1–96.

Rosenstone, Robert A.

    1995a   *Visions of the Past: The Challenge of Film to Our Idea of History.* Harvard University Press, Cambridge, MA.

    1995b *Revisioning History: Film and the Construction of a New Past.* Robert A. Rosenstone, editor. Princeton University Press, Princeton, NJ.

Sanello, Frank

    2003   *Reel v. Real: How Hollywood Turns Fact into Fiction.* Taylor Trade Publishing, Lanham, MD.

Smyth, J. E.

    2006   *Reconstructing American Historical Cinema: From* Cimarron *to* Citizen Kane. University of Kentucky Press, Lexington.

Sorlin, Pierre

    1980   *The Film in History: Restaging the Past.* Barnes and Noble Books, New York.

Toplin, Robert Brent

    1996   *History by Hollywood: The Use and Abuse of the American Past.* University of Illinois Press, Champaign-Urbana.

    2002   *Reel History: In Defense of Hollywood.* University Press of Kansas, Lawrence.

Vankin, Jonathan

    2005   *Based on a True Story: Fact and Fantasy in 100 Favorite Movies.* A Capella Books, Chicago.

INDEX

ABOUT THE AUTHORS

□——————————————————————————————————□

After completing a bachelor's degree in cultural anthropology and archaeology from the State University of New York, Empire State College, **RANDY AMICI** began his career working for Colorado State University's Center for the Ecological Management of Military Lands. At present, Amici is the cultural resources manager at the Fort Eustis Army installation in Newport News, Virginia, and the Fort Story Army installation in Virginia Beach, Virginia. Currently pursuing a Ph.D. in cultural anthropology, Amici's research interests include prehistoric North American iconography, mythology, and red ocher ritualism.

STACEY CAMP is a doctoral candidate in the Department of Cultural and Social Anthropology and Archaeology Interdisciplinary Center at Stanford University, Stanford, California. For her dissertation, Stacey founded and currently directs the Mount Lowe Archaeology Project (www.stanford.edu/~scamp/mountlowe) in Los Angeles. This project explores the archaeology and history of "Americanization" and reform movements directed at Mexican immigrants in late 19th- and early 20th-century California. Her other research interests include heritage tourism, archaeological ethics, Chicano and Mexican American history, literature, and theory, and the historical archaeology of the western United States and Ireland.

Lauren J. Cook is senior archaeologist for DMJM Harris Planning in Philadelphia, where he conducts and manages archaeology for transportation projects around the country. His research includes urban archaeology, industrial archaeology, the archaeology of social class and status, and waterfront archaeology. He has been researching and working on the historical archaeology of the northeast since 1979.

James Delgado has led or participated in shipwreck archaeological expeditions and projects around the world. One of the authors of the international treaty on the wreck of RMS *Titanic*, he dived to the wreck in 2000. Delgado is the executive director of the Institute of Nautical Archaeology, headquartered at Texas A&M University, College Station. He was previously the director of the Vancouver Maritime Museum in Canada and the head of the U.S. government's maritime preservation program in Washington, DC. He is the author or editor of twenty-nine books.

Jon M. Erlandson is a professor of anthropology and director of the Museum of Natural and Cultural History at the University of Oregon, Eugene. His interests revolve around the archaeology of maritime peoples and the history of human impacts on marine fisheries and coastal ecosystems. He has been working on the archaeology and paleoecology of Viking Age sites in Iceland since 2001.

Charles R. Ewen is a professor of anthropology and director of the Archaeology Laboratories at East Carolina University in Greenville, North Carolina. His research interests focus mostly on the historical archaeology of the contact and colonial periods. He is currently undertaking a long-term archaeological study of historic Bath, North Carolina (the last-known residence of Blackbeard). Besides many articles and book chapters, Ewen is the author or editor of five books, the latest of which are *Searching for the Roanoke Colonies* (North Carolina Office of Archives & History, 2003), and, more recently, *X Marks the Spot: The Archaeology of Piracy* (University Press of Florida, 2006).

CHARLES HAECKER is an archaeologist with the National Park Service–Heritage Partnerships Program, based in Santa Fe, New Mexico. Haecker develops partnerships with federal and state agencies, Native American tribes, communities, and private citizens, with the aim of protecting places that hold national significance in our nation's history. In addition, he works with the NPS–American Battlefield Protection Program investigating battlefields associated with the Mexican-American War, the Civil War, and Indian Wars of the U.S. West. Haecker is presently working with other researchers to identify camp sites and battles associated with the 1540–1542 Coronado expedition and 1541–1542 conquistador battle sites in central Mexico.

PAUL R. MULLINS is associate professor and chair of the Department of Anthropology at Indiana University–Purdue University, Indianapolis. He is the author of *Race and Affluence: An Archaeology of African America and Consumer Culture* (1999, Kluwer) and *Glazed America: A History of the Doughnut* (forthcoming, University Press of Florida).

ROBERT S. NEYLAND is the head of the Underwater Archaeology Branch/Naval Historical Center for the Department of the Navy. He has worked as a research associate with the Netherlands Institute for Ship and Underwater Archaeology and the Institute for Nautical Archaeology. Neyland also served as the project director for the recovery and excavation of the submarine *H.L. Hunley*. Currently, Neyland is searching for the Capt. John Paul Jones ship, *Bonhomme Richard*, which sunk in the English Channel after engaging and defeating a superior British naval force.

Vergil E. Noble joined the National Park Service in 1987 and currently provides external technical assistance to the stewards of seventy National Historic Landmark archaeological sites in the thirteen-state Midwest Region. He holds an adjunct professorship at the University of Nebraska-Lincoln and previously served as director of the Midwest Archeological Research Center at Illinois State University. A native of suburban Detroit, Noble earned his doctoral degree in 1983 at Michigan State University. His primary research interest is the 18th-century French fur trade in North America. He is a past president of the Society for Historical Archaeology.

Julie M. Schablitsky's academic and research pursuits are launched from the University of Oregon, Museum of Natural and Cultural History, where she holds an adjunct professorship and directs excavations on American pioneer sites and Oregon Chinatowns. Within these projects, she identifies expressions of ethnicity, assimilation, and adaptation to foreign environments. Her recent research includes the investigation of the Donner Party archaeological site in California and John Paul Jones' birthplace near Dumfries, Scotland. Schablitsky is also known for extracting DNA from artifacts. She recently published an edited volume "Remains of the Day: Forensic Applications in Archaeology" (*Society for Historical Archaeology* 2006). Within this publication she introduces a new field of study, "genetic archaeology," and highlights successful projects using traditional forensic techniques to better understand archaeological sites.

Russell K. Skowronek is associate professor in the Department of Anthropology and campus archaeologist at Santa Clara University, Santa Clara, California. He is also a research associate at the National Museum of Natural History, in the Department of Anthropology, Washington, DC. Skowronek is the editor or coeditor of three books (*Telling the Santa Clara Story* [City of Santa Clara and Santa Clara University, 2002]; *X-Marks the Spot, The Archaeology of Piracy* [University Press of Florida, 2006]; and *Situating Mission Santa Clara de Asis: 1776–1851* [Academy of American

Franciscan History, Berkeley, CA, 2006]) and has published in *Historical Archaeology, Ethnohistory, American Antiquity, International Journal of Historical Archaeology, International Journal of Nautical Archaeology,* and *Research in Economic Anthropology.*

STUART TYSON SMITH, professor of anthropology at the University of California, Santa Barbara, is on intimate terms with mummies, having participated in and led excavations of ancient Egyptian cemeteries in both Egypt and more recently Sudanese Nubia, including Luxor's famed Theban necropolis. His research focuses on the dynamics of Egyptian imperialism and royal ideology, culture contact and the rise of the Nubian 25th Dynasty, death and burial, and the social and economic dynamics of ancient Egypt and Nubia. He has published three books, including *Wretched Kush: Ethnic Identities and Boundaries in Egypt's Nubian Empire* (Routledge, 2003), and, with Nancy Barnard, *Valley of the Kings,* a book for young readers (Oxford University Press, 2003.) He has three film credits as an Egyptological consultant: *Stargate* (1994), *The Mummy* (1999), and *The Mummy Returns* (2001).

MARK AXEL TVESKOV is an associate professor of anthropology and director of the Laboratory of Anthropology at Southern Oregon University in Ashland. His interests include historical archaeology, maritime cultures, ethnohistory, and colonialism. He has conducted field research in New England, Oregon, Alaska, and California, and, as part of the Mosfell Archaeology Project, directed the field excavations at theHrísbrú site in Iceland in 2002 and 2003.

BRYN WILLIAMS is a doctoral candidate in the Department of Cultural and Social Anthropology and Archaeology Interdisciplinary Center at Stanford University, Stanford, California. He is interested in the archaeology of overseas Chinese communities and the history of the western United States. His dissertation project is a comparative study of the Point Alones Chinese fishing village in Monterey, California, and the Market

Street Chinatown of San José, California. In this project he examines connections between race, masculinity, nationality, and material culture.

Rebecca Yamin is a principal archaeologist with John Milner Associates in Philadelphia. In the 1990s, she directed the analysis of the nearly 850,000 artifacts recovered on a block in Lower Manhattan that was once part of the notorious Five Points neighborhood. The Moynihan Federal Courthouse now stands on the site. In recent years, she has been working in Philadelphia, where her projects have included major excavations on two blocks of Independence Mall and the restoration of Independence Square in Independence National Historical Park. Yamin is currently writing an archaeological memoir of Philadelphia.